A PLUME BOOK

RESTAURANT MAN

JOE BASTIANICH opened his first restaurant, Becco, with his mother, Lidia, in 1993. He and partner Mario Batali have since established some of New York's most celebrated restaurants, including Babbo, Del Posto, Lupa, Esca, and Otto Enoteca Pizzeria, as well as restaurants in Los Angeles and Las Vegas, and Eataly. He also appears as a judge on Fox TV's *MasterChef*.

Praise for *Restaurant Man*

"[*Restaurant Man* is a] rambunctious memoir. . . . Mr. Bastianich writes in a vigorous, swaggering style . . . a cross between Anthony Bourdain and Holden Caulfield."
—*The Wall Street Journal*

"Enthralling . . . Funny, often surprising, and, if anything, illuminating."
—*The New York Observer*

"A fascinating, brutally candid look at the realities of operating your own eatery."
—*People*

"Compulsory reading for anyone who dreams of someday opening an eatery . . . The lessons [Joe] Bastianich has to offer are important and fundamental."
—*LATimes.com*

"[*Restaurant Man* is] a wild ride that ends with a richer, happier, healthier man amazed at his survival, emotionally reconciled with his past, and committed to nurturing his family and his culinary legacy."
—*Wine Spectator*

"Joe Bastianich tells it like it is. . . . *Restaurant Man* is a brutally honest account of his rise from self-proclaimed Queens 'punk' to a James Beard–winning restaurateur. . . . [*Restaurant Man*] serves as an education—and a warning—to anyone who is thinking of entering the restaurant business."
—*The New York Daily News*

"*Restaurant Man* [is] a terrific trench-level primer on the biz."
—Anthony Bourdain

Joe Bastianich

RESTAURANT MAN

A PLUME BOOK

PLUME
Published by the Penguin Group
Penguin Group (USA) Inc., 375 Hudson Street,
New York, New York 10014, USA

USA | Canada | UK | Ireland | Australia | New Zealand | India | South Africa | China
Penguin Books Ltd, Registered Offices: 80 Strand, London WC2R 0RL, England
For more information about the Penguin Group visit penguin.com

First published in the United States of America by Viking, a member of
Penguin Group (USA) Inc., 2012
First Plume Printing 2013

℗ REGISTERED TRADEMARK—MARCA REGISTRADA

Photograph credits: Insert page 4 (bottom), 7 (bottom), 8 (middle and bottom): Photo:
Barbara Kaufman; 5 (top three), 6 (all): Photo: Kelly Campbell; 5 (bottom): Photo: Lydia
Gould Bessler and Glen Coben; 8 (top): Photo: Evan Sung. Other photographs courtesy of
the author.

THE LIBRARY OF CONGRESS HAS CATALOGUED THE VIKING EDITION AS FOLLOWS:

Bastianich, Joseph.
Restaurant Man / Joe Bastianich.
    p. cm.
ISBN 978-0-670-02352-3 (hc.)
ISBN 978-0-14-219684-7 (pbk.)
1. Bastianich, Joseph.   2. Restaurateurs—United States—Biography.   I. Title.
TX910.5.B373A3 2012
647.95092—dc23   [B] 2011048874

Penguin is committed to publishing works of quality and integrity.
In that spirit, we are proud to offer this book to our readers;
however, the story, the experiences, and the words
are the author's alone.

For Olivia, Miles, and Ethan.
This is your legacy.
Embrace it.

Contents

Acknowledgments   ix

Preface   xi

CHAPTER ONE: **Restaurant Man**   1

CHAPTER TWO: **Queens Boulevard**   15

CHAPTER THREE: **Joe Stalin's Stratocaster**   30

CHAPTER FOUR: **Eat to Live/Live to Eat**   48

CHAPTER FIVE: **Be Afraid. Be Very Afraid.**   59

CHAPTER SIX: **From Blue Nun to Barolo**   78

CHAPTER SEVEN: **Don't You Know? Busboys Run the Show.**   93

CHAPTER EIGHT: **Babbo: Primi**   106

CHAPTER NINE: **Babbo: Secondi**   119

CHAPTER TEN: **Heroes and Villains**   132

CHAPTER ELEVEN: **Sour Grapes**   145

CHAPTER TWELVE: **Romulus, Remus, and Me**   165

CHAPTER THIRTEEN: **Pirate Love**   182

CHAPTER FOURTEEN: **The Curse of Restaurant Man!**   197

Contents

CHAPTER FIFTEEN: ★ ★ ★ ★   206

CHAPTER SIXTEEN: **Don't Shoot the Piano Player**   222

CHAPTER SEVENTEEN: **No, You Can't Sit Down**   231

CHAPTER EIGHTEEN: **That's Right, the Women Are Smarter**   242

CHAPTER NINETEEN: **Game Changer**   256

CHAPTER TWENTY: **Closing Time**   270

Acknowledgments

Writing a book, much like the journey of a Restaurant Man, is not a solitary venture, and I am indebted and grateful to everyone who has been so supportive and enthusiastic.

Mike Edison was invaluable in helping me get the story onto the page and keeping the energy and spirit cooking over almost three years of working together to make this book a reality. Mike entered the world of the Restaurant Man with a dinner of tripe soup and toxic white wine at the Istria Club in Queens with the original Restaurant Man—my father—and me, and since then his selflessness and total immersion in the project (not to mention his practically criminal love of food, wine, and Led Zeppelin) have helped me find the confidence in my own voice to write this book without compromise. Mike is a great collaborator, a great writer, and a great friend.

Alessandra Lusardi shared our vision and edited this book with a level of understanding, thoughtfulness, and sensitivity that I have rarely encountered in any business. Her own distinguished Italian restaurant lineage (and love of Led Zeppelin) helped to make writing this book an extreme pleasure. If someday the publishing thing doesn't work out, she could be a great Restaurant Woman.

Thanks to Rick Kot, without whose leadership and tenacity this book would still be living in the realm of ideas, and to everyone else at Viking.

As always, thanks to my tough-as-nails agent, Jane "Give 'Em Hell in Chanel" Dystel of Dystel & Goderich Literary Management, to whom I am more grateful than she'll ever know.

Thanks to Cass Bird for capturing the spirit of Restaurant Man in his stainless-steel lair, to Lisa Eaton for designing the cover (and most of my life), and to Jessica Meyer for finding order in chaos.

Very special Restaurant Man thanks to my assistant Kim Reed, whose patience, spirit, charm, and organization (and ability to persuade the manager of Duane Reade to carry Pabst Blue Ribbon tallboys) kept this train a-rollin'.

Love and thanks to all the busboys, coat-check girls, maître d's, dishwashers, hostesses, bartenders, cooks, waiters, sommeliers, captains, runners, and everyone else who worked with me over the years to create this incredible world, and especially to our fantastic customers, who supported our dream—you are the reason all of this can happen.

And of course special thanks, deeply heartfelt gratitude, and profound love to my mom, Lidia, for letting me fly and catching me when I fell; to my grandma Nonna Mima for everything she has taught me and for providing balance and family values to a stoned youth; to my partner Mario Batali for being a cheap fuck (and Led Zeppelin fan) from way back and keeping it real; and to my astonishingly patient and beautiful wife, Deanna, who stood with me from the Balkans to Babbo. I think you knew what you were signing up for. . . .

Preface

I never would have guessed that the New York tabloids would be so interested in Joe's story. The bildungsroman of a Queens boy growing up in his parents' red sauce joint who quit Wall Street, then scrabbled his way to open restaurants with a clogged chef starting in the '90s seemed interesting enough to me, but I did not suppose that it would be perceived as incendiary or as controversial. . . .

"Restaurateur Joe Bastianich minces few words in his new book *Restaurant Man*," started the *Daily News*. "Is it his *Heart of Darkness* or The Good Word?" wrote the *New York Observer*. "Dishing It Out," said the *Wall Street Journal*. And in what turned out to be a six-part serial in the *New York Post*: "Food Fight" and soon thereafter "Bitter Taste of Bastianich." (Not the headline team's best work, if you ask me.) Then the food blogs weighed in with "'Prick' (John Mariani) vs. 'Vile' (Joe Bastianich)."

Press is press is press.

In mid-May, we started receiving a voluminous collection of scathing letters written in retribution. "I wish I had a house account at some of your venues so I could cancel them after reading about your ungracious and unkind remark about Sirio Maccioni," started one missive. I'll wait another year or two before I present Joe with the scrapbook we made of his fan mail.

Being a partner of someone who lives in the public eye is somewhat of a two-way street. The obvious upside is awareness of the businesses and the volume the fans create; the downside is the silly scrutiny of every single thing we do in what we thought was private life. By now I have become accustomed to explaining what I *meant* to say in the press—to my family and to Joe and to our lesser percentage partners—but it was quite illuminating to see it happen from the other side of Page 6. In the end, Joe and I both realize that working together in a partnership is 99 percent about the positive attributes each brings to the table, and the mirth and laughs about the other 1 percent of the time one of us says something the other does not agree with or might not have said in any case. In the final analysis, we both agree on how to conceive, design, build, operate, and profit from a restaurant, and we both agree that the public space is a funny place to do business. In the world of media, we can both hold our own most of the time and feel pretty good about what we say and how we are perceived.

Now, a year after the book was released, no one questions how compelling Joe's story is. After selling more books than most autobiographies last year, Joe has gone on to headline an Italian spin-off of his perennial hit *MasterChef*. At present, there are rumors of a TV series based on *Restaurant Man*. It turns out the tabloids were not the only ones interested in Joe's tale . . . and with good reason.

Restaurant Man is the funniest, most truthful inside look at the restaurant business written in years, joining the bloodline of *White Heat* and *No Reservations*. Joe doesn't pull punches, but he also doesn't shy away from portraying himself (and me) in a sometimes less than favorable light. Restaurant dealings are not as glamorous as many industry aspirants are led to believe, and Joe tells it like it is. For those who know him, it's clear that the account couldn't be more real or true.

Joe is and has always been a keen observer. He has gotten a lot of press for his color, particularly the four-letter language with which he tells his story. But *Restaurant Man* is a veritable handbook to the restaurant industry that should be compulsory reading for anyone who hopes to someday open a shop of his or her own in any business, but especially ours.

Joe delves into the entire operation—how the money flows, who makes what, how it is sliced up, where the scams are, and how the success trickles down to each restaurant worker. These are the financial rules of the entire category, its mores and style and bravado, the joys and tribulations of the hospitality business, all of which are part of how our own operation has grown consistently for a decade and a half. The margins are tight, the stakes are played daily, and we work hard. But we love it; for all of its grit and chicken water there is now some bit of glamour.

It's a captivating story of the restaurant lifestyle that started between Joe and me with Babbo, which begat Lupa and Otto, then Casa Mono, and on to Vegas, Los Angeles, Singapore, and now Hong Kong. This may in fact be the first chapter of Joe's much larger book . . . *buon appetito!*

MARIO BATALI

•

CHAPTER ONE

Restaurant Man

Here's everything you need to know to open a restaurant. Your margins are three times your cost on everything. Some things you make more, some things you make less. You have loss leaders on the menu—veal chops and steak might cost you 50 percent of the ticket price on the menu. Pasta and salad you can run closer to 15, just as long as everything works out to 30 percent.

Bells and whistles like appetizers and desserts bring down the cost. Desserts are almost pure profit. Wine by the glass is usually marked up four times, although we don't always do that. At Babbo we get about three times cost for a quartino, or sometimes even two times, so our wine cost is 30 to 50 percent.

Thirty percent of your monthly take is going to be your food and wine cost. Thirty percent is going to be labor, 20 percent is miscellaneous, including the rent, and 20 percent is your profit. Your rent per month should be your gross take on your slowest day.

And that's it. Restaurant math is easy. If you need to gross ten grand in a day, then it's about having two hundred people coming in and spending fifty bucks apiece. And within that $10,000, you should have $3,333 going to the cost of goods sold, $3,333 going to labor to execute that, and 20 percent miscellaneous, including the linens and insurance and bug spray and anything else. That leaves 20 percent profit. Like I said, it's very simple. There are a lot of more complex models, but this is the basic way of doing it.

Anything you give away for free is bad. Linen is the number-one evil, because it is expensive and no one pays for it. Same with bread and butter. You don't mind paying fifteen bucks for a veal chop you sell for thirty dollars, but paying a dollar and a quarter for a tablecloth and thirty-five cents for each napkin that someone gets dirty before they even have their first drink is a drag.

In a typical Manhattan fine-dining restaurant, between 10 and 20 percent profit is an acceptable margin. Twenty percent if you're a stud, 10 percent if you're just doing okay. But every little thing will eat into your margin. A spoon that goes into the garbage is coming out of your pocket. A pot of coffee no one drinks costs you money. How close the chef cuts the fish to the bone will make a big difference. In this business, to make money you have to save money.

My dad taught me that. He was a restaurant man. That's what he called it: "Restaurant Man."

He taught me at an early age the enigma of the business—you have to appear to be generous, but you have to be inherently a cheap fuck to make it work. He taught me how to make money—it's a nickel-and-dime business, and you make dollars by accumulating nickels. If you ever try to make dollars by grabbing dollars, you'll never survive. It comes down to a very simple concept that my partner, Mario Batali, and I live by in all of our restaurants: We buy things, we fix them up, and we sell them for a profit. That's been our mantra since we started. We're not full of ourselves. We can't afford to be. This is a business that will always see more failures than successes. We are very passionate about what we do. We live to pleasure our customers. We want to bring them to gastronomic orgasm, and we want to be there to bask in the afterglow. We're the luckiest guys in the world to have this job. But really, what we do is very simple: *We buy it, we fix it, we sell it for a profit.* That's the restaurant business.

At Babbo, our first truly celebrated restaurant, we had a low fixed cost—when we started, our rent was only about $12,000 a month, and we had 110 seats. We were lucky; a comparable location could easily have cost two or three times that. We figured we'd take in about forty or forty-five bucks a person and turn the place one and a half times a night—that's 155 covers a night, which is $7,000 a night, about $50,000 a week. It's a nice little $2.5- or $3-million-a-year operation. If we're doing well, all told we make 20 percent, $600,000. But these days utilities cost more than rent. It's crazy— you have to have extremely high revenues. You have to be busy all the time.

Most people who open restaurants will fail, because they lack the fundamental understanding of restaurant math. Either they think they're superstar cooks or they think they're superstar hosts. They do it for ego, and they don't realize that without making money it's nothing but bullshit. You are in the business of marketing, man-ufacturing, and customer service, all at once, every day. If you don't break it down into these elements and take each one of them for what it's worth, if you think you're some sort of glorified dinner host or some artistic cook, you're never going to last a week.

If you're counting on your friends when opening a restaurant, you're fucked. That is not how you build a business. This is another lesson my father taught me: He always preferred the unmuddied Customer–Restaurant Man relationship—you come here because I give you a product at a fair value and, hopefully, exceed your expec-tations. You're happy to pay for it. I'm nice to you because I'm mak-ing money. You enjoy, you leave, you come back again. You say thank you, good night, and *maybe* I buy you a drink.

Friends feel entitled. They keep you away from what you should be doing with the customers who really matter, and you have to send them free shit. Friends fuck up your night—and your margin.

Walking into the restaurant every day, you're basically looking for opportunities to make money. And how do you make money? By stopping money from going out the front door.

First thing is, your restaurant has to have a scale at the front door, because every meat purveyor and fishmonger knows whether you do or do not—they all have a checklist of their restaurants that don't have scales. You weigh everything as it comes in, then check your invoices. Your chief porter is usually going to be doing that. In the case of most restaurants, he's a dishwasher, but he's evolved. He's your boy. You watch out for him—if that guy is on the take, you're totally screwed. He has got to be on your team, because he's at the pulse. And you have to make sure he's aggressive, not only weighing everything but making sure you're not getting stabbed for ice weight, or water weight on fish, or box weight on meat. There are so many ways that you can get fucked. You've got fresh produce and dairy, and if it goes bad one second before you're ready to sell it, that's coming right out of your profits. You're taking credits on the linen deliveries. You have to buy lightbulbs, toilet seats, stemware, flour, sponges, you name it, and if there's a way to skim on it, someone is going to try. If the vendor thinks he's going to be a wise guy, he gives your guy at the door an envelope, a couple hundred bucks in cash every week or every other week, and then your guy is going to sign for any kind of invoice. That's classic. You have to make sure your man is as incorruptible as a parish priest.

The magical point of the restaurant, where you make money, is not at the table when the check comes. It's at the door when you sign in that invoice, for whatever it is. Because when you get it and you're signing it and it's still on a double-ply receipt, if you mark a credit for dirty napkins or dirty tablecloths or weight on a fish, they're going to take back your marked receipt and you've still got an angle. When you sign off and take your half of the ticket and now you only have your invoice left and later you find out you've been ripped off, the road to getting that money back is much longer. So that's the real pressure point—when you still have the delivery guy there and your guy there and you can still mark that invoice and put up a stink if you have to—*Fuck you, I'm not gonna pay for this, fifty cents on the dollar for this*—you still have leverage. Once you sign off on it, you're done. People will try to cheat you all the time. It's like Monty Python's *Life of Brian*—if they didn't try to cheat you and you didn't try to haggle, everyone would be disappointed. It's part of the game. Once you have a relationship with vendors, you hope you can trust them. But it's definitely a crawl—they'll nickel-and-dime you until nickels become dimes and dimes become quarters.

Then there are the people who actually want to steal from you. Sleazy waiters like to steal cash, but these days when everything is done on computers, it's tough. It used to be that they could give a customer a fake check without running it through the register and then pocket the money off the books, but that's very risky. If they're in cahoots with the bartender or whoever is taking the cash, that's a better way to steal. That requires two people cooperating, though, and a little honor among thieves. But at least that way they might have a chance.

I remember closing up one night, at Buonavia, my parents' restaurant in Queens in the 1970s. I was about ten or eleven. I was about ten or eleven. My father would close the place himself every night, which was a real bitch. That's a lot of long nights, hanging out, waiting for the drunks to finish, having a couple glasses of wine, flirting with the coat-check girl. It's where good goes to bad. You've got to be supervigilant at a time when your instinct is to have a few and call it a night. Back then my job was to pull the gates down and put the padlocks on, usually around three in the morning, freezing my ass off. On this particular occasion, I looked over where the garbage was being picked up on the street, and the garbage bags were moving. It was like a horror movie, totally weird. We cut one open, and it was full of lobsters. It's very simple to sneak food out with the garbage, then swing back later and pick it up to resell for easy money.

Then there are the people who aren't actively stealing but are eating expensive product and wasting stuff. They're wasteful because they don't give a shit, and ultimately they're fucking you. They don't care if you lose money or make money.

There's an old joke in the business: The restaurant owner has just hired a new bartender, and it's his first night of service. The owner is up on the second floor looking down at the bartender, keeping an eye on the new guy. Some people come in and order two Budweisers, two shots of Jack Daniel's. It comes to thirty bucks, and the bartender puts fifteen in the drawer and fifteen in his pocket. The next guy orders a round and it's forty bucks. Twenty in the drawer and the bartender puts twenty in his pocket. The boss is upstairs watching the whole thing. The next big order comes in. Shots all around, beers, a few cocktails, sixty-dollar tab. The bartender puts twenty in the drawer and forty in his pocket, and the boss loses his shit. He says, "Goddamn it, I thought we were partners!"

That's the way it is—you're just happy to know *what* people are stealing from you. After that it's how much you're willing to tolerate.

Being Restaurant Man means being there in the morning. It's a drag—you closed late the night before, you were probably drinking too much and trying to lay the coat-check girl—but you have to shake it off and start all over again. You sip your espresso at the bar, maybe have a little Fernet-Branca to kill the hangover, and take a look at what happened the previous night. You survey the land. You check out what's been coming in the door and what's been going out. You look in the coat-check room, because that's where people leave the good stuff. You always go behind the bar, because that's kind of like the cockpit of the restaurant—that's where the cash register is, and usually that's where you can see the door. You check the bartender's tip jar, because that's where they leave the evidence— blow, money, theft, phone numbers. Whatever happened the night before, the story is going to be right there in the tip jar.

I go to the kitchen and pull open a couple of lowboys to make sure the inventory is being circulated. Restaurant Man is always following the product and following the money through the cycle— receiving, storage, processing, bulk processing, fine processing, application of heat. Customer comes, pays for it, leaves. The money goes in the register, you buy more shit. You have to be part cop, part paramedic—at every point in the process there are people who want to waste stuff, steal from you, make it less profitable, and ultimately throw it all in the garbage can, and your job is to keep it tidy. You have to be brutal to keep the margins from bleeding out. Ultimately, Restaurant Man's job is to stop the people who want to fuck him from fucking him.

The other thing I like to do in the morning is check the reservation book. See what's on for lunch, see what's on the book for dinner, see who's coming in, and start thinking about who sits where. The seating chart is very important. Is anyone famous or infamous coming in? And I don't necessarily mean celebrities. I mean customers who are either real heavies, meaning real spenders, or complete douchebags. You want to know. Famous film director is coming in with a four top. Likes to be on Table One. Fat opera diva is coming in at eight-thirty. She needs extra space. Ex-president and do-gooding rock star coming in together. Don't keep them waiting.

Just as a reality check, sometimes I'll mark a couple of random bottles before I leave the restaurant at night. When I come back in the morning, I'll check on the fill levels, see what the staff was drinking the night before. You need to know what the staff drinks, if they're drinking Patrón or Grand Marnier—that stuff is not free. If they're going to be drinking, you hope at least they're drinking from the rail.

You would like to have a no-drink policy, but the people who work in restaurants . . . well, they drink. It used to not matter quite as much. We made a lot more money on the bar—liquor was cheaper, and customers would drink more. Now everything is superpremium, and it costs superpremium. Back then it was gin, vodka, Canadian whiskey. A big shot trying to show off might say, "Gimme a Cutty on the rocks." You used to pay $7.00 for a bottle of Cutty, but even in 1978 you were getting $3.25 for that drink, so 50 percent of your bottle cost was in the glass. Not anymore. You sell someone a Grey Goose martini, even at wholesale, it's $32.00 a bottle, something like $2.00 per ounce. These days what's a pour? Three, three and a half ounces? All of a sudden, you've got $7.00 of vodka in the glass, and what are you going to charge? Eleven, twelve bucks? I hate those margins. It's not like it used to be, buying the bottle for seven and selling the glass for three and a half. Now you've got to sell three or four drinks to get your money back on the bottle as opposed to two.

I'll check out the bathrooms and the locker room, usually the most disgusting part of a restaurant. For me, restaurants are always about maintenance and cleanliness, about cleaning and upgrading, then upgrading some more. My father drilled this into my head from the time I was six years old. He used to say, "We don't run this place like a fucking Chinese restaurant." You know, down in

Chinatown sometimes they treat the restaurants as if they lived there. Have you ever seen three space heaters with the cords all duct-taped together, plugged into one cheap extension cord, along with the TV, which the whole family is watching at a table? And the boom box and the Christmas lights are also plugged in there, and the place looks like a half-finished basement that somebody's trying to make festive? It's like building a nuclear power plant on a fault line.

Before lunch you set up the dining room. My dad used to chalk the tablecloths to save a few cents—he'd go through the tablecloths from the night before, and for the ones that weren't so dirty he had a little piece of white chalk to chalk out the marinara stains and refold them and use them again. If one was too dirty to use as a topper, it could always get a second showing as an underliner. Linens are a sore point for Restaurant Man, because they're one of the big expenses for which you don't get anything back. My dad had a drawer behind the bar where he kept one napkin. He would use it for a week or two. The same napkin. No kidding, Restaurant Man *hates* linen. Bev naps—the square napkins you get from the liquor companies for free—are Restaurant Man's secret artillery. When the staff is eating, I make them use the bev naps. I take them home and make my family use them at dinner. I clean the windshield of my truck with them.

After lunch is over, when the last table leaves, you clear it off but keep the same tablecloth. Maybe turn it over. Back in the day, the owner ate first, maybe with the coat-check girl if he was banging her. Or the bartender, or one of the head captains, or the manager. To sit at that table, you had to be *made*. Sometimes Restaurant Man would have the cook fix him something special, which is a real kick in the balls, to force someone to cook after lunch is over, but even then he was watching the cost. He wasn't going to have a steak and a shrimp cocktail while everyone else ate veal scraps and spaghetti marinara, which was a typical family meal. This was Restaurant Man basking in his success but still living on the margins.

At Buonavia in the seventies, between lunch and dinner everyone would be either asleep or getting drunk. Here's an image for you: There'd be three or four tables put together, with people lying on top wrapped in tablecloths, sleeping in their underwear, with their stinking feet dangling off the table in their black suspender socks. The rest were smoking cigarettes and reading the *Racing Form,* also in their underwear, or they'd be out at OTB, hopefully with their pants on, betting on the ponies. All the lights are off. The first thing we did when the lunch customers were done was turn the lights off. Restaurant Man hates the electricity bill almost as much as he hates linens.

Between lunch and dinner was when the drinkers would start to get a load on, and then they'd basically stay drunk throughout the night, stealing a glass of wine here or there. One of my jobs at Buonavia as a kid was to salt the wine—if I didn't put two tablespoons of salt into every gallon of cooking wine, everyone in the kitchen would be completely shitfaced.

These days we have a formal family meal. We have a meeting, and it's a little bit more legit. At four o'clock at Babbo, we set up the upstairs, put a couple of picnic tablecloths down on the tables, and bring up some trays of food. At Babbo there's always a vegetarian option. Everyone sits down and eats together, and we have the waiter meeting. The manager comes up and addresses the staff, the wine guys come up, they pour a wine or two, they talk about the wine. The maître d' does the roll call—who's coming in, who's famous, where are they going to sit, who's who, what their deal is, what they need to get. Usually they're regulars, so it's pretty standard. Then the managers talk about the specials and anything else that needs to be addressed, and the kitchen will send in a couple plates of food. After the family meal, the chef will come up and talk a little more about the dishes.

Being a good waiter these days is all about communicating a lot of detail—the ingredients, the spirit of the dish, the expectation of it, why it's relevant to the restaurant. Waiters are how you communicate with your public. They're an essential part of the experience, the true bridge between Restaurant Man and the customer.

We have an arsenal of possibilities at our disposal, and it's the restaurant's responsibility to take that cache and custom-craft an experience that will match or exceed your expectations as a diner. Not every experience fits every diner, and it's the waiters' job to interpret the experience and match it to the diners' needs and expectations. That's a pretty high level of the game, but that's how we play.

The battle is always between the front of the house and the kitchen. Luckily, I'm in business with Mario, who is 100 percent old-school Restaurant Man. He is famous for policing the garbage— if you throw it out, you can't sell it. We're two cheap fucks from way back. He's a genius at being showy but not spendy. Show is free— baby carrots cost three times as much as big carrots, but if you carve big carrots down to look like baby carrots, it's the same thing. You have to pay the guy shaving them, but it costs much less than buying the baby carrots.

You have to strike a perfect balance between being a cheap motherfucker while still being selfless when it comes to the quality of your customer's experience, which is really our goal. But it's very delicate, because if you favor either side, it can throw off the whole equation. Being able to ride the fine line between them is one of the most important skills a restaurateur can have. You have to make sure your parsimony is invisible. You have to appear loose to the point of being opulent—but really, when you're giving from the front, all you're doing is pulling from the back, and you have to be careful. You can't win this game by giving stuff away.

Every time I put a price on a menu item, I think about it three times. And then I think about it at night when I should be sleeping. I think about the markup, I think about the margin, and then I think, regardless of the margin, what is it really worth in terms of the experience? I think about it in both directions.

My personal rating system for restaurants isn't really activated until I get my American Express bill at the end of every month. I go down the bill and see where I've eaten. Dinner at Da Silvano? Let's see, that was six hundred dollars, and there were four of us. I think we drank some good wine, but was it worth six hundred dollars? Was it a transformative experience? I'm deciding a month later. If it passes that test, it's a winner and I'm going back.

I think that people look at a menu and don't squabble so much about whether the veal chop was thirty-two dollars or twenty-eight. But when they sign that check, when the coffee and sambuca are done and the tip is in and then they're looking at it—a couple of bucks for a dinner for two, or five hundred or a thousand dollars for a dinner for four—that's the price of the experience, and I think that's really what it's about.

What fuels my mentality—from the perspective of being a Restaurant Man—is the all-in check average. "All-in" meaning average spent per person, including tax and tip. That's your *spend*. That's what it cost you for the experience. That's where the rubber meets the road, and that's how I look at my restaurants. I'm always thinking, Well, dinner at Del Posto these days is a hundred-and-eighty-dollar check average. Fucking A, if you're spending a thousand bucks for four people, we had better give you *some* kind of experience. You could buy a 1978 Buick LeSabre for a thousand dollars and have a great time wrecking it. You always have a choice.

Actually, at Del Posto, lunch we pretty much give away. It's the best deal in town—twenty-nine dollars for the fixed-price three-course lunch, no gimmicks. The duck breast is epic—and no supplement for that either. We fill the place—just fifty or sixty covers a day—but there's no motivation to do more than that, because we don't make any money on it. It creates goodwill and Internet chatter, a lot of people talk about it. But you've got twelve dollars of linen on that table. You have a dollar a head in bread, plus Italian butter and house-cured lard that takes two years to make. You haven't even ordered and I've spent fifteen bucks and two years on you, and that doesn't even include the fancy stemware, the lights, the sommelier who is going to take care of you like a doctor, a very large staff of top-shelf waiters, busboys who are like ninjas, not to mention a chef who's got more stars than Hollywood Boulevard and a pastry guy who talentwise is somewhere between Wayne Gretzky and Pablo Picasso.

And you're going to spend twenty-nine dollars for all this? Now, hopefully not everyone is a cheap fuck, and a twenty-nine-dollar prix fixe turns into a sixty-dollar lunch-check average. Still, this is not Restaurant Man's preferred formula for success. Actually, the best thing to do at Del Posto is go on Friday afternoon, make a one-thirty reservation, and stay till six. You'll drive everyone crazy, and they'll hate your guts, but it's basically like having an early dinner. You can have a couple bottles of wine and still get the full Del Posto experience without spending a Buick. Bring five friends, whoop it up all afternoon . . . Wait, I forgot to put the piano player on the bill. We have live piano music at Del Posto, even at lunch, and he's a hundred sixty bucks a shift, divided by fifty covers, so that's about three dollars a head in music. Guess maybe restaurant math *isn't* all that easy. But when you can do it, it works, although it reminds me of the Marx Brothers routine from *Animal Crackers:*

GROUCHO: What do you fellows get an hour?

CHICO: For playing, we get ten dollars an hour.

GROUCHO: I see. . . . What do you get for not playing?

CHICO: Twelve dollars an hour.

GROUCHO: Well, clip me off a piece of that.

CHICO: Now, for rehearsing we make a special rate. That's fifteen dollars an hour.

GROUCHO: That's for rehearsing?

CHICO: That's for rehearsing.

GROUCHO: And what do you get for not rehearsing?

CHICO: You couldn't afford it. You see, if we don't rehearse, we don't play. And if we don't play, that runs into money.

●

CHAPTER TWO

Queens Boulevard

My parents opened their first restaurant on Queens Boulevard in Forest Hills, Queens, New York, in 1970. Queens Boulevard is the magic road that goes from near JFK to midtown Manhattan, and more people get killed trying to cross it than any other street in the world. Forty years later it looks almost exactly the same.

The restaurant was called Buonavia, and it started as a typical seventies red-sauce joint, with velvet wallpaper and fake paintings of Venice and women with large breasts playing violins. The first incarnation was small, maybe thirty seats. My dad, Felice, ran things, both in the front of the house and in the kitchen. He made the deals, he bought the food, he hired and fired. For me he was the original Restaurant Man.

My mother, Lidia, never came on as a player when they started— she was the cashier, she worked the bar and kind of stayed in the background. She had a great interest in food and in cooking—she'd learned to cook from her grandmother in Italy, and we made these fantastic trips to Italy every summer that always involved seeking out great local specialties—but she really only evolved as a chef after the restaurant had opened. Later, of course, she would become quite famous.

The food at Buonavia was the typical Italian-American stuff of the day. We had a chef who had a mustache like Juan Valdez who could make piccatas, veal parmigiana, chicken scarpariello, hot antipasto, and, naturally, spaghetti with meatballs, but better than the competition's. It was all very good.

The place instantly drew long lines. Forest Hills had a large population of Jewish folks who appreciated a good meal and a good deal. Many of these people were immigrants themselves, so their affinity for a hardworking young couple making delicious food is easy to understand.

Once in a while, Lidia would get in the kitchen and whip up dishes that were more ethnic and authentic to her. My parents came from a kind of unusual place in Italy, near the city of Trieste in the northeast, on the Adriatic, not far from Venice, at the top of the Istrian Peninsula, bordering what is now Slovenia and Croatia. Besides their Italian heritage, they had also been exposed to lots of Slavic and Austrian cuisine as well as some Hungarian and Jewish influences. That region had always been something of a cultural crossroads, what was sometimes called Mitteleuropa.

Lidia would braise some tripe or make gnocchi or a guazzetto sauce, and she began serving that to people. Polenta and risotto seem so common now, but in 1971 this was the first time people had ever tasted dishes like these in a restaurant. And there was a great clientele for it in the early seventies—everyone in Forest Hills had, or was, a Jewish grandmother. A lot of them came from Central and Eastern Europe and had a real sensibility for this kind of homemade European food and a real taste for what was authentic.

We made wine and vinegar and grew tomatoes in the back. My mother always reminds me of the time when I was three or four and cut all the flowers off the new tomato plants to give to my grandmother as a present, pretty much killing all the tomatoes from our garden for that year. She's laughing now, but you can bet that there isn't an Italian mom in the world who would have thought that was funny at the time. So it was a good dose of the Old World right there in Queens.

Eventually she took up the role of chef and my dad stayed in the front of the house. He was a hard-core Restaurant Man, a real blue-collar restaurateur. He woke up every morning and got into his truck and headed out to Hunts Point in the Bronx to the meat markets and downtown to the Fulton Fish Market. He'd buy the vegetables, buy the chickens, he knew how to save money on paper goods, you name it. We bought black-market cigarettes from the mob—my father would empty the cigarette machine in the restaurant and fill up a canvas bag with the quarters, and he could tell just by lifting one exactly how much money he had collected. He'd just pick it up and tell you: "Thirty-seven fifty." He never missed.

I was born in Astoria in 1968, and moved to Bayside, Queens, a few years later. But we didn't go home after school—we'd go to the restaurant in Forest Hills. I had a little desk on some tomato boxes in the dry-storage room, and I'd sit there and do my homework. Sometimes I would take a nap on the flour bags and then go upstairs and have dinner.

I had my first job at eleven years old, washing dishes, and I loved it. Eventually I graduated to the dining room at night, seating people. After hours I dug into the banquettes to find coins, making a few bucks on the side. I liked hanging out with the cooks. They were these bad-ass motherfuckers, much cooler than me and my grade-school friends. They always had the best cars, with eight-track stereos. One guy drove an Eldorado. But that's all they were—cooks. They didn't have any fancy names. There was no sous-chef. There was a salad man. And a grill man. I was always friends with the salad man, since he was also in charge of desserts.

Forest Hills was a classic Queens neighborhood. Sam Heller owned the Knish Nosh across the street, next door there were Koreans who owned a stationery store, and there was a beauty salon, and a Sterling savings bank on the corner. Eventually Buonavia got so popular that we expanded, first taking over the stationery store, then the beauty parlor. We could seat 120 people, and there were still lines outside waiting to get in.

Ethnicity was very important when we were growing up. My father taught me that the Jews worked in the banks and the Italians worked in the restaurants and that the Irish were cops, and you never wanted a Jewish doctor, but you wanted a Jewish accountant and make sure you have an Italian lawyer. It was a simple view of things, but we lived in a diverse neighborhood of immigrants, and the first thing you knew about people was their religion and their ethnicity. Everyone got along, but this is what you used to size them up. I realized that there was us and the Jews and the Irish, and then there were the Puerto Ricans, who were somehow different from us. But I was hanging around with a pretty mixed crew—Angelo Sorrentino was Italian; the Grimaldis, Italian; Brain O'Flaherty, Irish; Paul Putski (known as the "Polish Hammer" for his ability to pound a six-pack of Bud in record time), Polack. Eric Vilando, Filipino. Havel Blapk, Czech. Nicky Vakovic . . . I don't know what the fuck he was. Maybe Serbian.

My Jewish friends were more affluent. They belonged to pool clubs, they had the nicer cars. They lived in the nicer part of town. We were different. The kind of crew I ran with, we all went to Sacred Heart, a Catholic school. The Jewish kids were more society than we were; you got that feeling at a very young age. They were the shop boys—they hung out at the shopping center, what we used to call "the shop." Sometimes we'd cross lines to play roller hockey together, but not really too much, not until later when we all discovered that we liked to smoke pot together. That was a great unifier.

And then there were other Italians. They weren't Mafia, but definitely more well-to-do people. They had swimming pools and these Mock Tudor castles, and at some point you had to know that it was all about money. That's what distinguishes how well people live.

Of course, the identity politics of little kids in Queens in the 1970s seems like something out of the Stone Age, but it was a different world. We were all very much defined by our last names. Later, in a much different way, this would become one of the most positive messages my mom could teach me: Being tied to where you came from makes you who you are, and with a strong family there is nothing you can't do.

I worked hard, and I learned about how food travels, from hoof to plate. I would go with my father to the market early in the morning. Up at Hunts Point, they were slaughtering veal and beef. There were a lot of carcasses, thousands of pounds of meat hanging from those rolling racks of hooks, vats of blood everywhere. It was the complete process—the good, the bad, and the ugly. It could be very intense.

Hunts Point was a three-ring circus, the land of wild dogs roaming the fields where the mob buried people. In the middle of the night, there would be bonfires in barrels on the street corners. Did you ever see *The Bronx Is Burning*? You better believe it. I'd see dozens of toothless prostitutes on the corner, naked. I mean, really naked. It was unbelievable. Truly a meat market in every sense of the word.

At the Fulton Fish Market, it was no less crazy. This was one of the biggest fish markets in the world, and it was largely mob controlled back then. I met a lot of characters in those days. Herbie

Slavin was one of the masterminds of the wholesale-fish business, and he was there every day shaking hands and kibitzing with anyone who would listen. A little guy, a multimillionaire who would fuck your sister for a two-pound grouper. He sounded like Popeye. He used to tell people, "I'm like the pope. . . . People see me and bend down and kiss my ring. I don't have a ring, I have a fishhook, so they kiss my hook."

I learned from my father that when it came to buying food, it was mano a mano. They were out to fuck you, and you were out to fuck them. That was how you got your product; that's how the cycle began. It was about negotiating the best price and getting the best margin you could. It's like being a commodities trader—in many ways that's what the restaurant business is all about. As I say, it's not a trick: We buy it, we fix it, we sell it for a profit.

In the summer we would go buy chickens, and thanks to my dad I now have this incredible aversion to poultry. We would drive to the market in his Jeep Cherokee—the big ol' family car with the Apache heads on the side and the full wood paneling—and in the back was this giant stainless-steel tray to put cases of chickens in, which were packed in crushed ice. If you didn't catch the melting chicken water in the pan—which was the foulest liquid in the world, all greasy and bloody, real butcher-shop effluence—not only would it get into the truck, it would rust out the bottom. It was a disaster waiting to happen. Never mind that it smelled like rotting death. Naturally, it was my job to ride in the back of the truck with the chickens and all that disgusting, melting ice, with all that crap floating in it. Just imagine a giant pool of bloody red chicken juice on a ninety-degree day—and then Dad would hit the brakes and a tsunami of that shit would come splashing out of the tray, completely submerging me. It was like the last ten minutes of *Carrie*. Welcome to the restaurant business.

My other job was to manage the loading and unloading of the truck back at the restaurant. My dad was also very big on cleaning the sidewalk with lye. To give you an idea of how nasty this stuff was, Brad Pitt uses it to burn Ed Norton in *Fight Club*. It is part of the same happy family as lime, which is what the mob uses to decompose bodies. It would burn through your Timberlands. If you weren't careful, it could blind you. And this is what we used to keep the place clean. We had a big deck brush, and I scrubbed the sidewalk and the curbs until they were bright. I don't even know if this is legal anymore.

I was always at the restaurant. Monday was a big night. We'd close the restaurant and go out as a family to eat at someone else's place. It was always the same five or six joints. I had two uncles, actually close family friends, who had restaurants. Ezio Vlacich had Piccola Venezia in Astoria, Cesare Dundara had Giulio Cesare's on Ellison Avenue in Westbury, and Bruno Viscovich had the Café Continental in Manhasset. And since we were closed on Mondays, Ezio closed on Tuesdays and Bruno took off Wednesdays.

A few years later, Felice and Lidia bought their second restaurant, Villa Seconda, in Fresh Meadows, and then in 1980 they sold them both to open Felidia on Fifty-eighth Street in Manhattan. That's when Lidia became more of a public figure and eventually a media star and a genuine celebrity—an icon, really. But my father was never particularly interested in that kind of life. When he started, you would never want the customer to even see you. Being a restaurant owner, a *Restaurant Man*, was like the bluest of the blue-collar jobs. There was a servile mentality. We were servants to the people who came into the restaurant—it was a venerable place reserved for customers. No restaurant owner would ever want to be seen enjoying food in his place the same way customers did. Back then the owners wouldn't even eat in their own places, not when anyone was there—you sat there between lunch and dinner when there were no customers and had your family meal on dirty table-cloths. Now to run a restaurant you have to be media-savvy. Chefs have become like rock stars. It's all about glam and glitz. But back then restaurants were for customers, period. Just regular people. This was hard-core, blue-collar work. It wasn't fabulous. People worked their asses off. I can remember being embarrassed telling my friends that my family was in the restaurant business—that my father was a Restaurant Man. It involved a lot of sweat and hard work, and your hands were always burned and bleeding. It was not a job that anyone could possibly aspire to, certainly not me.

We never really had friends come to the restaurant—it wasn't encouraged. My father always said that friends made lousy customers. But there were a few customers who over the years crossed the line and became close to the family. There was this guy Gino who was just tremendously, flamingly gay. This was in the early seventies when it wasn't really accepted for a man to prance around the outer boroughs. He hung out at the bar at Buonavia drinking Canadian Club and 7UP and ended up becoming a close friend of my parents'—he even came over for holidays. But he was one of the few. There was another customer, a fat guy who smoked White Owl cigars with the white plastic tips and drank Cutty Sark all day who was with us when we went to see the first *Star Wars* in Times Square. I think he sold stereo equipment. I remember he sold my dad a Betamax player, which is how I saw my first porno movie, *The Analist* (which was also a life-changing experience). *Star Wars* in Dolby, and *The Analist* on Betamax in my living room. Yeah, the world was changing very quickly.

My mother came to the United States in 1958, when she was twelve. My dad, who was seven years older, came over a couple years before she did.

After World War II, and after a lot of haggling over the border, the Istrian Peninsula was given to the newly formed Yugoslav Republic. The Italians, through Mussolini, had sided with the Nazis, so when Italy was carved up after the war, the Allies gave huge swaths of land to Tito in Yugoslavia, since he was instrumental in fighting the Nazis. Italians from the region fell under Communism and became political refugees. My mom and her family were forced to live in a political refugee camp for two years.

They were eventually brought to New York by the Catholic Relief Services, who got them their first apartment in New Jersey and got my grandfather his first job there at the Chevrolet plant. Soon after, they all moved to Astoria, where they found a large community of displaced Istrians.

My father was an accordion player, and he would hang out at the Istrian social club. When I was a kid, he'd take me there on Sundays, and there'd be Italian and Austrian oompah music. Everyone would get really drunk, and there was a lot of dancing and singing. All the children were taught how to waltz. There was a boccie court in the back. Those were the things that were important to Felice.

My mother's values were a little different. My father was very practical. You want to be a Restaurant Man? Then you had to get up really early in the morning and go to the market, fight to not get screwed, and beat your competitors on quality and price. My mother was more educated and terribly smart. She had a full scholarship to Hunter College, no small feat for a woman who didn't even speak English when she'd arrived in the States.

Eventually, when my parents had a bit of success with Felidia, I was able to go to a private high school, Fordham Prep in the Bronx. There was an early-admissions program, and if you got in, you got to skip the eighth grade. I was still going to Sacred Heart in Bayside with all my pals, and I had no idea why we needed to skip the eighth grade, but I took this admissions test and somehow got in and started to go to high school in the Bronx.

Fordham Prep is located on the campus of Fordham University, and that was my first formative experience of the world outside Queens. People were very different. There were always Jews and Italians and Irish in my neighborhood, and Puerto Ricans and blacks—but I had never met preppies or Wasps or people like *that*, guys wearing wide-wale cords and moccasins. Top-Siders? What the fuck was that all about? It's not like we went to school on a fucking boat.

The standard uniform in my neighborhood was black jeans or blue jeans, white thermal shirt, and then the blue hoodie zip-up sweatshirt under the painted jean jacket for the summer, under the leather MC jacket for the winter, and Timberlands. I wore the same outfit every day. My jean jacket had the cover of the Doors' *L.A. Woman* painted on it. I bought it at a head shop and paid a lot of money for it. It was *sweet*.

I was a well-accomplished pot smoker before arriving at Fordham Prep in 1981 for the ninth grade, and since I skipped a year, I was only twelve years old. I remember that the same day as the first time I got stoned, I heard about a guy getting a blow job, which really kind of blew my mind. I had actually seen that before in a porn movie on the Betamax, but I didn't really think it actually happened to real people. Someone said, "Hey, did you hear that Colleen O'Shaughnessy gave Mike Moresky a blow job?" I thought about it for a really long time.

We'd buy cigarettes and go down to the Cherry Valley store— back in the day, the first Koreans who came here to open up delis and bodegas would sell beer to a twelve-year-old. They didn't give a shit. We carried a big boom-box cassette player and listened to *Morrison Hotel* and a lot of Lynyrd Skynyrd. Then touch football in the park, just horsing around, and then home to try to act normal for dinner. It was pretty harmless, actually. But when I came home, my grandmother was there waiting. Soft and corny as it sounds, there was always a sense of love and warmth, of coming back to a home that's really a home. And you still couldn't wait to get the fuck out, to go back to the park and get wasted the next day. But the economy of the lifestyle was clear—there was a lot of value to both things.

For my lunch Mom would make real Italian food, the kind her mother made when she was a kid. Fried zucchini and eggplant sandwiches, all of this ultraethnic food. The other kids up in the Bronx had roast beef and peanut butter and jelly; we had tripe and innards. We ate everything, and that was another important lesson: Nothing was wasted. Years later, after we opened Babbo and Mario had become somewhat infamous for rescuing celery tops and other flotsam that he deemed delectable, it didn't seem weird to me at all.

Every Saturday, while my buddies were out playing stickball by P.S. 41, I'd take the bus from Bayside to Fresh Meadows to go to work at Villa Seconda as a busboy. The kids used to call me Bus Head—I had the black polyester pants, the shiny black shoes, white shirt, pressed, also polyester, and a black bow tie with an elastic neckband. That's what I looked like. Fucking Bus Head. And I used to have to walk across the schoolyard, taking their abuse, with my lame crumber in my pocket.

By then the novelty of working in the restaurant had worn off. I wasn't a little kid anymore, feeling like a big deal because I got to work around adults. The whole thing had become my personal family nightmare. Some days I felt like I was going to be the fucking Bus Head until the day I died.

But I was always thinking about how to make money. When I was ten, I had a paper route delivering the *New York Post*. I had to buy the papers from Turtle, this guy who had stubs where his fingers were supposed to be. His office was a wooden shack with no electricity and broken floorboards and a leaky ceiling, and all the paperboys came around to see what they could hustle. I'm sure most of these guys are now in the Fortune 500. It was like the Aspen Institute for up-and-coming *machers*.

Turtle chain-smoked Pall Malls, lighting the next one from the last, and he always had a bottle of whiskey on his desk. He was the distributor. You bought your papers from him, and then you were basically in business for yourself. When you started, he'd float you the papers, but he charged you a vig. Fucking cocksucker—loan-sharking to grade-schoolers so they could run a paper route. But then when you turned it around and you became cash-positive, you'd get a discount for paying up front.

I started with the *Post* and then moved up to the *New York Times*, but eventually I did both. I was in seventh grade, and I delivered two routes. The *Post* I'd have to pick up at Turtle's place, but the *Times* was actually delivered to my house—a truck would come and dump off the papers while it was still dark outside, and my grandmother and I would get up and start wrapping them.

On Fridays I went out collecting. Some people would give good tips and some wouldn't. How could you not tip the fucking paperboy? It is incomprehensible to me. There was an interracial couple who were the biggest tippers. The paper cost $2.35 a week, including the big Sunday paper, and they would give me a fiver. I remember I had so much love for them, just that little act of humanity. I used to deliver to the Bagel Den in Bay Terrace, dropping off all the papers for the shop. It was run by a young guy who would get me stoned in the morning. It was my first stop, and he would already be completely wasted. I used to take a few hits to get through my run. I wound up working for him. One morning we were smoking a joint, and he asked me, "How much are you getting for the paper route?" I was like, "I don't know. Eighteen, twenty bucks a week?" He said, "Why don't you come bake bagels for me?" He told me he would pay me twenty bucks a shift. I told Turtle to go fuck himself and got started in the bagel business.

The Bagel Den was the first food-service job I had that was not for my family. On Saturdays and Sundays, I'd wake up at five in the morning and go to work. Back then it was all hand-rolled bagels. We used to roll them on the wooden tables and put them in the refrigerator. I wanted to do the baking, but that was for the more advanced stoners. It was the classic seventies bagel shop—we sold Philly cream cheese in the different-size silver packs, coffee, we'd cut the bagels and put either butter or cream cheese on them, wrap 'em in waxed paper, mark the prices with a grease pencil, and it was never less than ninety degrees in there.

There were lines of bitchy old ladies who always suspected that you were trying to get away with something, like shorting a dozen, as if there were any percentage in that—bagels cost ten cents each. Plain bagels got the biggest bin, because they were the most popular. After that it was a dead heat between onion and sesame, followed closely by poppy, and then trailing were salt and garlic bagels—the garlics had to be put in a separate bag unless you wanted one of these old yentas to come back to the store screaming to chop your fucking head off. Eventually I was stoned enough that they let me start baking.

There is no doubt that I invented the "everything bagel." This is where stoner mentality meets Restaurant Man's instinct to be cheap and find ways to use shit you would normally throw out in order to innovate and create a superior product.

When you bake bagels, first you boil them, then you put them on wooden slats, and then you blast them with whatever is their destiny in life: poppy seeds, sesame seeds, that weird onion shit, whatever. Underneath the slats is like a big metal trough that catches everything that doesn't stick to the bagel, which quickly becomes a mess of poppy seeds, sesame seeds, that weird onion shit, and everything else. You can see where this is going. One stoned day your newly minted bagel baker was just stoned enough to see the future—and voilà, everything bagels. Thank you.

Even then I realized that to make money in the food business, you needed to sell things that had greater value than bagels. You sell a bagel for ten cents, how much are you really going to make? There's no margin in bagels. I realized then that selling dinner for fifty bucks a person might be a more interesting proposition than selling bagels at a dime a pop. Maybe there was something to the restaurant business after all.

But I liked the bagel gig. I used to bring free bagels home to my grandmother every day. It was a good perk—as many bagels as you could take. And there's nothing like a garlic bagel with butter in the winter when you're young and stoned. Plus, it was my first time tasting one of those store-bought soft-baked cookies. That was kind of mind-blowing, too.

After being brought up by immigrants who lived through wars and faced starvation, I felt incredibly decadent getting wasted. Well, decadent or stupid. It's so far from the values you've been taught. You think you're getting away with something that your parents would never understand. This is the beginning of the generation gap—the immigration gap, really—and this is how it starts. It's the first hard right turn off the bridge. The hope is that you will expand your mind and it will bring you back onto the path with a few lessons learned. If you're smart enough to let it, I guess. Some of my friends and family started the same way, except they never came back. Now they're like forty-year-old degenerates. One of them specifically could never seem to reel it in. It happens. I've seen it a lot.

People get stoned and they stay stoned. My favorite antidrug commercial of all time is, "I've been getting stoned for thirty years, and so what? I haven't done a thing."

It's all balance, right? I lived with my parents and my grandmother, and I saw how hard they worked, and I knew I had to work and go to school every day. We got wasted on weekends, but there wasn't a whole lot of fucking around—no one could afford it. I always had the idea I was fighting for something, although I didn't yet know exactly what. I was no genius, but I learned pretty quickly that I had to perform at a certain level, that there was no other choice—it was the mandate of every immigrant's kid: Do better than your parents. Restaurant Man was the Old World, and I was the next generation, headed for something different—I could feel it every time I listened to the Who or Zeppelin, something my parents would never understand. I didn't know exactly where I was heading, but there was definitely money and girls involved. This is what you got by working hard, I was sure of it. And when all the cylinders were firing, the weed and everything else were lubricants that enhanced the overall performance of the machine. When I got to college and got into the whole *Doors of Perception* thing, that didn't hurt either. Years later, when Mario and I were walking around Greenwich Village reimagining Italian food and trying to guess how a Sicilian lifeguard would cook his calamari, then basing an entire restaurant around that concept, just a touch of imagination went a long way. So I'm a bit of a hippie. So what? Just don't tell my kids. And besides, as my friend Sharky likes to say, a little madness keeps the big madness away.

•

CHAPTER THREE

Joe Stalin's Stratocaster

When I was a child, every summer we'd pack up the car, drive out to JFK Airport, unload the car, drag all our bags through the old Pan Am international terminal, which always seemed to me like where Batman kept the Batplane. My sister and I followed my mother and father like chubby little ducks, complaining the whole time, getting ready to fly off to Italy for the summer.

We'd been doing these trips since I was at least eight years old, but by the late seventies, things began to change. My parents had the idea of doing an ambitious, high-end, authentic Italian restaurant, which would become Felidia. They sold both of the Queens restaurants—Buonavia and Villa Seconda—more or less at the same time in 1980 and bought the building in Manhattan at 243 East Fifty-eighth Street, between Second and Third avenues. It had been a white stucco Spanish restaurant, with wrought-iron window bars and brick accents. This was their dream.

Felidia would open up in 1981, so there were two years in between with no restaurant and not much money. That's when the trips to Italy started getting really intense. We'd rent a car and drive all around the country—it would not be abnormal for us to start in Rome and drive every day, stopping at restaurants and wineries over the whole peninsula, and wind up in the northeasternmost city in Italy, Trieste, then wander across the border to Communist Yugoslavia, where some of the old family still lived. It was about total immersion—my mom was into exploring this incredible culture of Italian food, absorbing it, and then executing it back home. She knew exactly what she wanted to do. She was a pioneer, bringing back wines that were mostly unknown outside their regions, and re-creating that authenticity in New York. That was the action—she wanted to be a gateway to Italian culture. Felidia was going to be about creating the experience of real Italian food, just like what you would have in Italy. She figured that everyone had had enough veal parmigiana and spaghetti and meatballs for a fucking lifetime—that was the bet.

We'd eat and drive, eat and drive, for two or three weeks without a break. We would be looking at several gigantic meals a day—I love to eat, but this was fucking ridiculous—plate after plate of food, and the whole time you could just see the wheels in my mom's head spinning. We'd have a four-hour lunch at a restaurant, meet the owner, take notes, get in the car, drive, and then sleep on the side of the road in the car with no air-conditioning. It's 120 degrees in Italy in the summer. We were exhausted and didn't have a hotel room, and we were on our way to another dinner in three hours.

Spending all day in restaurants was torture for a little kid. My sister is four years younger than me, and we'd fight constantly—it was only the threat of serious physical violence from our parents that made us sit at a table and eat everything in front of us, day after day. But we were going to incredible places—Sicily and Amalfi and Sardinia—and meeting these fantastic, larger-than-life people. Some of them wound up having a big impact in my life. This was like the upper crust of seventies, eighties Italian restaurants. It wasn't family style—this was fancy shit. In that way Italy was kind of like America at the time. Taking root in Italy was this nouvelle cuisine, it was all about painting plates and what was of the moment and trendy. Of course, that's not what my folks took to Felidia, but it was definitely what was happening in Italy during that period. Seems kind of silly now.

One person would introduce you to another person. The wine-maker would take you to a restaurant because they made this salami or they made this special ravioli, they braised this beef a certain way, they cooked the tripe like this, they knew the ins and outs of every part of a pig. I was twelve years old when I went to my first three-star Michelin restaurant. What the fuck did I know? But you can always feel it when something is that good. Quality tells.

The first people who made a strong impression on me were the winemakers—we met the gods of that world. It was the late seventies, and there was this transformation happening—the Italian wine industry was becoming very commercial and producing a lot of industrial crap, but there were still people producing great shit. Angelo Gaja and Bruno Giacosa were making great Barolos. Carlo Mastroberardino was making soulful wine in Campania, and we were out there visiting all of them. The first time I saw a white truffle was at the house of Giacomo Bologna, another wine baron. Now when I buy white truffles (which is kind of like a drug transaction—the guy comes in with Ziploc bags filled with them and weighs them on a gram scale), I always think about that. I didn't know what the hell they were then, but I could tell they held some magic.

Going to visit these men at home was very much a holy-shit experience—forget about what my parents were doing, I wanted to be *them*. They had this incredible life. The places were beautiful, they entertained guests, they were like the Pablo Escobars of Italy. It was obvious that they were very powerful. They made wine.

.　　.　　.

My parents came from two separate towns in Istria. Mom is from Pula, which is a city and has lots of tourism, and my father's family came from a very poor part, very rural. It was a town called Albona, on the coast, anchored by a giant cement factory where everyone worked—a Soviet-era behemoth that spewed dust 24/7—and everything there was covered by a white film. They carved out the whole mountain and mixed the limestone with chemicals to make cement. Ships would come in and transport the cement all over the world.

Truthfully, none of them were exactly killing themselves at the factory. Everyone kind of got taken care of by the government. This was Yugoslavia in the seventies—these guys would hit the bar at eight in the morning and start drinking nickel beers. There was a lot of alcohol abuse in the culture of Communism.

We used to stay with my father's grandfather. In 1976 he was a hundred years old, but more than that he was just fucking old in a way you could only be in Communist Yugoslavia. He smelled funny—there's nothing in America that can remotely compare. At night we'd sleep on the roof of the outhouse, which was actually pretty awesome. You couldn't see stars like that in Queens.

My mother's grandmother was still alive, too. Her name was Rosa, and she lived in a house that was the size of the bathroom at Babbo, on the outskirts of Pula in a town called Busoler. The fireplace and the bed were in the same room, and the mattress was made out of fucking corn husks. No plumbing, no running water. There was a metal piss jug—I don't know what they called it, but she would get up in the middle of the night and piss in that, and I don't know which was worse, the sound or the smell. In the morning I had to empty it out.

My great-grandfather's next-door neighbor lived with his sister. He had like three teeth, and he was hammered morning, noon, and night. He used to beat her, and I'm pretty sure there was some fucked-up incestuous shit going on. Just by looking at this guy, I realized at a very early age how much excessive alcohol consumption and nonstop cigarette smoking could ravage a human being. I was only a kid, but I had seen better-looking—and more charming— turnips. Nevertheless, I also started smoking cigarettes on one of those trips—all the kids started smoking when they were nine years old there. These German girls gave me my first cigarette. I remember the brand—HB, in a red and yellow pack. I was a real delinquent in Yugoslavia. Everyone was. It was a long way from Italy and the land of truffles and winemakers who drove sports cars and lived in villas with their fancy wives.

My father's brother, Guerino, was a crazy musician. He used to play the accordion professionally and was pretty well known around town. During the day he was a mailman, and sometimes he made me come with him—I rode on the back of his farty little moped, and we would drive around and deliver the mail to all the women who were home alone while their husbands were getting drunk or working in the cement factory. He was screwing half of them—we'd stop so he could have "coffee," and they'd give me a Coke and tell me to get the fuck out, go play in the yard. Meanwhile, down the road, his wife used to walk around in her bra and apron, snorting tobacco. And when I was playing, she would want to clean my face with her apron, into which she had blown her nose. She'd spit on the apron and then fight me to clean my face with it. That was some nasty shit. I'll remember the smell of that wet-snot tobacco on her apron until the day I die—it is one of the defining olfactory experiences of my life, and in a perverse way it probably opened up my head so that I was able to smell and taste wine.

The best part of those summers was always the beach; that saved it no matter what. The beaches on the Adriatic were gorgeous. We'd go to the sea every day and play with the other kids and do stupid kid stuff. The big thing was to see who could jump off the highest rock into the shallowest water.

There were still water mines and land mines left over from the war everywhere. All these people, even the little kids, were out of their minds, and a lot of crazy shit happened. It could be a little scary—the factory was right behind the beach, spitting out noise and dust like some kind of monster—but at the same time it was so great because everything was supercheap. Communist-era beach-side resorts cost practically nothing for an American with a few dollars.

When I was about twelve, I got into hustling electric guitars to the Commies. Before we left home, I'd go to Manny's, a guitar shop on Forty-eighth Street, and buy a new Stratocaster—I'd say it was mine to get through customs and then tote it around the beach until someone noticed and eventually sell it to some musician who would pay me a shitload of money for it. *Hey dude, I'm from America. Check it out, I got a Stratocaster for you.*

My grandfather was in on the deal. He counted the money—he and my dad—so it wasn't like I was running around with a wad of dough, but I used to make two or three hundred bucks every summer doing that. When you had a real Strat in 1979 in Yugoslavia, you were fucking badass. You were like the king of rock 'n' roll. I bought a lot of ice cream, and later lots of beer.

But outside of everything else, pretty much the whole time we were there, we were eating. I was tasting flavors that would last a lifetime, flavors I would bring with me into everything that worked later. Like what *real* grilled calamari tastes like—you have to burn it just right until there are freckles of black, blistered char. It was sweet, caramelized, and tender, then doused in this angry, bitter olive oil laced with unbelievably stinky garlic, then hit with chopped parsley, then shot into outer space with this lemon that was so sweet and tart it made you screw up your face.

I remember risotto with crabs. The risotto was just a vehicle for the sweetness of the shellfish—it was somewhere between fish candy and ocean butter—you could taste every individual kernel of rice. All the fish was grilled over wood. For the most prized fish, you had to drive twenty miles to this one dude in Albona, which is now part of Croatia. Again, it was like a drug deal—I guess when the fish is that good, it always is—and you got a little plastic bag that looked like it had a dozen eggs in it, but it was a bag of red mullet, three or four inches each, that this cat had caught with a primitive handheld line made of twine and a bent wire. It was like something out of a comic book, or a fucked-up Italian version of *Huckleberry Finn.*

Back in Queens we were eating ghetto fish. We went to Marino's Fish in Astoria, a gangster joint—the boss was one of those guys who had a gun under his apron—and bought porgies for like ten cents a pound, real gutter fish. Now we sell them at Esca for thirty bucks a plate. Back in the day, no one would touch them, too many bones. No one wanted mackerel or calamari either, but my father knew what to do with all of it. He loved the mullets especially, though. He put them on the grill when it was at its hottest and the leftover-food residue was starting to hiss and smoke and fume, and he'd hit 'em with a little salt and olive oil. The fish would blister and curl up and turn from red to orange. I still do it the same way, but when you're on the coast and it's the summer . . . *that's* the flavor that I have in my head. I remember my uncle building fires with vine clippings and grilling these calamari that they'd just bought from the fisherman and covering them in the olive oil that they made right there, with garlic that someone had brought over from his farm or garden, with tomato and cucumber salads. I can remember what the bread tasted like. There was this one style of bread that they baked only there—they had a knack for burning everything perfectly. The impressions of the flavors of my childhood are indelible. The Communist-era ice-cream cones I used to buy at the bar and the kind of soda we drank—now I drink a chinotto and it brings me right back to that. It is so ingrained in me, it is actually kind of heavy. It may sound like a cliché, but so what? It makes me really happy.

The big tourism draw in Istria was camping. There was a campground near my father's old house that held dances at night. Germans, Dutch people, Italians—the Germans were hard-core, they were nudists with a propensity for having group sex in their tents. Everyone would go to the beach with their flippers and rafts. After a whole day of that, all night there would be a band show and a grill where you could buy ćevapčići, which are little nuggets of meat made out of a combination of beef, pork, and veal. You grilled them and ate them with ajvar, which is like roasted-red-pepper puree.

All of that was great. And talking about it now it seems like a dream, a really good one, but honestly, at the time it didn't seem like such a great privilege to go on a European vacation, if you even wanted to call it a vacation. It was like another world that I lived in for three weeks of the year. There were magic moments, of course, but seriously, the conditions were pure squalor—you had to sleep in a house with no plumbing and go out and shit in the grape fields in the middle of the night. There was nothing really charming or fun about that element of the experience. And meanwhile all my Jewish friends in Queens were going to camp and making out with girls. My Italian friends in New York, none of them worked. They just fucked around all summer until they eventually got lifeguard jobs. It was always strange coming back to your friends after being away—it was culture shock in a very real way.

I was embarrassed by my family. My grandmother lived with us, walking around in her bra watering the plants, yelling at me in Italian. I was trying to figure out how not to be all that. How to eliminate the ethnicity. How not to be Italian, or blue-collar. How not to be Restaurant Man.

Going to school at Fordham Prep was a big lesson in breaking away. I was being let loose with a student subway pass into the world of New York with zero supervision. It was living in the city for the first time in a real way. We'd go down to Eighth Street to buy clothes, then go to the head shops to look at bongs. We'd go to see *The Rocky Horror Picture Show* and watch the freaky girls throw toast at the screen. We went to Canal Jeans and ate at Wo Hop. We'd go to the Bowery, to CBGB's for the punk-rock matinee shows and try to sneak in. I was playing guitar, and I had a little band with this Greek kid who lived up the block and wore a dog collar— he fancied himself a little bit like Sid Vicious, so we would do "God Save the Queen" over and over in my basement. I wasn't really a punk, but I used to play with them because I knew all the songs on guitar.

We slept outside on line for tickets to see the Police at Shea Stadium. It was the Synchronicity tour—R.E.M. and Joan Jett were the opening acts. Michael Stipe wore a white wedding dress onstage. Incredibly, now we're all good friends.

Fordham had a pretty serious academic curriculum. They were very tough on the classics—I took Latin and Greek every year—but there were a couple of cool, hippie professors there, too, both Jesuits. There was one guy, a deacon, who looked like Dom DeLuise, which was perfect—that's what all Jesuits should look like. And then there was Mr. Beck. He was this quirky, crazy theology and philosophy teacher who turned me on to the concept of freethinking and intellectualism, thinking for the sake of thinking, away from pragmatism and that sort of monoexistence. Coming from the background I did, I had seen everything as very much cause and effect. You worked to make money so you wouldn't starve to death, so you had a place to live. We didn't do nuance.

I started thinking about politics for the first time, and the thought processes that created the situations we were in. The weed, school—it was all coming together. A package deal. Just meeting young guys who were professors who taught during the day and were jazz musicians at night—it was pretty amazing to realize that the people who were teaching you actually had other interests and were actually interesting. I think that's the first time I realized that my teachers had something going on, that they weren't just robots, that there was more than meets the eye to pretty much everything. That helped wake up my brain, too. I loved the people who helped me break down the walls I had built in my head and to think about things a little bit differently.

The summer between my freshman and sophomore years, 1982, we went on a trip with Father Sloan. He used to smoke More 120s, the green packs. Fucking strangest cigarette ever, those long black things. And like all good Jesuit priests, he was really fat. He drove about ten of us around France for five weeks. This was my first time going to Europe without parental supervision. I'd never really been to France, and I don't speak French. But it was like the highest exchange rate for the dollar ever—it was ridiculously cheap so we'd go to bars and buy beers for everyone—and I loved every second of it. We went to Strasbourg, and I remember seeing Normandy for the first time. Eating crepes on Mont-Saint-Michel. We were in Paris when Italy won the World Cup.

It wasn't a big foodie trip. It was low-budget. We were eating a lot of jambon on baguettes, a lot of cheese, and these premade frozen crepes stuffed with cheese and mushrooms that we would buy in the *supermarché*. One of the guys with us was a couple years older, a real Queens tough guy, the kind of guy who smoked Marlboro Reds and kept them in the rolled-up sleeve of his T-shirt. He scored some hash in the Paris subway, which we smoked with a couple of blond Dutch girls. We were camping in the outskirts of Paris, near the Seine, trying to smoke hash from under a cup—you know, you put a piece on a needle, like the pin from the Clash badge you were wearing on your denim jacket, then put the cup over it to trap the smoke. Except all we had was this shitty collapsible cup made for camping, and it kept falling down on the needle. I don't think the girls were too impressed.

All of our family trips were paying off for my parents. My mom especially was soaking everything in, and not just on the level of revisiting the old country. My father, I think, went out of some sort of obligation, but my mother saw it as a chance to explore. It was like she was bringing rare jewels and silk back from the other side of the globe. She knew what she was doing.

When Felidia opened ("Felidia" = "Felice" + "Lidia"), it was like the birth of modern Italian restaurants. Suddenly we went from charging $8.95 for a spaghetti-and-meatballs dinner with salad and dessert at Buonavia and dealing with the old Jewish clientele—they would ask, "What comes with the veal parmesan?" You get some pasta. "What else do I get?" You get a salad. "What else do I get?" You get dessert. "What else do I get?" You get a Motorola fucking television. That was my father's big joke—to selling risotto for twenty-five bucks a plate and hundred-dollar bottles of wine.

In America risotto was born in 1981. Before that no one had any fucking risotto here, no one knew what the hell it was. No one had puntarelle; there were still parts of a cow no one had even heard of. This was the birth of real Italian food in New York. A lot of these things were facilitated by overnight delivery. FedEx was born in that period, too, and it was the first time you could overnight buffalo mozzarella, which is one of those magical Italian ingredients that everyone now takes for granted.

Felidia came up just when, for the first time, the boys in the back mattered. It was happening everywhere, a new kind of kitchen culture. People were going to restaurants not because the food was good or because you liked the guy running the joint but because a certain chef was cooking there, and where these guys came from, their pedigree, and their art form became topics of discussion. This was the beginning of the culture of chef worship, and that was a game changer.

There were times, when Felidia was first getting ready to open and my parents were overextended, that I gave them money from my paper route. These were some down-and-out times. In the late seventies, interest rates were 18 percent and higher, and my folks couldn't borrow money, and everyone pitched in. It was a wartime mentality. I remember eating frozen chicken wings for dinner for a while. You have to remember, my family was starving in Europe before they came here—going through something like that will change your whole value system. My father's sense of affluence is directly connected with the food that you eat. Once you've been hungry, things are never the same again.

People always ask me, "What motivates you?" and I say, "An acute fear of poverty. That's what motivates me." Because the alternative to having money is not having money, and I know what that's like. Not that I was ever truly starving to death, but there was always this sense that being in business—our restaurant—was the only thing that kept us from being destitute. It was very real. Maybe it's amplified by recollection, but it certainly wasn't amplified when I was living through it.

My dad was such a classic restaurant guy, even after Felidia became successful, that for the rest of his life he lived in a time warp, caught in 1976—he thought that two hundred bucks was a lot of money. But he taught me the one immutable fact of running a restaurant: To be successful in the business, the best instinct you can have is to be a really cheap fuck. My mother was more romantic—she went from being nothing to being a chef. She was never trained, she was just a *cook*. She learned from her mother and her grandmother, and then somehow in the early eighties she became a *chef*. She realized where it was all going—she was young, she was ambitious, she was smart.

The whole nouvelle cuisine thing began in France in the 1970s and migrated to New York like the fucking plague. Barry Wine's Quilted Giraffe in the Sony Building was *the* place, the coliseum of soulless painted dishes. Anne Rosenzweig and Jonathan Waxman bowed to the trend in 1984 with Arcadia and Jams. And Italian was coming in, real Italian. You had the big French grande dame places firing on all cylinders, and the Italians kind of snuck in there in the late seventies. You had Da Silvano, New York's first truly authentic trattoria, and it kind of dovetailed with the art boom in SoHo in the early eighties. It was Wall Street and the Masters of the Universe at that point in time—misguided Reagan and cocaine optimism, bright lights, big city.

Where Felidia was, on Fifty-eighth Street, it became like Restaurant Row for Italians—there must have been fifteen Italian restaurants. La Fenice, Tino's, Tre Scalini, Gian Marino, Nino's . . . They were all doing high-end food—and charging for it. These guys were hard-core guineas—they would line up their Ferraris out on the street on Saturday nights, and after work they'd race down to

Atlantic City to go whoring. During the week they hung out at Club A, underneath the Fifty-ninth Street Bridge, where the topless joint Scores was later. It used to be a major gangster hangout—bring in some hookers and magnums of Cristal; the Italian restaurant boys loved to show their largesse.

For Felidia my mother recruited two brothers, Dante and Nino, who worked at Brussels—a very fancy restaurant at the time. They brought legitimacy to the whole deal—at home Dante made prosciutto, vinegar, and wine. He was bona fide. He made everything kosher.

The big thing at Felidia was that all the pastas were finished in the dining room, each pan made to order. We'd do three pasta plates—later I would amp that up at Becco, my first restaurant, and people always loved it.

The first course was the antipasto table, which was the centerpiece of the room. You didn't serve yourself, but there it was to worship and choose from: shrimp in white bean salad, steamed mussels with roasted red peppers, dried cod with olive oil, and the grilled octopus and potato salad, which was famous. Seafood salad, clams, monkfish floured and fried in olive oil with wilted white onions and peppercorns, then classic mozzarella and peppers. We had cima alla genovese, which was veal pounded flat, then rolled up and tied with string around a big fluffy frittata. It was incredible. Felidia had good authentic antipasto when most places were still doing ginzo shit.

Dante was a classic character from the Old World. He had some kind of problem with his leg and moved kind of slowly, and he wore this butter-stained tuxedo that would get increasingly dirty over the course of the week because he was finishing pasta tableside in the dining room every night. But what he lacked in dry-cleaning receipts he made up for in spirit, bringing real Italian flavor to the table.

He was from a small town near Bologna. His family owned a

hilltop trattoria there, and we actually used to visit him when I was a kid. He took me foraging—it was a real entrée into the culinary culture of high-altitude Italy. My people had come from near the sea, but the mountain food is a whole other thing, and I learned to love it.

Now he was a real live Italian country man living in Queens. He would go to Cunningham Park and find porcini mushrooms. He could compose a bitter salad out of weeds he pulled from the service median of the Cross Island Parkway. He had the ability to re-create the flavors of the hills around Bologna—he had a way with food, a magic touch, and even though he was a captain at Felidia, he had a lot of influence on the kitchen.

He worked there until he couldn't walk—they literally carried him out, and then Felice built a ramp for him in our garage. Dante would wheel himself over and direct everyone how to make wine and vinegar—"put the grapes in there, squeeze that, okay, stop." In a very real way, he gave everything he had to Felidia and was a big part of its success. He'd hand you the menus to look at for a second, then hobble back to the table and take the menus away from you and say, "Justa tonight I make-uh sumpthin-uh very special for you." That's how he did it, every night. He really knew how to pour it on. He made a career out of that.

At the beginning everyone in my family worked at Felidia. My grandmother would put on a shirt and go in the morning to take care of the plants and answer the phones. But pretty soon my mother was starting to happen. Felidia was obviously becoming successful—there were some good reviews, and it was catching on—and little things started to change in my life. My mother took me shopping at Bloomingdale's. Fucking *Bloomingdale's*. She bought me *real* clothes. I used to get all my clothes at the army-navy before that, my basic uniform of thermals and hoodies. Now all of a sudden I had a two-tone Calvin Klein denim jacket and a pink-and-gray argyle wool sweater. It was

getting a little gay, but I was going to the dances at Fordham Prep trying to figure out what would impress the ladies. At that moment it was
like guido preppy. We wore Capezio dance shoes. I swear, of all the
things I'm going to cop to in this book, that is probably the most
shameful. White fucking Capezios. And I wore them with parachute
pants. And a white turtleneck. Ugh. Think Morrissey 1982.

But on the weekends I was still fucking Bus Head, working as a
grunt at the restaurant. Now, however, I was learning about wine.

Lidia and Felice started buying wine in quantity, really *investing*
in wine. They had this massive cellar at home, and every day they
came home with a carful of wine. And before school in the morning,
after the paper routes, I had to unload it all and bring it into the
house. The wine started in one corner of the cellar, and before you
knew it the whole ground floor of the house was full of wine and
getting fuller. Every day we'd put more cases in the house, pull out
some for the restaurant, and bring more in. It was massive.

Once in a while, I'd steal a bottle of port to drink with my delinquent friends, but most of what I knew was Barolo and Barbaresco.
I knew the names, the places I had visited, and I knew it was expensive.

Pretty soon I wasn't just busing tables. I was only fourteen, but
I might recommend a bottle of wine at a table and then run and get
it. I still wasn't thrilled with working in my parents' restaurant
when I could have been out getting fucked up and chasing girls with
my friends, but pouring wine was definitely a step up. And, more
important, I was *really* tasting wines—for the first time in a professional setting. I'd been drinking wine my whole life because it was
part of the meal, but this was the next level. Maybe it wasn't speaking to me just yet, but it was definitely whispering in my ear.

Nino was the sommelier at Felidia. He would take a bottle of 1947
Barolo and open it up behind the bar, I used to pour some off the top,

and we'd taste it. And then he'd say, "Now we gotta freshen it up a little bit." He'd pour some of the house wine back into the bottle, top it off to "give her a little more body," he said. I'm still not sure if he was doing that so we could have half a glass of really good wine each, and then we could bring a full bottle of the wine to the table, or if it really benefited from a tiny dose of cheap swill just to give it some body.

He was always saying, "Hey, kid, check this out. This is a '47, a '51, a '53. . . ." Even then I was drinking thirty- or forty-year-old wine, fifty-year-old wine, and I could tell the difference. My mother always said I was a born taster. Nino was just trying to take care of the boss's son, but I was getting an accidental education.

And then there was Sam the bartender. He had his picture in *Playboy* with a martini shaker and his big, bushy, flavor-saver mustache. He was an operator, too. He used to make the best martini in Manhattan—people would come in special for it. He would pour the martini, shake it, put the glass in front of you, and pour it so it bulged over the rim without spilling. And he said that if you could move the glass without spilling any, he'd buy it for you. That was his MO. I used to shoot the shit with him, asking him about brands of spirits, Cutty Sark, Galliano, what sells, what doesn't, what's in what cocktail, what's hot this year. There was always one bottle of Rock & Rye or some disgusting old shit that no one wanted—I was always fascinated by that. He made a Pussycat Parfait, an eight-layer drink—all the liquors have different densities, and he would pour them over the back of the spoon. That was like the perfect drink for a teenager, like the rock concert of cocktails—I tried to make it several times without much luck. And then there were all the trendy drinks: grasshoppers, something called a Comfortable Screw Against the Wall (which was just a screwdriver with a shot of Galliano added), a lot of girlie garbage.

But I was learning the bar business, the markups, what goes into what drinks, what the costs were. And I'm tasting all kinds of wine and learning everything I can about them. My father is making wine at home, and I'm tasting wine in Italy in the summers and tasting wine in the restaurant. Thankfully for me, there was always a clear distinction between guzzling jugs of Boone's Farm and Riunite in the park, listening to Led Zeppelin and smoking weed, and tasting wine in a restaurant. I never really confused the two. It was always very clear that one was professional and real and the other one was just getting fucked up.

In 1984 I was a junior in high school and still going to Italy with my family every summer, but I was getting sick of it. I didn't realize what I had. The whole driving-around, going-to-restaurants thing became a drag, because you couldn't smoke in front of your parents, so I'd have to go out and sneak cigarettes all the time. When you're an accomplished teenage smoker, you're trying to smoke your pack a day because you feel that's what you need to do, and when you're with your parents the whole day long, it's a pain in the ass. It all became about getting away from them to find where the booze and cigarettes were. Finding the Dutch and German girls who were a little bit slutty and just trying to get some action.

At some point I'm saying to myself, *Fuck, my Jewish friends, they go to pool clubs, and I'm working as the Bus Head, and I have to go to Europe and live in a cowshed with my degenerate great-grandparents.* I was whining—*Why can't we go to fucking Florida? Why can't we belong to a pool club? Why can't we eat hot dogs?* My mother set me straight: This is who you are, and fucking deal with it. Get used to it, because it's never going to change. You're never going to be a Goldstein, and your father is never going to be a lawyer or a doctor, and you're never going to belong to a pool club, and your grandparents don't live in fucking Florida. You belong to a restaurant family. You gotta work. This is who your people are. Embrace it.

•

CHAPTER FOUR

Eat to Live/Live to Eat

My friends at Fordham Prep mostly came from families that had all gone to college. There were a few exceptions, but everyone seemed to be on The Path—you got decent grades, you went to a good college, you got the dope smoking and keg parties out of your system, stopped fucking around and found a nice girl who looked good in tennis shorts, you got a white-collar job, joined the local country club, made babies named Troy and Whitney, drank too much scotch, and lived happily ever after. This was their version of the American dream, and after looking in my rearview mirror at a bunch of toothless Communists, no matter how successful my mom had become representing the old country, I was beginning to buy into it. The reefer and Jesuit philosophy went only so far.

Everyone I knew seemed to be applying to Georgetown or NYU or fancy Ivy League schools, the next chapter in the preppy handbook, so I sort of took their lead. It was still a little strange to me—you know, you can take the boy out of the painted denim jacket and the hoodie—but I was doing my best.

I decided that Boston was the right place for me. It had something to do with reading *The Catcher in the Rye*—I know, it took place in a boarding school in Pennsylvania and then New York City, of course, but the whole scene at his preppy private school and the bit where he goes to see his old teacher with the grippe just felt like New England to me. I really can't explain it, but once I got it into my head, that's where I was going. (And by the way, when did people stop having the grippe? I didn't even know what the fuck that was until I got out of college—it was the only part of the book that confused me. I even knew where the ducks went in winter.)

Somehow I got it together to take the train up to Boston by myself to visit some schools—Boston University and Holy Cross. I kicked around the campuses, checked out the girls, tried to rate the possibilities of getting laid (I was smoking Benson & Hedges 100s Ultra Lights at the time, which probably killed any chance of *that* happening—but there were a lot of Irish girls in Boston so I thought I might have a shot). And one day, just for the hell of it, I took the T from BU up toward Chestnut Hill, to Boston College. I wandered into the admissions office, just kind of kicking the tires, and wound up meeting one of the heads of admissions, a guy named Father John Acres, a Jesuit who later left the society. And I told him my story.

I told him the story of my family, the restaurants, our crazy fucked-up background, what my life was like in Queens and up at Fordham with his brother Jesuits. He took a real interest in me—he might have heard of the restaurant—and for some reason he seemed to think he had a stake in my future. He guided me through the admissions process, and I got into Boston College, pretty much just like that. I literally just walked in off the street on a whim. I wasn't even planning on visiting there. It all happened pretty fast, but it felt right. And that's how my whole experience at Boston College began.

Fordham Prep was just the opening act. This was the main event. I thought I had some freedom before, but this was a license to really run wild. Though, ever the entrepreneur, I was there for only a short time before I started promoting for-profit keg parties out in the woods by the Newton campus.

Boston was an even greater departure from the very ethnic, son-of-immigrant upbringing I'd had in Queens. I thought maybe I could get the Bus Head DNA out of my system, that maybe there was a parallel universe where if I went to college I could get a job on Wall Street and get the fuck out of guido Queens. I was determined to prove that my life wasn't snagged in the manifest destiny to work in a fucking restaurant.

It started in freshman-year dorm, hanging out with these guys who came from different parts of the country, from Ohio and Texas, with big bags of pot and money to buy beer. These guys got stoned every day—they just didn't give a fuck. They were complete suburban Deadheads. I remember this guy Randall Huffington. His dad would come to Boston to visit and take us out to some stodgy, oak-paneled restaurant, and after a couple of perfect manhattans he'd start proselytizing on the virtues of fine living in suburban Indiana. "Joe, you gotta come out here. We got a pretty good lifestyle out here. Me and the family, we go out and shoot some ducks, then come into our very large home and sit with our very preppy children and discuss how fabulous life is as the snow falls outside, while you inner-city folks go out and murder each other and live in the filth and grime. Yes, we're doing all right." This was during Reagan's second term as president of the United States—the whole culture was kind of blah. His kid would just roll his eyes, but of course this was his future; he didn't even really want to escape it. As soon as he got done playing in the sandbox, he'd end up right back where he started from, in some horrible house in the middle of fucking nowhere with needlepoint pillows and completely undistinguished children, fucking his stupid Stepford Wife when she would let him, and selling insurance.

Randall was one of those guys who came to college with an army trunk full of cassette tapes of every Dead show from 1968 forward, all labeled supermethodically, all superanal. A lot of Deadheads were completely overorganized in their drugs and music—they'd have enough pot and psychedelic mushrooms to get through the week, and then it was all about budgeting it. They really were their parents, but they were just doing it in a different way. They were trust-fund Deadheads then, and now they're bona fide rich dudes. They were never part of any counterculture, not really, but they pretended because they could afford to buy into the romantic part of it without having to make any sacrifices. Then, the second they got out of school, they went back to who they really were, because money and comfort are the ultimate draw.

But at the time there was something very alluring about that whole specific situation of the Grateful Dead and their road show. It was a very good time for me, the drugs and the euphoria of having no real responsibility, and at the heart of it was this music, which has affected all my musical taste since then—Hank Williams and lots of roots music, and bluegrass and blues and folk. Classic hippie rock. It really wasn't that far from the southern rock I used to listen to in the park in Queens. Funny thing is that I knew a lot of Deadheads who would flat-out say, "I don't like country music," or "I don't like the blues." I should have known right then that these people were full of crap.

Twenty-five years after being in that scene, I still take the good parts with me. The effect was profound; I just learned how to separate the good shit from the bullshit. It was all very earthy, and it was right at the time. The girls were loose, the weed was good, and it was a fair enough rebellion for me, against all my parents' values—and it was the ultimate waste of my heritage, my culture, and my mom's money. It was very liberating. The whole scene was a little bit cultish, maybe a little creepy, but there were Deadheads that no matter where you went, there they were, and they were welcoming. Now I could be part of my own community.

One of the good lessons of being a hippie was to try not to affect the world in a negative way. You wanted to be conscious of your consumption and keep it all natural. That opened up the sensibilities to organic food and wine, which stayed with me forever. Whether you can maintain those values once you get out of college and have to work to make a living and have kids to feed is another question, but I have certainly tried. You won't be eating any processed crap in any of my restaurants, and without a doubt, no matter what became trendy in the food world later, for me those values began with my family and were reinforced in my hippie phase. They stirred a sentiment in me that I had already known very well—that having what you need should be enough. It was a strange nexus of hippie and immigrant survival instincts: You don't need more food than what can sustain you. You needed only one pair of jeans. You needed only one Hacky Sack.

I began to prioritize things in a different way. You take all the stuff that the Jesuits had taught me about free will, throw some magic mushrooms into the mix, and you're starting to get somewhere. Once you move away from that primal urgency to survive passed on by immigrant parents, then instead of being stuck in the politics of personal survival, you can open up to the politics of the world at large and the smaller world around you, and start thinking about how the decisions you make affect the world that you live in beyond immediate choices, like what you're going to have for dinner. Living out of the moment. So instead of thinking about next week, or next month's rent, you're thinking about the next ten years. Thinking about the planet.

But then I started seeing that there was a false bottom—you

know, the doors of perception swing both ways—and of course the obvious first thing you become aware of is the bullshit of mass corporate capitalist culture and authority. Eventually I saw how the entire 1980s Dead scene, no matter how earnest it seemed—and it was genuinely positive, for me, at least—was a world pillowed by more levels of financial stability than I could have imagined. These were people who'd had money for generations. They never had to think about anything—if one generation fucks up or doesn't work . . . well there's enough money in the trust funds to keep it going for another generation. It wasn't anything like hand-to-mouth; no one had ever even conceived of the possibility of starving. The alternative to life was not death, the alternative to life is a slower life, or an easier life, or a lazy life. The life of a Deadhead.

The irony here is that it got me right back onto the fast track toward douchebag preppydom. I started kicking the Top-Siders and gave up the dirty blue jeans. People thought I had gone over to the dark side, but I was still just trying to find the right track for me. I didn't all of a sudden give up on my hippie values; I only wanted to get focused and quit screwing around, maybe put up a wall between me and a bunch of people who I figured ultimately weren't really helping my cause. I bought my first pair of khakis and started rocking the pink Brooks Brothers shirt. Do you remember the multicolored Brooks Brothers shirts? There were a bunch of different striped patterns, and then there was one that had some kind of quilty pattern, and each patch of it was a different color? Ugliest fucking shirt ever, but back then it was the signal point of my transition. After that I was doomed.

I ran for student-body president and almost made it. Man, I hated losing that election. It was the first time I did anything like that, putting myself out there, really trying to bust free of the herd. There was a certain amount of ego involved—it was really just a popularity contest—but I asked people to judge me, and I lost.

Dave Lynch was my campaign manager. I met Lynch in my dorm. He lived downstairs in a cryptlike basement room, and I lived upstairs with this complete Masshole—he used to get dressed before he went to bed, in his Members Only jacket, acid-wash jeans, and Reebok white high-tops with the Velcro straps, the same kind that yuppie women wore to go to work, and he went to sleep like that. Fully dressed. When the alarm went off, he'd just sprint out the door.

Lynch, on the other hand, was an aspiring stoner who had a giant poster of Jimmy Page hanging on the wall—the one with Jimmy in the dragon jumpsuit playing the big double-neck guitar— so I figured we had an understanding. Pretty soon we fell in with the trust-fund Deadheads and became great friends, even though we weren't really cut from the same corduroy—he was from Glastonbury, Connecticut, and I was from Queens. But we were both always a little bit outside looking in; we never had the sense of entitlement that a lot of these other kids brought with them. We shared a lot of insecurities about where we came from.

The first night in my new apartment sophomore year, we had a bit of a party. He passed out on the couch and woke up covered in puke. After that we called him Dave the Wave and used to hum the theme from *Hawaii Five-O* to make fun of him. Later, of course, he would become a James Beard Award–winning writer, not to mention the wine director and general manager of Babbo, and truly one of America's greatest wine professionals.

Meanwhile, I hadn't completely abandoned the values that the Jesuits had taught me—I was getting more serious, but I still clung to their nonpragmatic freethinking approach. I was still rebelling, but the form that my rebellion took was becoming a bit more rarefied—I wasn't fucking around with phonus-bolonus faux hippies anymore.

I became a philosophy and political-science major and was lucky enough to run into even more astonishing Jesuits—Frank Kennedy and James Bernauer—in a program called Modernism in the Arts, a four-year curriculum with an ultra-liberal-arts focus. It was modeled after Allan Bloom's *Closing of the American Mind*—he even came and lectured. The concept was that a fundamental and profound education in the classical liberal arts—through the major art forms of music, fine art, literature, et cetera—is really all you need in life. At the time this was pretty out-there thinking.

Bernauer was a freethinker in the very spirit of the Jesuit tradition. He embraced a type of postmodernism and was able to open me up to the music of Wagner and the philosophy of Foucault, to help me learn how to make the transition from an ideological to a nonnarrative way of thinking. He was the leading expert on Hannah Arendt, the German-Jewish political theorist who had escaped the Nazis during the Second World War and went on to write about freedom and authority. He talked about Germany and how anyone could possibly reconcile a God-driven world with the atrocities of the Holocaust.

He introduced me to a very powerful strain of heavy philosophy that I spent a lot of time thinking about—I was really interested in the intersection where philosophy meets social science, writers like Rousseau, Locke, Hobbes, Tocqueville. It was a kind of applied philosophy, and the idea was how modern society and the structure of government both enslave and liberate man simultaneously. What is true freedom? The immigrant who comes and fights for survival and succeeds in an immigrant world? Or is it the person who comes through a well-to-do family with lots of education? These were all "states of nature," but you could change your circumstance, and you could sacrifice or gain advantage based on what state of nature you put yourself into.

In my senior year in the program, I had to do two semesters with a focus off campus—they were very serious about the applied part of the philosophy. It could all have been a lot of lip service, but they really wanted to walk the walk.

I went to a jail for violent juvenile offenders in Roxbury, to talk to people who were in a very different state of nature from anything I ever could have imagined. Going into a high-security prison, getting strip-searched, locked down, locked in, locked out, and being in a room with a seventeen-year-old kid who had bashed in another kid's head with a crowbar—holy shit, it was the exact opposite of anything I could call into my experience. These people were not trying to quell their pussy-shit inner struggle of being a spoiled trust-fund hippie versus their natural disposition toward upper-class complacency and capitalism—this was the wild, the truly untamed jungle of people totally stepping out of any prescribed laws and limitations.

It was very emotional. No matter what you see on television or in the movies, it's hard to believe that this level of humanity could even exist. I remember taking the T to Roxbury every day and walking across these frozen fields on December afternoons when it was dark at four o'clock. And then the glaring fluorescent lights, and the baby-blue-painted jail halls with Newport cigarette butts on the floor, and the desperate, stale smell of the place. I felt like it was the loneliest place you could ever find yourself on earth. It was hopeless. It was very powerful, very moving. When I was there, I kind of felt that I shared in the isolation and desperation of the place. It was the extreme opposite of all these other influences—with the Grateful Dead everything was so optimistic. Drugs, music, and dancing were the answers. The experience made me determined to work harder and head relentlessly into the next phase of my life.

From hoodies and Timberlands to Capezios (never to be mentioned again), to then trying to find myself in the Grateful Dead world—and learning a lot and gaining a lot of values that I still keep with me, but ultimately finding it about as shallow as a fucking puddle—to my new role as khaki cowboy, this was obviously the fucked-up trajectory of a guy from Queens trying to find himself. But at least you could say that I had an open mind. And I had successfully removed myself from my parents' world. Well, more or less. When I was in full hippie mode, we'd go see the Dead in New York or New Jersey and then we'd roll into Felidia, superstoned, for dinner with eight people—a bunch of unwashed, privileged kids eating piles of antipasto off the table and washing it down with Barolo. Thinking about it now, I am completely fucking mortified. If I were my mom, I would have thrown us all out on the sidewalk. We rolled like we owned the world, no respect. But my mom was always very hospitable. She didn't know we were stoned. She just thought we were happy young boys, and she wanted to feed us.

A little later, after I had ditched the tie-dye, I would take my Wasp girlfriends out to restaurants in the North End of Boston, where a few people knew Felidia and would give me the VIP treatment, maybe a free bottle of wine. I still wasn't beyond using my pedigree in the New York restaurant world to take advantage up in Boston and act like a big shot.

What the hell—as much as maybe I pretended to fight it, I knew the power of good food. I knew that it could turn dark into light—a bit of perfectly grilled fish and a bittersweet soda could make you forget all about Grandma's piss bucket. Food could blow minds and dissolve your problems, at least for a while, and I had a strong suspicion it might help get girls into bed. In college, cooking was second nature to me. We had a kitchen, and I'd make family-style pasta, simple stuff, with a lot of cream and butter. Stoner food. Spaghetti carbonara and shit like that, and it made me very popular. It always shocked me what incredibly poor food culture the people up at college came from. How they ate—or didn't. Robert Mancusi would sit there with a can of Cheez Whiz and spray it on his finger and eat the whole thing—that would be his dinner while he watched TV. That was how he was raised—I think my mother would have had a coronary. A lot of these people I met up in Boston had no ethnicity, no tradition of family dinner, no experience or love of the matriarchy that was based around the hearth of the kitchen, which put into stark contrast the food background that I came from. It was a shock to me how little food could mean to otherwise affluent, intelligent folks. They basically ate to live, while we lived to eat. The larger significance of that still didn't hit me, though. I thought that to be successful I had to work on Wall Street. I was so fucking dumb.

CHAPTER FIVE

●

Be Afraid. Be Very Afraid.

In the summer of 1989, I had just graduated from Boston College and applied for a job at Merrill Lynch, listing "wine buyer for Felidia" on my résumé as my current job, which was, of course, complete bullshit.

I probably could have tanked my career on Wall Street right there—I was definitely overextending. Rightly or wrongly, I had gotten into the habit of playing the Felidia card to gain access to all sorts of things, beginning with trendy restaurants in Boston in order to impress girls. Then I got into an internship—a very big deal, actually—at Lehman Brothers during my junior year. The guy who ran the program was an old Felidia customer, and that was enough to get me through the door—or at least my foot in. I had to have something else going on besides parents with a three-star New York restaurant to get my ass through. You could say Felidia got me the interview and I got the job myself, but I was learning an important lesson: I could use everything I knew about wine to gain access to people who were impressed by my very specific expertise. I could leverage boutique knowledge and trade on my microspecialty to create opportunities.

The guy at Merrill Lynch who read my application and called me was a corporate bond trader who went out for client dinners every night. He was a big wine guy, and he knew I was basically full of it. "Listen, kid," he told me, "don't pull my dick. I don't give a fuck if your parents run the joint. You can't be in fucking college and be the fucking wine buyer at fucking Felidia." Everyone spoke like that back then; it was expected. It was one of the few endearing features of the entire era.

He tried to call my bluff and asked me about some specific vintages—I remember it was an Aldo Conterno Barolo. Would I recommend the '82 or the '85, the '78 or the '82? It happened to be a wine that I actually knew—and I nailed it. I knew more about them than he did. I wasn't even twenty-one years old. And that's when it turned into a laugh. He invited me down for lunch at Sparks Steak House, and that began the whole process of getting into Merrill Lynch in this crazy investment-banking program.

There were about sixty full-fledged M.B.A.'s in there with me, thirty-year-old men who had already worked as interns on Wall Street for two years, then gone back to get their master's at Harvard, Wharton, you name it, the cream of the crop. Into that group had been randomly stuck eight undergraduate kids, to shake things up, I guess, of which I was one. They just sneak you in with all these people who are ten, fifteen years older than you and expect you to do the whole training program—it takes a year and a half to complete. You get licensed to trade stocks and commodities, get to go on all the corporate retreats, the complete shebang. It is very intense— basically it's an indoctrination to ice-cold capitalism and a ticket to print money. At that point there was a tendency not to hire business majors exclusively, the idea being that successful liberal-arts students might bring a new perspective to the stock market's particular brand of paganism, as if reading Milton would give you an insight into banking and finance. Well, maybe. It's a tough call—it doesn't always work out, but when it does, it does big, or at least that's been my experience in the restaurant world. Sometimes you hire people for their ideas and not their on-the-job experience and you hit a home run; sometimes they melt down, because no matter how many times you've read *Democracy in America,* it will never prepare you for being reamed by a Wall Street douchebag for real. But a few of the guys who went through that program with me are the top cats on the Street right now, so there has to be something to it.

All of a sudden, I'm no longer living in a dorm room surrounded by filthy hippies—I have a two-bedroom apartment on the thirty-eighth floor of a building in Battery Park City, overlooking the Statue of Liberty. After having eaten lentils in a parking lot at a Dead concert, I felt delusional—whether this was all an illusion or a delusion, I'm not sure—but something was definitely not right. The money was big, people were out every night, there were a lot of drugs, a lot of partying. A lot of rich guys living in nice apartments, buying great cars, and wearing custom-made English banker suits.

There was definitely a ton of competition when it came to dressing. It was like *American Psycho* without the chain saws. I started rocking the braces, Hermès ties were making an early entry onto the scene, and I was totally overpaying for suits. I guess I was just playing the role—from hoodies to tie-dye to questionable pink preppy shirts to Brioni, I was still trying to get out of the ginzo ghetto. And I slept with my first Jewish chick.

I brought her to Tribeca Grill, which was then the hottest restaurant in the city. It was Drew Nieporent's place, which he opened with Robert De Niro. I knew Drew through my mother and through the restaurant business, and we became great friends. Later, of course, he became famous for rolling the dice on David Bouley and for opening Nobu and turning it into a brand, but he is as old-school as they come, a real Restaurant Man, a fucking Restaurant Mensch, who came up doing every shit catering and kitchen gig you can think of. He didn't have it in his blood, so he earned it, and he is as hard as they come.

Drew was always great to me. I was a young kid, but he made me feel like a real big shot. So I brought this girl there, and De Niro came in, and it was totally awesome. He showed us his dad's drawings that were hanging on the wall over our table, and she just couldn't believe it. It was like we were movie stars. She was blown away. *I* couldn't believe I was going to get lucky with her—she was the totally hot secretary, I had no idea what she was even doing with me.

It happened because Drew treated me like a restaurant big shot even though I was a Wall Street nobody. This is where I finally bridged the reality of the new Wall Street playground with my upbringing in the restaurant biz and whatever advantage I was able to leverage because of my Felidia connection and my secret knowledge of wine. It was when I was banging this otherwise nice Jewish girl that I truly had my epiphany, with angels singing, the whole nine yards (although I was pretty shitfaced, and it might have been a combination of vodka, Billy Joel, and the orgasmic wailing of a Wall Street secretary), and I realized, what the fuck, in the whole world of finance I'm really nothing, but the New York restaurant and wine world was something the Masters of the Universe wanted to be part of but really didn't understand, beyond trying to palm the maître d' a Franklin to get a table. I was an insider, with a commodity.

One of the head traders—and this is about as big a dude as you were ever going to find on Wall Street, a guy whose bonus could fund wars (he's in rehab as I write this, by the way)—his big thing at the end of the trading day was to shout, "Spark me!" Which meant he wanted to go to Sparks Steak House, and when they couldn't get him a table, I would call Walter at the door and set it up, which made me the belle of the ball.

The other lesson I learned from the Jewish girl is how to go to work with a blistering hangover. I remember the next day after our night at Tribeca Grill I was hurting. Real pain. But I had to be at the desk at 7:00 A.M., seriously fucking wounded. That was the worst—it almost killed the good memory of the night before, but not quite. Anyway, misery loves company. And pizza.

On Fridays they would pay the kid at Lombardi's Pizza a grand to go in at 3:00 A.M. and fire up the pizza ovens. They'd have fifty pizzas delivered at six in the morning to the trading desk, because Thursday was the night everyone went out, and they would come in the next morning completely wasted, like I was. You've seen it in *The Bonfire of the Vanities,* all these guys standing around thinking that they really ran the world, with medical oxygen tanks under their desks to clear their heads. They used to have their boys come in and give them shoeshines, like two shoeshines a day. They'd send out for back rubs. If you've ever read *Liar's Poker,* you'll get what I mean. I watched that happen. These guys were playing liar's poker for hundreds of thousands of dollars a hand. That was a long way to come from where I started.

But it's funny—life is such a cycle. Wall Street was really more Queens than it was intellectual Boston—it was back to the Machiavellian politics of the street. Real survival technique, what I learned in schoolyards in Astoria. It was more relevant than the philosophers at Boston College even though that—and my Felidia pedigree—had gotten me the job in the first place. The competition among the traders wasn't even intellectual, it was almost physical. The rage and violence and competitive nature of these guys exposed them as being no more evolved than the worst street kids growing up in Queens. The pecking order was that raw and rudimentary. They were thugs. The investment bankers were a little bit more hoity-toity, maybe a little bit more intellectual, but the traders, they were the real deal.

Wall Street brought me back to those primal instincts, the core values I grew up with, which prevailed in that environment. Survival of the fittest. Eat or be eaten. Fuck or be fucked.

I was young enough to think, *Okay, this is what I need to do to be successful. Let's see how far it goes.* But I obviously wasn't committed to the lifestyle, because very soon there would be a point where I'd wash my hands of Babylon, put my dirty jeans back on, get a one-way ticket to Italy, and spend the next year and a half of my life living in my car.

For the entire year and a half I was on Wall Street, I felt like I was in a movie, just barreling along into the third act—I was on a full-flight trajectory to become a titan. My next move was the NYU Stern School of Business Executive M.B.A. Program. I was accepted, and I was going to be a made man.

But what was I really learning? I was learning the culture of *skimmers*. People who didn't really make or do anything. I found it disheartening and soulless. It was just so fucking empty—creating nothing of value, living on a small percentage of other people's transactions. And the office politics were idiotic. I was never good at being a kiss-ass—no one from Queens ever is, and I realized that having someone else decide how successful I would be and how much money I would make was not a way I could live my life. I needed to take that into my own hands. My entrepreneurial instinct started flaring up.

I was returning to my roots. I would come home from work and hang out at the bar at Felidia and talk to Sam the bartender and eat

some reheated bar pizza that my dad used to make. It was his big
marketing idea to go behind the kitchen line and get between the
chefs and make bar food—he thought it would draw more people
in. He used to make little chicken nuggets and pizzas with pita
bread and give them out to people at the bar. He made them spicy
so they'd make people thirsty enough to buy another drink. Even
though my mom wasn't a star yet—she had written her first book,
but she wasn't on TV—Felidia was famous as one of the best restaurants in town and was always filled with a very moneyed crowd. But
Restaurant Man never stops hustling. He can't keep himself from
trying.

The turning point was fairly simple—I just looked at my boss
one day and said to myself, *You know what? This guy's a fucking asshole.* He was the kind of tool who would walk around the trading
floor all day with his golf club pretending to practice his swing.
Total douchebag—I would have been happy to shove a three-wood
up his ass. He was married to this Barbie-doll blonde with zero
personality—she probably didn't have any genitals either, just like
a real Barbie doll—and they both had fake tans that made them look
like the orangutans in the original *Planet of the Apes,* all Dr. Zaius
orange, like a combination of Tang and beer puke. They made me
sick, they were clearly full of shit, and I needed to get the fuck out
of there.

And then, on my twenty-first birthday, there was a party at
Odeon. All my so-called pals were drinking whatever the trendy
vodka was at the time and snorting their paychecks, completely
oblivious to the fact that they'd come stumbling out of the bathroom
with white powder on their noses, looking like complete morons.

I was never into doing coke, but I knew that it was everywhere.
The thing was, if you weren't into it, no one said to you, "Hey, c'mon,
we're gonna snort some rails in the men's room." The cokeheads

always pretended it didn't exist—as if everyone else didn't know exactly what the fuck was going on when they were motormouthing a hundred miles an hour.

I realized that I had nothing to talk to these guys about. It was always about money and deals and what car you bought. I was happy in the beginning, with the novelty of it. But when it wore off, there was the stark realization that the paradigm of success that made you a big swinging dick on Wall Street was definitely not what I aspired to. I didn't want to be that guy, and I didn't want to fuck clueless women. I'd go home with a girl and everything in her house would be brand new, no style, just straight out of some catalog, and there were no books and no music. Their refrigerators were always empty—most of these women didn't cook, they hardly even ate. But they were easily impressed by expensive restaurants. It was all complete bullshit.

A lot of guys would buy an apartment right away with their first couple-hundred-grand bonus, and suddenly they were stuck in a vicious circle. Always having to make more to buy more to make more to buy more, and they didn't have the balls to get the fuck off the treadmill.

Looking back, I can see that it's almost as if I were triangulating all my past experiences—Queens, Fordham, and Boston—to come to this point, but it was more visceral than intellectual. It was real life. Sure, part of it was those few years of studying philosophy and shrooming rearing their ugly head—the road to excess, I was learning, probably does not lead to the palace of wisdom—that for me brought down the Wall Street myth, hard. It felt very physical. Everything about it. Very real.

When it was time to collect my end-of-year bonus, I just figured enough already. I tried to make it work, but fuck it, it was a big world, and I was going to get my ass the hell out of there. I remember I was just pacing around, and every half hour I'd go down to the ATM to see if my six-digit bonus had cleared—it was an obscene amount of money they were giving me, especially for someone who was about to leave their church. And as soon as it showed up in my bank account, I hit the ground running. *See ya.* No shit, I went right to a travel agent and bought a one-way ticket to Italy. Then I felt like I could breathe again.

I'd been thinking about Italy for months by then. I wanted to do something with food and wine—it was becoming clear that it was my destiny. Who was I to fight it? I had plenty of dough—Wall Street was at least good for that. I'd go over to Italy. I'm just thinking *explore.* See what the options were. It wasn't a directed trip, like I was going to go out and find a business. It was my escape route back into myself.

Truthfully, I missed going to Italy. And this was me, once again realizing how fucking stupid I was not to appreciate what I'd had in the first place. I wanted to get back to that juncture in my life where I knew people, where it felt safe. Italy was alluring. It was the antidote to the poison. I wanted to clear my head and get back to the garden, if you know what I mean.

My mom was very encouraging, of course—she didn't bat an eye before she said, "Great, go"—and picked up the phone and started calling people and making some connections for me. Felice was not so enthusiastic—he didn't like my quitting Wall Street. He felt he had worked his entire life to earn me the opportunity to do this, and now I was leaving it to rediscover the life he'd left behind, which had sucked.

I started out with our friend Bruno in Trieste. He was a successful young restaurateur in his own right, and hanging out with him I got a taste for the lifestyle. He helped me buy a car—a gray VW Rabbit hatchback with an Alpine cassette player. By that time I had already been there for over a month and was very much immersed in the culture, and I set out from Trieste to begin my journey. I did a couple of days in Friuli with Livio Felluga, a local wine producer. And then I went down to Tuscany and stayed with a family called the Cinelli Colombini in Montalcino, who made a Brunello called Fattoria dei Barbi. I lived in their forest house and got my first adult taste of Tuscany. There are very few wines that can make you taste a place the way Brunello di Montalcino can.

Montalcino is a great fortified hilltop town. I used to go to town every night and just hang out at the bar in the piazza. During the day I worked in the Cinelli vineyards, I worked in the cellar, whatever they needed. It was a medium-size winery. The Cinelli Colombini family is Sienese, with a very old lineage. They took me to Siena. I was just kind of sucking it in—they brought me everywhere and embraced me as part of the family. My Italian started getting better—I was learning how to speak Italian for real, and that's where the adventure really began. Doors were flying open.

I remember it as being very spiritually uplifting. It was a stark contrast to the emptiness I'd left in New York. The people I was with now truly believed in what they did, which was so life-affirming. It felt very rich and positive. You get immersed in some very serious stuff with these families that have made wine for twenty generations. Some of them were part of the Renaissance nobility and I was loving being part of it. I was feeling it—I was kind of fantasizing myself as being one of the landed gentry, not Bus Head from Queens.

Which was bullshit, of course. I am what I am—but the important thing I was learning is that even though these people were landed gentry, at the beginning and the end of every day they were *merchants*. They had to sell their wine, and they were really being nice to me because it's good business to make an investment in young people as potential ambassadors for their wine, people who will sell it and talk about it around the world.

I didn't get that then, but they certainly knew what the fuck they were doing—it paid them back in spades, because I've become an ambassador of their brands for thirty years, and all it cost them was a couple of kind words and a few dinners. Maybe a little patience. I've always tried to use that same lesson, to invest in young people. Give them your time, share your knowledge, try to impart to them some of who you are. The Italians understood this very well—it's a sensibility in their culture to treat young people that way. It's just a practical means of getting what you do out there into the world. If you can bring one person to your cellar through a tasting and a dinner, really turn his or her lights on about your wines, that person will go out and preach it to everyone. And the message is always better coming from an enthusiastic third party.

There were a lot of holy-shit moments on this trip—we did a vertical tasting of Brunello going back twenty years, which means tasting the same wine from the same vineyard, going back vintage by vintage.

This was at the Barbi estate. They were crusty and noble, friends with my mom, and they took great care of me. The whole time I was there, there was this nervous sexual tension between me and this older woman, a journalist who was hanging out and tasting wine, working on a cookbook, I think. She was about forty, American, and she was pretty in the way your friends' moms are pretty—but now, out in the Italian countryside, there were some real possibilities. Imagine the raging hormones of a twenty something kid, especially when he was getting no play from the twenty-year-old Italian girls, and the tawdry desires of an older but very vital woman, mingling without allegiance or responsibility in the soft air of Italian wine country. It was about all I could do to rub one out and play it cool.

It was a beautiful spring morning when the winemaker took us down to the cellar for the tasting, with the cellar master and his gimpy assistant. It was very ceremonial, very ritualistic, as if I were about to be admitted into a secret society, a combination of *Eyes Wide Shut* and joining the evil fraternity in *Animal House*.

The sunshine streamed through the cobwebs covering the windows, and I can still see the pattern of shadows it cast. There were twenty bottles set across a table, perfectly spaced, each with its own glasses. I remember that when the sunlight hit the bottles after they were opened and some of the wine had been poured, you could see their beautiful imperfections, of the green glass, of the labels beginning to crumble. That was nice.

That morning we tasted young to old, although these days when I do tastings we do old to young. The first wine, the current vintage of the Brunello, still unreleased, screamed of flesh—bloody raw meat. And violets. It is very carnal and very pretty at the same time.

The final Brunello was a '71, a great vintage, and it was a spectacular example of what twenty years can do to fruit juice. The subtlety and finesse, when the tannins became like the spiderwebs, superfine and silky. Those wines for me are all about that carnality even now, and as they mature, what was flowers and flesh turns into juicy tobacco, like a plug of Red Man, and the smell of a wet forest, like a carpet of rotting pine needles.

But the '71 was no longer wet or damp, more like dry leaves in December, leaves that have been there for a few months, maybe a bit crunchy and crackling when you rake them up for the final time of the season, and the tobacco had become more like blackberry brandy and cassis.

This woman and I were sleeping in adjoining rooms in the farmhouse. We shared the same bathroom, which meant she had to walk through my bedroom to wash up, or whatever it was that women did. I was in my early twenties, and when it came to real women, I really had no clue.

The smell of mature sex was very much in the air. It reached the point where I was tasting it in the Brunello. She had really gotten into my head. I was horny as hell, but I think sometimes when your senses are tweaked like that, it is a good time to taste wine. It was transcendent, the wine, the cellar, the woman—it was the perfect tasting. The big stinky Brunello and her musk and vulnerable me. It all came together.

On this trip I was learning in a very tangible way the subtleties of Italian regional varietals. I was getting very deep into the specific profile of the local terroir. The wines of Montalcino were incredible with Tuscan foods—it was all making a lot of sense. Not that it was so complex, but the first time you have Tuscan bread, which has no salt in it, it's almost like eating food with a void in your mouth. Very strange. But it is an important part of the experience, and you come to sense how everything about these places goes together. Like the first time I had a true bistecca alla fiorentina—it's just a piece of grilled steak, straightforward, but the way they cook it on the wood-fired grill outside brings out all the flavors. I still have very vivid taste memories of that moment in time, whether it's the green, peppery vibrancy of Tuscan extra-virgin olive oil or those perfect Tuscan tomatoes picked off the vine and tossed on a plate with a little basil and a glass of Rosso di Montalcino. The impact on a young palate of these products in their very primal and pure state was indelible. There were no tricks. It's all about ingredients—zucchini and eggplant picked from the garden by grandmothers, or my first Tuscan ribollita, which is like a vegetable soup that's cooked down and reduced to an eye-opening essence.

It was an intellectual journey, but also a very primal, sensory trip. Each place had a specific smell and flavor, each had its own products, which really fit in with the local wine—and that's when I realized that Italy is about small places. In fact, the best meal you will ever have in Italy will not be in a restaurant, but in someone's home. But tasting and smelling and seeing helped me become a better restaurateur and winemaker. What I do in my restaurants, when I'm cooking dinner, or when I make a bottle of wine in Friuli, is really about re-creating those simple flavors. The important thing is that the wine and the food exist together in space and time—there's not a distinction. They're one and the same, because wine is food and food is wine. More important, when they are consumed together, they speak directly of the place they come from. I don't think there are any hard-and-fast rules on what you can and can't do—no one is going to die from drinking Rioja with the risotto—but to be in Spain and to have a great white anchovy with a good *vino fino,* there's nothing quite like that. It's the same thing in Italy.

Celebrating that localness is when you really get into the spirit of *Italianness.* For young cooks and people who want to do this, what Mario and I have always said is, "Look, you can work here, you can do this, but ultimately you have to go live in Italy, because there is no way you can have that profound experience here. And then you'll know."

I went to Chianti for a while and hung out in and around Florence. In Chianti I stayed with the Stucchi Prinetti family, who are direct descendants of the Medici. I was flying in some rarefied air— my mom totally hooked me up. But here's an example of "if I knew then what I know now": If you're a dude backpacking through Italy, you have to go for the low-hanging fruit—generally Dutch and Australian chicks are the easiest to get some action with when you're on the road. Hippie backpackers, they like to share the wealth. They're not afraid about putting it out there. But locals, no way. Italian girls are like the Virgin Mary. Don't even waste your time. At least for the first go-round. The second time, then they're giving it away—I mean the second time around, like after they've been married once already, then they throw it to the wind. They might as well be from Queens. But at least for their first time, it's very sacred. I wish I'd known that then.

My mom also set me up with some gay restaurateurs in Rome who tried to romance me, to put it politely. I guess that was about par for the course for Rome, but believe me when I tell you they didn't have much luck. They were still supernice to me, though. The one fellow had a very famous restaurant in Rome—he was like the Italian Liberace, very flamboyant—and he had a younger boyfriend, and they used to take me out to dinner. They had a beautiful apartment near the Colosseum on via dei Serpenti, Road of the Serpents. I remember I got to this house on a Friday, and the next day was the first of the Three Tenors concerts, which took place at the Baths of Caracalla. The whole city was silent while they sang. It was one of those summer nights, really hot, and the sunset was perfectly epic. With the window open, you could hear it all. I was just sitting there in my room listening, lamenting this girl I had left behind in another town, and it all got very heavy very quickly. This culture had so many thousands of years of history, and I was coming from New York where everything is so immediate and shallow—so five minutes ago—and it just hit me that I was in a building that was five hundred years old, in a city that was three thousand years old, near a coliseum that was two thousand years old, where multiple civilizations have lived and died and coexisted. It was very humbling. Where I came from, the here and now was all-important, and what I was experiencing, from the romance of the place and its physically imposing nature, from being in Rome by myself day after day, was the weight of everything that had come before. I was nothing. Cities got built over cities. Cultures build themselves on the bones of those that came before them.

Later I found out that these guys, aside from running their completely flamboyant restaurant, were professional Etruscan-artifact thieves. They had this astonishing place out in the country—it was like half house, half tented palace, and all the men wore linen genie pants and Roman sandals, shirtless with ornate golden chains and sideburns. If you were to imagine gay porn being shot in Italy in the late seventies, this is what it was like.

They were also eating the best mozzarella, and the best ricotta, and the best olive oil, and the best tomatoes. Those guys knew how to do it. No cheapness. It was all about indulgence, on every level. The hedonism began with the location—just the splendor of it. And then the food and wine. They had this way of going about fulfilling their wildest desires. I think because none of them had kids or were really responsible to anyone but themselves, they were able to create this insanely indulgent lifestyle.

And the whole time they were out there, they were also excavating for Etruscan ruins. Stewardesses would come to these crazy parties with their Pan Am bags, and then they would exchange bundled-up packages of totally illegal artifacts. My two new friends were basically funneling them into the black market in New York to pay for their food and sex orgies in Italy.

It seemed as if everyone in Italy had some sort of hustle. Later on in Rome, I fell in with these Yugoslavian gangsters. It was in the heat of the war in the Balkans, and they needed to import toilet paper there. I actually formed a company that was going to do that—I figured everybody poops, right? They said if we could get paper at this price, we could make a lot of money. So they were my partners. When I eventually got back to New York, I called up all the various people who make toilet paper and figured out how to buy it and get it shipped to a war zone, but after some quick analysis I realized I didn't really trust my partners. They were more into smuggling cigarettes than they were into doing legitimate trade. The toilet paper was a front, and they were just going to use me to set up an import-export business—a pack of Marlboros in Egypt cost like twenty cents, and all you had to do was get it to New York in a container filled with worthless toilet paper, then hustle the cigarettes in the city for a buck-fifty. There was a lot of money to be made. They were preying on my dreams of being a legitimate merchant, ha-ha.

Aside from these get-rich-quick schemes, all of which failed before they even got started, I was eating and drinking the entire time, of course, and traveling a lot, sleeping in the car the way we did when I was a kid. My mom set me up at a place in Umbria, a very fancy restaurant hotel. In my room there was a chef's jacket over the chair, and I thought, *Great, my mom told them I'd work*, and I was actually ready to go do whatever they needed me to do in the kitchen. It was a nice change from the smugglers. So I come down, and everyone salutes me as I walk into the kitchen. They're like, "*Ça va*, chef? *Buongiorno*, chef." And I'm like, "Huh?" I'm looking at them. They're looking at me. They want to know, "So what's today's special?" It was like an episode of *Fawlty Towers*—they thought I was the new chef. I had taken the wrong room, and the other guy hadn't shown up yet, and I was wearing his jacket. It took a few minutes to defuse that situation. I guess for a second I was thinking about just taking the job.

My mind was very open to everything, and I tried to absorb as much as I could. I knew what authentic Italian food was, I knew the difference between chanterelles and porcini (which weren't so common then), pappardelle and risotto, and the then-almost-unheard-of magic of balsamic vinegar. I was just building on the foundation laid between Queens and Felidia and all those trips we'd taken when I was a kid.

Wine culture was very different in Italy, though. Italians never looked at any wine list—that was for German and American tourists. Italians drank the "wine of the place." They generally don't fuss much over big important bottles of wine. But I realized that understanding the rare and expensive wines and the people who made them was how I would eventually make my living.

So I focused on the top-end wines and the names that I heard, because I knew that's where the money was to be made in New York, whether it be in a restaurant or retail. I learned those wines and met the people who made them and at the same time immersed myself in the world of hyperlocal consumption. Really, none of it was that fancy, just simple wines, simply served, with simple local food.

Getting back to New York was major culture shock. While in Italy I had lost all that post–Boston College preppiness, the crunch, the Deadhead tie-dye, left behind Wall Street and the pinstripe suits and gotten a little Euro, hitting the disco scene in Sardinia and the beaches of Rimini, running around with crazy Albanian prostitutes. There's a summertime Euro-disco vibe that happens in Italy and the rest of Europe. I was working it.

I came back at the beginning of '92, the year before Clinton came rushing into office with all that Fleetwood Mac–driven optimism. There was a bad real-estate recession at the time; I remember things were not great at Felidia, times were tough. And here I was coming back with the bright idea of opening my own restaurant. But starting a business in such a shitty market ended up being to my advantage. I was able to get a space at a great price, and I adapted these ideas that I had about food and wine from an intellectual and passionate level into something highly practical, to make sense in the business realm. If anything, I'm very much a marketer, and my strength is to take ideas of passion and purity and turn them into a sellable product. And that product at the time had to be something that could appeal to people in a major economic downturn yet still be a good deal when things turned around. Better, in fact.

Here was the pragmatism that my dad had taught me. I'm back to ground zero. I've left all the different phases in my life behind me. I'm done fucking around. The academics are over, the Wall Street stint is over, I proved I could do it and took a lot of lessons with me, and now I'm going to make money in food and wine. I'm going to *be here now*. I went back to my primal instincts and bought a 1978 Suburban—a 100 percent Restaurant Man–approved vehicle. I thought, *Where can I get the cheapest rent? Where do people have to eat?* The Theater District. People have to eat in the Theater District. I found a location and built the restaurant myself.

I was like Jeff Goldblum at the end of *The Fly*, when he is suddenly becoming more insect than human. He was turning into a monster. This is what was happening to me—I could no longer suppress it. This was my biological imperative.

The DNA of Restaurant Man had finally taken over.

Be afraid.

Be very afraid.

CHAPTER SIX

From Blue Nun to Barolo

When I first got back from Italy, I was crashing in a room upstairs from Felidia, in a storage closet, basically. This is what passed for my post-hippie, post–Wall Street bachelor pad—I'd pick up chicks and bring them back to the restaurant at 4:00 A.M. after the bars closed, open up the kitchen, make spaghetti puttanesca, put some prosciutto on the slicer, and try to get laid. And then the skies opened up, for real this time, and I met my future wife, Deanna. Maybe I should let her tell the story. . . .

"Joe was just back from his year in Italy. He was wearing black pants and a black turtleneck and chain-smoking, and mostly he was just happy to be back with his boys from Bayside. I was definitely not impressed. I got to know him slowly, and somewhat unintentionally. I kind of blew him off that New Year's Eve—I was with a bunch of friends, and one of them got too drunk and got thrown out of the bar where Joe and I were supposed to meet. A few nights later, we finally made plans to go to a movie alone, but after he picked me up (in his dad's car), he decided to change the plans and took me to his 'uncle's' restaurant instead—Angelo Vivolo's place—where of course we were treated like royalty. Now I was impressed.

"Later that month I took him up to Westchester, where my

family was celebrating my grandmother's birthday. I introduced him to my grandparents, and he spoke Italian to them, and they were really impressed by his knowledge of food and wine and how he understood them perfectly. On the way home, he pulled off the road unexpectedly and kissed me. It was love, all right. Now I just had to convince my parents he had a future. They didn't believe he was the wine buyer for Felidia, and they weren't exactly convinced that he was going to make it selling toilet paper in war-torn Yugoslavia."

It kills me to think that I was still considering the toilet-paper business when I first met her. I had an office, maybe I had a computer. Spent a lot of time making phone calls. I looked at a lot of toilet-paper samples. And for the record, I was not testing the toilet paper. I was looking for a volume product to send to the Balkans. Anyway, as anyone who has ever had to take a shit in Bosnia can tell you, they have a different way of thinking about toilet paper. It's not exactly Mr. Whipple's Finest over there.

But basically I was wasting time all day. Smoke cigarettes, drink coffee, wait for Deanna to come home from work. Go out to dinner, nurse my hangover on her couch, try to get Deanna to sleep with me, then mooch money off her. (See, I could have been a great musician.)

But it was time to get back to my inescapable destiny. I was twenty-three years old.

My grandmother was the first investor in Becco, my first restaurant. It was a pretty big leap of faith for her—there was no real business plan. We were at dinner at my mother's house, and I pretty much sat her down and told her, as best I could, what I wanted to do. She loaned me eighty thousand dollars to get started. "Spend it wisely, kiddo, because that's all you're going to get." She was doing all right, Grandma was. She'd been saving money her whole life, and when my uncle started working at IBM fifty years ago, he got her to buy stock in the company every year, and she became a big shot over at the International Business Machines Corporation. Who'da thunk it? Hard to think of her like that when she was walking around the yard in her bra watering her garden.

Drew Nieporent was the kind of restaurateur I wanted to be, someone I looked up to and wanted to emulate. Of course! He had the hip, cool restaurant in Tribeca. He was partners with Robert De Niro. But I was going to go a different route. Becco was never going to be trendy—it was going to be *consistent*. So what if people thought I had a schleppy Italian place in the cheesy Theater District? So what if Drew was getting movie stars and I was humping it out with Mary Schleneggen from Morristown and Bobby Lipshitz from Larchmont—they wanted to get to the theater and they didn't want to have to spend a lot to get a great meal and a great experience, and it worked. This is a lesson I learned early, and we stuck with it for all our restaurants—it's better to be lukewarm for twenty years than hot for six months.

Despite the economy, Broadway was still bustling—*Miss Saigon* had just opened and was pulling them in with that oversize hydraulic-helicopter gimmick—and there was no question those crazy theatergoers had to eat before all that excitement. A couple of years later when Becco was up and happening, *The Who's Tommy* was the big thing, and we used to hang out with Pete Townshend after the show at O'Flaherty's bar, shooting pool.

We were right in the heart of the action, on Forty-sixth Street, Restaurant Row, and I had managed to score a triple-net lease for three thousand dollars a month. But there was no real business plan—my plan was basically my truck, an out-of-work Mexican construction worker, and a Croatian sociopath named Davor. This was my team. We had no contractors; we did the whole job ourselves. We were taking over a space that was previously a barbecue joint called Caroline's that had been popular for about five minutes in the late eighties. It was a great room with a 1930s Deco bar imported from Paris for whatever restaurant had failed there before Caroline's fleeting moment came and went.

Davor was a character from my childhood—he used to hang out at the bar at Buonavia. He was a good-looking young guy, and he dated this Irish barfly who hung around there, a woman named Pat. She was a bit androgynous—they were a very strange couple; it was hard to see the chemistry. He helped me build the restaurant. Later, after I got married, he built an illegal porch on my house, which I almost got arrested for, building without the right permits. Even then I was trying to get away with doing things on the fly.

Making Becco out of a BBQ joint was no little feat—there was an old BBQ pit that had to be cut into pieces in order to take it out of there. I decided I was going to do it myself, so I rented my first blowtorch and had at it. I didn't know what the fuck I was doing— I cut the thing up but managed to start a fire in the process. I could have burned down the whole building, and the last thing I wanted to do was call the fire department. Somehow I managed to put it out myself with a garden hose. Of course, then the place was flooded and I had that problem to solve. Another time I was down in the old walk-in refrigerator. They used to have these wooden walk-ins— they were okay for beverages back then but not for food. I couldn't afford a new one, so I bought sheets of aluminum and was going to use those to line the insides of the wooden ones. I had all this industrial glue, and I was shut up in there, and at the time I was smoking three packs of Marlboros a day, drinking like twenty-two cups of espresso, and not really in the best shape to be working with highly toxic adhesive in a closed-off area. Anyway, the fumes overtook me. I passed out and started convulsing. Davor and the Mexican had to drag me out by my heels or I would have died.

But somehow it got done.

Becco was a wing-and-a-prayer project, and the whole concept had to be recession-proof. The idea was a fixed-price menu—antipasto and pasta, everyone eats the same thing. It was my interpretation of the communal table in Italy, but for the Theater District in Manhattan. So everyone had some grilled vegetables and a little shrimp and calamari, and then we had three pastas every day, maybe some butternut squash ravioli with toasted almond and pumpkin oil, and rigatoni in spicy tomato sauce with soft-braised cabbage and salcice picante, perhaps some risotto in sweet crab stock with moist lumps of lobster. We'd put them on platters, bring those to the table; they would all help themselves. We kept the food cost low and charged sixteen bucks for lunch, a bit more for dinner. It was the textbook example of another concept that we'd try to lean on for everything else we did—Keep It Simple, Stupid. (Although by the time we got to opening Del Posto, that idea had pretty much sailed right out the window. More on that later.)

Here was the real kicker: Along with the value concept of our menu, we had a couple hundred wines, all at fifteen bucks a bottle, including Barolos and Barbarescos, wines that were traditionally very expensive.

For years, growing up working at Felidia, I had always seen people reading the wine list from right to left—reading the price first, then figuring out what they would have *based solely on the price point,* which always struck me as contrary to the whole point of ordering wine. I thought, wouldn't it be great if we could eliminate price as a factor in choosing a bottle and make it incredibly affordable so they could concentrate on enjoying wine with their food, rather than its being this status symbol? With the wine at fifteen dollars a bottle, how could I miss? We took price away and made the wine a central part of the experience. It was no longer a nightmare to choose a bottle of wine. It was now a pleasant part of the trip.

The wines were all Italian, and they were selected regionally. They covered the whole map of Italy, they were interesting, they paired well with the food. I really sank my teeth into being the value-wine guy in the market. In a way the recession actually worked in our favor—in a bear market, people are desperate to sell. You can make deals, and we were very aggressive.

Becco math was based on "seventy-two bucks a case"—that's six dollars a bottle, and we sold each bottle for fifteen, a 40 percent cost, which isn't so bad. Usually in restaurants the rule is to charge for a glass what you paid for the bottle, and the bottle usually gets marked up three times. Of course six times three is eighteen, so we weren't making as much as we could, but the percentage still had integrity. And we thought we'd make it up in volume. You'd see this incredible list, how could you not buy a bottle? Or two? And it worked. People would order a bottle of white, then a bottle of red, and then they'd try another bottle of red. Consumption increased, and we got a lot of attention for this great, affordable list that was making good wine accessible to regular people without giving them sticker shock or stressing them out over the list. People loved it, and they kept coming back.

Before Felidia, New York had been drowning in a completely unevolved Italian-food scene. Wine options in the United States in the 1970s had been fairly limited—there were some knowledgeable people, of course, and French wines were largely revered, but what most people knew was Fazi Battaglia, Riunite Lambrusco, and the Pescevino in the bottle shaped like a fish, and of course the Chianti in the straw-covered bottles, maybe a cheap Valpolicella, some thick Carlo Rossi "Burgundy" in a jug, and Boone's Farm for the Frisbee tossers. Leisure-suit-wearing swingers drank Mateus with an air of faux sophistication (I remember they used to advertise that shit in upscale hi-fi magazines), and Blue Nun seemed to be the favorite of the drunken clergymen I'd see hovering around Times Square. The Italian wines were mostly very industrial, driven by government subsidies. They made a lot of it and flooded the market with it. It was mass marketing and all about volume—the more you produced, the more money you made, and since most people couldn't tell Montepulciano from motor oil, it didn't make a difference.

But by the time Felidia opened, there was a shift in the culture of Italian restaurants in America. And by the late eighties and early nineties, things were changing in Italy as well. People were getting away from industrial wines made by these huge companies and turning to the history of their own terroir and their own varietals, making wines that were more regionally significant, that had historic, real Old World value.

My mom was my partner. She was there, helping me with menu development, she helped me hire the chef. We were business partners, but she had the sensitivity to be there when I needed the help and let it be mine, on my own, when I didn't. It was that sensitivity that allowed me to create a project that was my own vision, one that I could feel good about and keep my independence. She definitely had her followers, and that didn't hurt. She knows the business, she's got names, contacts, she was on the verge of becoming a star, but she never tried to take over or dominate or pretend that we were one big happy family where she played at being a contrived Italian matriarch for marketing purposes. She is far too down-to-earth for that. It was practical—I was just a kid, and I had some idea of what I was doing, but mostly I was just busting my ass. Working there together, we realized that sometimes it was best if we weren't in the same restaurant at the same time, another lesson that would be invaluable later.

From a business and cultural point of view, the idea at Becco was to change the role of the restaurateur, to become an advocate for the customer as opposed to just being a tool of the food business. We were rejecting the corporate themes, and over time the trend we created became the standard.

We had two hundred wines on our list, 70 percent of them red, and we invented the concept of wine service in a very affordable setting that anyone could enjoy. Call the guy or gal who brings you the list whatever you like—the wine director, the sommelier, the wine rat—but this was the birth of smart wine. We distilled all the marketing and corporate bullshit out of wine selling and wine branding and got to the essence of finding the right wine and putting it on the table. This was wine for the people. It was much more ambitious than what my father was doing back at Buonavia, but it was still completely true to Restaurant Man's hard-core mentality. We were adding value without adding expense.

Eventually the wholesalers and the distributors saw the volume we were doing and the impact that this was having and they got behind it. We were buying closeouts and doing direct imports— everyone wanted to be part of the Becco wine program. It was the first time anyone had really done anything out of the box with a wine list. The standard then was still this absurd, giant, bound behemoth wrapped in plastic or God forbid, *pleather.* It was supposed to be like the Holy Bible—very intimidating. It thumped like a drunken rhinoceros when the waiter dropped it on the table. And it was useless. Page after page of pictures of pretty bottles, and all these wines listed without vintage. This was the absolute apex of nonintellectual, distributor-driven, supremely dumbed-down wine marketing. Our list was one of the first steps to helping customers get smart about choosing a bottle of wine and for the restaurants to stop looking down on customers as if they were easy marks. We wanted them to enjoy it, we wanted them to enjoy the entire experience.

We started buying wine for Becco before we opened in '92, and we got lucky—1990 turned out to be a benchmark vintage for Italian wine. At Becco we caught lightning in a bottle.

Now it is harder to find good wines to fit the price-point parameters, but we've become such a big player that we can still do it. It was fifteen dollars a bottle when we started, and twenty years later it's only twenty-five. When you confront business decisions, you have to stay true to what you believe is right. Really, it's just about being honest with what moves you. We knew that quality always paid dividends—whatever you're doing, it will pay off, exponentially. Always. Your customers will take care of it. Guaranteed.

Well, you can believe that if you want. That's what I want to believe, that's the way it should be, and we have been supremely fortunate, but I can remember some pretty sweaty moments at Becco when the cash flow wasn't going right. There was at least one time when the power was about to be shut off during dinner service and I had to come up with a check, stealing from Peter to pay Paul, getting caught in that bad circle of owing yourself money just to stay open, but we made it. Restaurant Man is made of some pretty stern stuff. I was making business decisions based on instinct, but I was buying everything myself, and you *know* I was being a cheap fuck—I was the one writing the checks.

Every day I'd get up, buy two packs of cigarettes and two cups of coffee—this was before Starbucks, so they were fifty cents each—and get into the Suburban and cruise the produce market for the loading-dock specials, which is produce that is one day bad, so they pretty much give it away. So we'd have pallets of asparagus and raspberries, and we'd have to pick through it to get to the good stuff, and it would be great, ripe and perfect, but it took a little bit of work. Then we'd see Fat Sal, who ran the broccoli rabe mafia; he was the only guy you could get it from, and you'd have to bring him coffee, light and sweet, and a cherry-cheese Danish every day for six months before he'd even talk to you. Then the fish market a few days a week. You have to pick out fish one by one. You have to know what a bad fish looks like—that's where the battle of margin begins—and you have to love the nervous energy you feel in your stomach when you get a good deal on a three-hundred-pound swordfish and you're taking it at four bucks a pound, and you have to know that even if you're selling fifty portions a day, you're going to just get through it before it goes bad, but you're going to make so much money on it. It's a risk-reward scenario, but it's all about getting good product and cutting a good deal and making your customers happy.

I saw Becco as this apocalyptic, I-gotta-make-it, end-of-days scenario, because I felt that if I failed, I'd roll off the cliff and into oblivion and poverty. This was my last chance at doing something with my life. It sounds extreme, but it was that black and white for me. It was also where the hard-core, blue-collar Restaurant Man had to grow up and become supermedia- and client-savvy, too. I'd spent so long with the construction boots and the buyer's jacket on, with the fishhooks at Fulton Street, building the restaurant from surplus I found in lumberyards and going to restaurant auctions and ripping out used restaurant equipment, and suddenly I was a guy putting on a suit and rescuing my Hermès ties from the back of the closet. "*Buona sera, signore.* Can I get you a drink?" That's what I did every night. Greeting every guest and seating every one of them personally. We were definitely a front-of-the-house-driven restaurant. My goal was to make every customer happy at all costs. Whatever it took. The Becco mantra expressed the enlightened version of Restaurant Man: Overdeliver, exceed expectations, every day.

Tableside service, which became the successful hallmark at Becco, was actually a very successful accident. We had a packed house one night—including Gael Greene. We were overwhelmed and didn't want to get into the weeds and screw everything up with such a heavyweight critic in the house. We couldn't plate the pastas fast enough in the kitchen, so we sent waiters out with the pasta pans and let them plate it at the table, just keep it moving, and that's how it got started. It was a total smash—everyone loved it. Where else could you get that kind of service at that price? Gael gave us a good review, although I think she was a little bit doubtful—maybe she thought that since I was my mother's son, somehow all this had been given to me. I was out of my mind working so hard, and I kind of resented that. These days she calls me for a table.

And then Bryan Miller at the *New York Times* gave us two stars. My first two-star *New York Times* review! Two stars is very good, three stars is nearly impossible to get, four stars is like a blessing from God. For Becco a two-star review was as good as I could ever have hoped for. Honestly, when Bryan came in, we totally jacked up his meal. I remember recognizing him, and we did everything we could within our power, including cooking every dish twice to make sure it was beyond criticism, making the portion size bigger, really laying it on thick. I waited on the table myself and made sure the check was low. Whatever I had to do to guarantee he had a great time. A lot of the guys who actually printed the *Times,* the print-run managers, ordered lunch at Becco, and that morning they brought the paper by, literally hot off the press. Ever pick up a paper while it's still warm and smells of ink? It's another wonderfully Old World thing in itself. And they gave me the original plates from the print run on that review. It was huge. Probably in today's terms Becco is a one-star restaurant, the rest of the world having caught up to us— but that review definitely set us on our way.

And then there was John Mariani, a food critic who was still important at the time. He berated me. I served him a red snapper I'd bought from Herbie Slavin, and John said it was the most rancid, disgusting piece of fish he'd ever had. He told me, right there, sitting at the table, looking up at me with laser beams for eyes, that he'd broken the head open and it stank of rotten fish and almost made him vomit. I felt all the air leave my lungs. I thought I was going to pass out. I was standing there, emasculated, in front of an entire dining room full of people. He just sliced my balls off, right there at tableside, and let me bleed from my crotch as his guests smirked and laughed on. That was our first meeting.

How did that red snapper get past the Young Restaurant Man? That son of a bitch Herbie Slavin must have had the best of me that morning. He probably pulled out one snapper, showed it to me on the hook, then swapped it for another fish. It was a bait and switch, literally and figuratively. That was typical frontline warfare at the old Fulton Fish Market. My idiot chef didn't notice it. He just cooked the fucking fish and served it to the food critic, who proceeded to take me down.

He made me feel that I had disgraced my entire hardworking immigrant family by serving him an inadequate snapper, and that my entire lineage of forefathers were rolling in their graves at this egregious error that I had committed. It was brutal. Since then pretty much everyone who's had to deal with him knows what a self-righteous, condescending prick he can be. When Mario and I opened Babbo, I was a little unsure how to handle Mariani—my dad told me, "John eats for free." But Mario set me straight. This was the kitchen talking to the front of the house: Fuck him, he pays. Everyone pays.

After I started making a couple of bucks, I decided that Deanna was indeed the woman of my dreams. This was December 1993, and I basically emptied the coffers at Becco, trucked down Forty-sixth Street to see my friend Howard Weisberg the Jewish Diamond Guy, and I bought a beautiful engagement ring that cost more money than I ever dreamed I'd have.

I proposed to Deanna on a Friday night in December, right in the middle of pre-theater dinner service.

At the time we were living above Becco, and Deanna was working during the week as an assistant buyer at Bloomingdale's and as a coat-check girl at Becco on the weekends. Coat-check girl is one of the best jobs you can have—you make a lot of dough for doing very little, and you're in with the boss, which comes with its own perks, even if you aren't fucking him. The coat-check girl knows everything. She's the first to arrive, last to leave. She's always near the bar, always near the boss. And you can tell what people are really about by their coats, don't doubt it for a second. She's not an on-the-books employee—you don't pay the coat-check girl, she pays you for the concession. She makes her deal directly with the house. The old way of doing things is she takes the first fifty and then everything from fifty up is split with the house. It's easy money. Or she guarantees you three or four hundred bucks a week and after that she keeps it all. Every deal is different. But you never have to buy information from her—she's not an official employee, she's clandestine, and she knows who's fucking whom and what everyone is doing. She knows who's coming in and who's going out. She's your girl.

The night I proposed to Deanna, we were fully booked. People were waiting to sit down. Packed. I had the ring in my pocket. I was going to take her on a trip to Cape Cod for the weekend, but I couldn't wait. The ring was burning a hole in my pocket. I was really gaga in love. During the pre-theater rush, I ran upstairs to our apartment—she was just getting back from Bloomingdale's—I dropped to one knee, proposed, gave her the ring, and then ran back downstairs to get everyone the fuck out by seven forty-five so they wouldn't be late for their show. My whole family was there waiting to celebrate with us, and when she came down, everyone applauded. There were tears, there was lots of backslapping, the whole Italian works. That night we went out to Sparks to celebrate.

My mother turned our wedding into a sort of industry event. She invited food and wine journalists, winemakers and restaurateurs from Italy, guest dignitaries, kitchen superstars. Five hundred and fifty people. My wife probably knew eight people at the wedding, not counting her family. The food was major—we did all the traditional stuff like baccalà, sauerkraut and pork, caviar, stuffed cabbage, Italian wedding-pillow pasta, octopus and potato salad. . . . Most affairs have one hour of hors d'oeuvres; we kept it on for three. We had wine made special for the wedding—five-liter bottles of Brunello with custom labels printed to commemorate the day. And then we gave everyone who came a bottle of the same Brunello as a gift. It was a little bit more of an industry event than I might have liked, but it was very cool, a lot of fun. People still talk about it.

And naturally we moved back to Queens. Where else was I going to go? Down the block from my mother's house, which was kind of a mistake. It's another one of those things I can't really explain; after years spent trying to bust loose I was right back where I'd started. Maybe I shouldn't be ripping on the guys I knew in college who wound up becoming their parents? Whatever. I'm still not selling insurance. But it just seemed like the right thing to do.

We bought a nice house, but we'd go to my mother's house to eat all the time. It was a little weird for Deanna, but seriously, if Lidia Bastianich wanted to cook for you, you'd go, right? And then my father would show up on a Saturday morning, in his underwear, playing the accordion. And he wasn't shitfaced or anything like that, it was just that kind of neighborhood. My father would be walking around in his bathrobe singing these goopy Istrian love ballads, and meanwhile there would be six police cruisers parked outside my grandmother's house. The first time I saw that, I freaked the fuck out—"Oh, my God, what happened?"—and ran inside, where she's got all these cops sitting at her kitchen table, including some of the top brass in Queens, and she's making them espresso and giving them tips on how to farm radicchio and tomatoes in their backyards. Yeah, I was back into it, all right. There was no escape.

●

CHAPTER SEVEN

Don't You Know?
Busboys Run the Show.

R unning a restaurant isn't just about making the food. You have an entire army of people working for you who have nothing to do with food prep or cooking, but they're the people whom the customer is most likely to come into contact with, the people who at the end of the day are going to make the place sing or make it crash no matter how good the stuff coming out of the kitchen is. If Restaurant Man only cared about the fancy-pants chef, he would be out of business before he even got started.

The lowest man on the totem pole in any restaurant is the dishwasher. It's *mucho trabajo, poco dinero.* And dishwashers take a lot of shit. *Saca la caca.* They start on pots and pans. That's the bottom of the barrel, worse than dishes and plates—they have to scrub the pots and deal with the cooks who rush them—"We need the fucking pots back, Chachi"—who are all drunk lunatics, throwing hot pans at the dishwasher, under a lot of pressure. So pot washer is at the bottom—for a guy who's just off the bus, it's where he cuts his teeth. When he gets promoted to dishes and plates, at least he's dealing with busboys, and he can call them names—*Maricón! Te gusta la pinga?* There's a lot of fag joking going on in a kitchen.

That's going to happen in any male-dominated locker-room-like situation. There's a lot of that between the guys in the kitchen and the management, too, but you really have to strike the right balance, because these guys are generally very hardworking and you need to let them know how valuable they are to the team. Mexicans probably work the hardest, but the Ecuadoreans and Peruvians have more culinary aptitude—except, of course, for Mexicans from Puebla. Puebla is the one place you could always pull a good Mexican cook out of. The first thing you do when you interview your dishwasher is ask him where he's from. The ones from Puebla can cook. All of them. I don't know what the fuck goes on in Puebla, I've never been there, but everyone who comes from there can cook like a motherfucker. You can get them out of the sink and off the pots and put them right on the line.

Otherwise, from dishwasher a guy can move up to clean the restaurant and become a porter, which is really the head dishwasher, but it's a nicer title. The chief porter is the key job—not only is he in charge of cleaning the whole restaurant overnight, he accepts your merch. If you don't have the right guy, that's the weak link in the chain—he's the guy who's got the scale in the front and checks everything in, and therefore you have to hire carefully. He has to be incorruptible. So pot scrubber, dishwasher, restaurant cleaner, porter. That's kind of the hierarchy. And in our restaurants you can absolutely move up the chain. At the point when you're cleaning the restaurant, either you aspire to become a porter or you go to the front of the house and become a busboy.

Busboys are like the blood of a restaurant. With a good team of busboys, you can take over a small city. Busboys really run the place—they do most of the work in the front of the house. They clean the front of the house, they clean the tables, they deal with all the shit that waiters don't want to do. The old axiom is that busboys work for you, waiters work for themselves. Busboys love Restaurant

Man, because Restaurant Man allows them to enter the world of tips. That's where life changes. Imagine if all of a sudden someone decides to double your salary—"Okay, kid, tomorrow you're making twice as much money as you made yesterday." That's pretty good. Workaday, uninspired waiters hate Restaurant Man, because they see him as the oppressor and they see the job of being a waiter as something to pay the bills while they pursue whatever other things they think they're going to be successful at. Sing, dance, be a chorus boy—they wait tables while they're failing at their art. Professional waiters are generally overeducated, artistically deprived, bitter people who feel that every dollar they earn is blood money, and they resent being there.

But the better example of the waiter is the person who truly wants to work in one of our restaurants. My thing with waiters is that I want to keep them here in the restaurant working for the shortest time possible so they don't burn out, I want them to make as much money as possible, and I want to educate them as much as I can. The waiter is my voice when he speaks to my customers. He communicates what our philosophy is, what our menu offerings are. He's the interpreter for the back of the house, which is the production engine. He's the orchestrator of the meal. He's the conductor. And it's the waiter's job to take the experience and customize it for each consumer. What a waiter does is curate: A restaurant has the capacity to produce a fantastic experience, and the waiter's job is to take that experience and custom-fit it for every person who comes in to spend money with us. Nothing is taken for granted.

The waiter is the intermediary in the battle that goes on every night between the front of the house and the kitchen. It's classic—Mario and I live it each day. It is epic, and it will never change. His world is a world of black and white. Right and wrong. Good or bad. Rotten or fresh. The world of the front of the house, with customers, is entirely gray. There's no clear right, there's no wrong. The customer is right, the kitchen is wrong, the kitchen is right, the customer is wrong. Everything is subject to interpretation and perception. This is the classic battle of all restaurants—the mentality of Restaurant Man versus The Kitchen, and the waiter can easily get caught in no-man's-land.

I think it says a lot that our waiters stick around—we create a positive work environment. It is a good job, with benefits, and you can learn a truckload if you're tuned in. Many of the people who get hired as waitrons are very passionate about food and wine and probably very good cooks in their own right, or aficionados who can see it as an academic pursuit leading to the next level of food consciousness, and that is no shit. Work at Babbo or Lupa for six months and you will leave having seen things few others could even imagine.

What we're really looking for, simply, is people who enjoy giving other people pleasure. Once you have that, that's the skill set you need to be a great waiter. If you have a passion for learning about food and wine, even better. Everything else we can teach you. To get the gig, you have to have carried a plate before, but I'll forgo experience any day for someone who is willing to learn, listen, and get satisfaction and joy out of creating a memorable experience for the customer. That's the most fundamental quality a great waiter needs to have.

We're also conscious of creating a situation where waiters can pursue their other aspirations, encouraging them to stay with us as long as they can, so if they fail at their singing career, they'll still dig working for us, and they become part of our family. The restaurant in its purest sense is truly a family. We have waiters at Becco who've been there for twenty years, since the opening. Jason Denton—who is our partner and now owns eight restaurants—was a waiter at Po working for Mario. That's how he started. We always take care of the people we like.

And then there is the bartender. He's like the bunk sergeant of the waiters—when you come into a restaurant, you always assume that the bartender knows something more than the waiters do. He's a stud. Usually it's a job that makes more money. Depends on the restaurant, but in our restaurants the bartenders handle the cash. They handle the booze. They decide who is going to get drunk and who isn't. They really need to be your ally, because there are so many things that they can control, including the spirit or philosophy of the restaurant, even when they're just bullshitting with customers.

Babbo was where we launched the bar-dining craze, so the bartender position at Babbo was always the key thing, and then it went over to Lupa and onward. Bartenders became almost a hybrid management position. In many ways they are the figurehead of the restaurant. So you always want to pay special attention to your bartenders. You want hot-looking guys, good-looking girls with a nice set of tits, you know. It's a tricky thing, because it's not cool to talk about how attractive your staff is, but it's a reality. There's a lot of that in the restaurant business.

Hostesses are functionary. There's no magic power. They're usually college students. We've had a lot of hostesses who have gone on to greatness in our company, running wine divisions and becoming general managers, but generally the hostess is a pretty blah position. It's an hourly gig for a pretty girl, but she can turn it into an opportunity if she knows how to hustle a little bit.

Service director is one of those catchall phrases—basically it's the guy who makes sure that everyone plays nice. He's like the playground cop. He's on the floor, he kind of acts as a manager. He makes sure that the standards of the restaurant are kept up, hiring the right people and seeing to it that they're trained properly, ensuring that the level of hospitality and technical service is everything it should be. He sees that the restaurant is set up correctly, that waiters know the menu and the wines, that everything happens in the way that it's supposed to happen. A lot of service managers are promoted from their gigs as waiters.

Entry-level manager is someone just out of restaurant school. It's a weird thing, because even though a waiter makes two or three times as much as the manager, the manager is his boss. But if a waiter's acting career doesn't pan out or if he doesn't become a rock star and he figures out he's got to make a living in the restaurant industry and doesn't want to be the waiter whore for the rest of his life, he has to step into management, and that's the great injustice. The managers work harder than the waiters, sometimes for half the pay—but if you're a manager or a service director, you're supposed to be a career guy. You're supposed to work for the house, investing in a career, taking a salary. You're not a tip employee. It's a whole different trajectory.

Now we come to the wine director and the sommelier. A wine director would be in a restaurant where there is more than one wine person, so the sommeliers work for the wine director. The wine director is responsible for writing the wine lists, buying the wines, figuring out which wines are going to work by the glass, working with the bartenders on the liquor, and ensuring the wine quality and service in the restaurant. Wine director is more of a management position than the jobs of the sommeliers and wine waiters who work for them on the floor, opening bottles and making recommendations.

Usually people on the wine trajectory have a specific passion for wine. Some are ex-waiters, some are people who just happen to fall into the wine world. It's a lot of work for low pay, but it is tailor-made for people who love wine. You get to live in the world of wine. There are plenty of perks—you go to a lot of tastings and meet a lot of rich people. Wine is that great social oscillator that can drag you down to the bottom level and maybe give you a quick rise to the top.

I've seen many people through the years take the wine ride to the top very quickly.

To be the wine guy—or gal, I shouldn't have to say it, but obviously there is no job in the joint, including Restaurant Man, that is somehow gender-specific—you need to be a good taster, and you can't fake it. Do not give me any of this medium-body, fruit-forward bullshit if you expect to work for me. If you talk like that, I don't even want you *eating* at one of my places. Seriously—if I invite someone to taste wines with me and ask about his or her perceptions, I can tell if that person is a good taster. If I'm going to hire a wine director or sommelier, I am definitely going to taste with any potential candidates and have them talk to me about the wines. It tells me a lot.

In my places, wine directors are especially important, because wine is so important to our brand, and each of our restaurants has a stylistic direction for its wine service. Lupa focuses on wines mostly between forty and fifty-five dollars a bottle. Not the grand terroirs, not Barolo, Barbaresco, or Brunello—more labels from Mezzogiorno, Lazio, Campania, Abruzzo, or Sardinia, wines that are appropriate for the kind of food served at a trattoria. Babbo is more about full coverage, every wine from every region, with deep vintages of grand cru wines, Barolo, Barbaresco, and at a much higher price point to categorically cover Italy. But within that list, Babbo is also about offering a lot of good deals. You can pick gems out of the list at Babbo. We haven't always updated the pricing, and the price of wine has gone up astronomically in the last ten years. If you really know what you are doing, you can make a big score.

And of course I have my own wines on the list, and the members of our wine staff are the de facto representatives. Our wines get positioned front and center. We use the restaurants to position and promote them, and the wines are great. They're totally appropriate for the experience we create in the restaurants, and they're not very expensive. But I've never, for the sake of selling more of my wine, sacrificed the integrity, the intellectuality of a wine program, and you can see that in every restaurant you go to.

If you ask the sommelier for a recommendation, he might start with one of my wines, but it depends on the individual's personality. It varies. Sommeliers are as guilty of ego and bravado as anyone else—sometimes the wines they recommend have to be wines they have found and they take ownership of. They may perceive my wines as being the wines of the Restaurant Man, their corporate master, so they rebel. There are all sorts of different scenarios. But most intelligent wine people will understand that promoting the wines is part of the job, and why not? If you thought my wines sucked, you shouldn't have taken the job as a wine director. It's kind of cut-and-dried that way. The sommelier carries the flag, so it's kind of a representation of me personally and my reputation in the market. The wine world is a small world. It's old school—you have to teach these young people who just got into the game to respect their elders, not act like punks, shut the fuck up if they don't know what they're talking about, behave intelligently, act on behalf of the restaurant and the economics of the restaurant, check their ego at the door, and not be a schmuck.

Selling wine is all about sizing people up, and it takes a certain amount of chutzpah. The tableside bottle sell is a very funny thing—you take a look at the guy's blazer, what kind of shoes he's wearing, what kind of broad he's with. Is he trying to be a hero? Is he a cheap fuck? Who does he want to impress? Maybe he wants it to seem like he's spending a lot but he's actually cheap, or maybe he actually wants to spend a lot of money but doesn't give a shit what he's drinking. Does he need to impress the table? Is he a boss, is he a date, is he fucking around on his wife? There's all sorts of variables you have to size up, because these people have come here to part with their money and your job is to take it and turn it into a great experience for them.

So now you're the customer. You're fortyish with a pretty girl your age, sharing the first two plates and having separate entrées—that's pretty good. I'm guessing based on the way you dressed—you bothered to put on a jacket, but obviously you don't do that every night; you're trying to impress your date—I'm going to get you for a couple glasses of sparkling wine or a cocktail in the beginning and maybe two white quartinos. Split them between you with the app. Maybe a heavier white wine going into your first plate of pasta, and then I have you marked for something solid but not too insanely expensive, maybe a Barbera in the eighty-, eighty-five-dollar range, but if I'm feeling it, I'll upsell you to a Barbaresco for a hundred twenty-five. But I will never rip you off—that would be suicide. You need to leave singing, "Holy shit, I never knew that a two-hundred-fifty-dollar bottle of Barolo could bring me that much sheer fucking joy!" And then you'll come back and do it again.

The general manager is kind of like the step into darkness when you reach the top of the league. As GM, you're responsible for everything, including the maître d's and the sommeliers—all these people who have their own agendas. But you probably make less than the maître d' and have a lot more work and a lot more headaches.

It's a career job. You go to restaurant school and the school of hard knocks, but you do the job because you know it's going to bring you other stuff in the future—career, security. It's for people who are tipping off the end of the industry and trying to make it to someplace else. The GM winds up opening his own place or being a manager for big companies opening *their* own restaurants.

The paradigm of pay versus work, headache, and responsibility kind of goes off the charts with general managers, because often they don't balance. Being general manager is like being the de facto owner. It's like wearing the crown of Restaurant Man without *being* Restaurant Man. You're trying to run the business, but you're running the ranch without riding the big horse. You're in that weird position where you have the responsibility—and the liability for all the performance—but you don't own it. It's a tricky job, and usually thankless. If you're going to be a general manager, you try to take a step up into the next world or the next reality, but it's tough.

In a funny way, the maître d' is the most important and the least important position in the restaurant. Maître d's are at the financial spigot of the restaurant, meaning they control who gets in and who doesn't, but aside from that they don't do anything. And yet they get paid as much as the highest-paid people in the place.

Maître d's make the big salaries, because unless you yourself as the owner are going to be at the door, your maître d' is the face of the restaurant, and choosing one is a big decision. But he is definitely not Restaurant Man. In fact, there is always a lot of tension between Restaurant Man and the maître d', because the maître d' has his own agenda. Usually he's kind of a semifabulous person who thinks he's hot shit and has his own thing going on, and eventually his psychosis will expand until he believes that people come to the restaurant to see him. But that's not true. The people come to the restaurant to see Restaurant Man.

The skills of a maître d' are the same skills a hooker has—to please the clients. Make them come. Make them feel like they're the only one. Extract as much money as you can.

Maître d's are all on the take. They get paid a salary, but then there's the palm variable. A fifty-dollar bill might get you noticed. Depending on the restaurant, they might even take a twenty. For an Upper East Side rip-off joint or a busy midtown steakhouse a hundie should get you in the game, but it's just as likely that if they don't know you, they're going to think you're a douchebag. It's not about the cash flash, it's all about the implicit value of your relationship. People send thank-you notes to the maître d'—not even thank-you notes but cash-value surrender trade. Before and after. It's an ongoing relationship.

John at Babbo has been there pretty much since day one. He's the guy in New York that everyone loves to hate, but if we didn't love him, he wouldn't have been there all these years. He could have this gig for fucking ever—in the world of New York restaurants, twenty-year employees are a rarity. He's a classic New York story. Love him, hate him, buy your way into his heart, or tickle his Prince Henry—however you can figure out a way to get into his good graces, do it—because unless I'm there or Mario is there and we're feeling generous, at the end of the day he's the one who decides whether you sit or not.

I micromanage him. I stay on him and keep him pure. He's selling real estate, and I know he's on the take, it's part of the job description—if he weren't, something would be wrong. Say my sister-in-law wants to come in with a four-top at eight, and it's full, and he thinks he's going to sell that table for a hundred bucks. You know what? Fuck you, not if it's full. When there are no more tables, there are no more tables, for anyone in the world. That's my struggle with the maître d'.

The other side of it is that there is always a table for Bill Clinton. Some people might wait a little bit, but it'll all be good. There's a lot of fungibility in our world. Once in a while, you bump somebody or walk them to the next restaurant. Or you make them wait—the first thing you do is placate them with a glass of cheap bubbles. An extreme example is when you end up buying them dinner, and you know how Restaurant Man feels about that.

The maître d' and the coat-check girl are the closest to each other in terms of being in control of their own gigs—they don't work for you, they have inventory that they sell. The agenda is, you get a base salary to keep the restaurant full and run the book, but they feel it's their right to sell and trade. So they make money on your back, all the time. The skill set is definitely knowing who matters in New York, how to prioritize the people who come to the door, and how to kiss the boss's ass properly. He's got the hot seat between the customer and the boss; this is his own little world, that seesaw right there, which is his balancing act, the place where he makes out extra big. And that's the maître d'—they're the biggest prostitutes in the business. About half the time, our interests are aligned, when the customer is truly fabulous, one of those people you want in that room, but more often than not you have to allow the maître d' a bit of latitude. He's the guy you're paying to do the job you would do if you were lucky enough to be in your own restaurant all the time. You want to hate him, but you couldn't do it without him.

I think it speaks well of Mario and me that we have a very low turnover in a business famous for going through more bodies than Charles Bronson and George Romero combined. We try to be good employers, we've always offered health insurance, we always try to be fair. We have our moments—we're passionate Italian men—but I think if you look around, you're going to find very few people in this industry who've had the kind of growth that we have. We've made partners out of employees. We've very rarely had those situations backfire—although today we almost had a "Waverly."

A Waverly is when we whack someone. If Mario or I ask you to have a cup of coffee at the Waverly Restaurant, a diner near Babbo, don't go, because you won't come back. Today it was a guy who had been with one of our restaurants for about ten years and was now in a management position, hiring people. He would find ten great people—sommeliers, managers—interview them, and they would accept the job, and then they wouldn't come to work. Or they would come to work for one day and never come back. And we were like, what the fuck's the problem? I think what was lacking was charisma; he just couldn't convey it to the people he wanted to hire. A job is not always only about the salary position. You have to be inspired by the aura and energy of the person you'll be working for, and if that person doesn't impart those qualities right at the beginning, then people might just find another job or go in another direction. This is a very good guy, intelligent and smart, customer-focused—just not inspiring. Not evolutionary. I don't think we're going to fire him, maybe just move him along to a different job. But we had an interview with someone who worked under him, and this person extolled so many of his virtues that now we are rethinking it. We value good people and all we really want is for it to work.

But if I had to, if it came to that, I would fire him and I wouldn't lose any sleep. It doesn't make me happy. I used to get very upset to have to fire people, but I learned a long time ago—and this is something my mother told me—that when you're firing someone, you have to look at it not as if you're eliminating someone's job, you're securing and enforcing the position of everyone else in that restaurant. Your average restaurant has 80 employees, and 3 people live off the salary of each employee—that's 240 people who exist because of the economic reality generated at one restaurant. And once an employee gets in the way of maintaining the vibrancy of that reality, then that single person is jeopardizing every one of those people's worlds. Think about it that way, then it's easy. Sit down at the table and say, "Your performance is jeopardizing the well-being of the restaurant and everyone who makes a living off it. You have to find something else to do."

•

CHAPTER EIGHT

Babbo: Primi

I had been hearing about this guy, Mario Batali. Ours was kind of a small world, and I knew that he'd been living in Italy around the same time I was, in a little town south of Bologna, and then gone on to be something of a hotshot chef on the West Coast before going back to Italy, kind of like I had, to get himself sorted.

He opened Po in 1993, which is what put him front and center. He borrowed twenty-five grand from a few friends, including his wife, who was still his girlfriend then, and he and this guy named Steve Crane opened up on Cornelia Street. He was the chef, and Steve was the front-of-the-house guy. It had thirty-four seats, and it was always busy—he was cranking his take on Italian food and earning a very loyal following.

Mario was a pioneer of cooking with an unapologetically Italian sensibility, even if the food was something out of his own fucked-up brain. He was fierce in not diluting the real spirit of Italy. His strength is being this interpreter of the authentic. Not an imitator but a very inspired, strong interpreter of the experience and making it stand out in the New York restaurant scene.

Po was a three-man operation, and it was always packed. The waiters there made like six hundred dollars a night. It was quite a machine. I was at Becco—I had the midtown Theater District restaurant that was kind of square, and he had the hipper, downtown West Village restaurant that cool people went to. I was a little bit jealous of that.

I didn't go to Po until after I'd met him, which was another *shidduch* (as my Jewish friends would say) made by my matchmaking Italian yenta of a mother. She was coordinating the James Beard Foundation Journalism Awards dinner, with the theme of Italian cuisine. She called Mario to curate the culinary side and to bring in the new chefs, the young guns, the up-and-comers who were challenging the old guard, and she asked me to work on the wine side and bring in some young wine punks to make the mix. So we met at this awards dinner and became fast friends, fucking around, getting stoned, acting like hooligans. Neither of us was married yet, and we still owned the night. We'd go out to eat all the time—after I finished up at Becco, I'd go down to Cornelia Street, and we'd hang out in front of Po and polish off a couple bottles of white wine outside on a bench, shoot the breeze with the neighbors, give the drug dealers a hard time, and head out for dinner.

We were always checking out what the new restaurant was. We'd philosophize a lot. We'd go out, critique other restaurants, study the menus like a couple of forensic scientists. Most of those places from the early nineties are probably long gone, but I remember that Jean Claude was big. Odeon. There was a restaurant called Boom. It was very early on in the new restaurant scene, and things weren't really even that chef-driven yet. We leaned on the classic steak joints—we went to the Old Homestead, Sparks, Frank's. But more often than not, we'd head to Blue Ribbon at, like, two or three in the morning. We met Bobby Flay there, and Tom Colicchio when he still had hair—there aren't that many of the gang who were around then that are still doing it. We used to sit around eating until five. An assortment of strippers would roll in after work, and we'd hang out and drink with them, maybe end up in an after-hours club. This was Restaurant Man spreading his wings.

I felt like part of the club. I had a successful restaurant that paid the bills. I had enough money to do whatever I wanted—travel a little bit, take my girlfriend to Paris. I was living in Fat City, and Deanna was definitely on board. She had to be. There was no choice, even after we got married. That's who I was. The funny thing is, she's not a big eater—but she humored me. I was still smoking three packs of cigarettes a day, something she put an end to the very instant our first kid was born, but back in the day we'd drink three bottles of wine. Well, she'd have half a glass and I'd mop up the rest.

Mario was totally irreverent in his style, kind of a hippie like me, but a lot farther out than I was willing to go. He was from Seattle but had gone to school at Rutgers in New Jersey. He used to wear a robe and genie shoes, and he worked at a place called Stuff Yer Face Pizza. He wasn't wearing the clogs yet, but always the shorts. That was his signature—cargo shorts and sneakers. By then I had eased into some kind of post-bachelor urban-contemporary bon vivant. Mostly I looked as if I owned a successful restaurant. Mario looked like he was on his way to a Phish concert. We made a good pair.

One night we were coming from dinner somewhere and were walking down Waverly Place in Greenwich Village, by Washington Square Park, and we saw the old Coach House restaurant all boarded up with a big For Rent sign.

We were just having fun, not really planning on opening a restaurant, but somehow we got the inspiration to start what we thought would be the perfect restaurant, where we would have no economic ambitions and just kind of fulfill the pure aspiration of creating the ideal environment for eating and drinking and expressing our passion for Italy and all things Italian. You can bet that Restaurant Man has a few in him when he starts thinking like this. And that was the birth of Babbo Ristorante e Enoteca.

We didn't need to make money, we were flush—both of our restaurants, Becco and Po, were doing better than we could have dreamed—and so suddenly there was a purity of spirit and ideas, a freedom, almost an irreverence toward what was standard or expected. Sometimes the greatest commerce comes from a lack of commerce, we declared, contrary to every truism that Restaurant Man has ever preached or lived by. We didn't exactly have our feet planted too firmly when we got to blue-skying this fantasy—we were just thinking about this great new idea for an Italian restaurant, wine and food in the perfect setting, and the Coach House was calling our names. We were convinced that if we were thinking about money while we were jamming ideas, then we would have been doomed. When you're trying so hard to get rich, we reasoned, you forget that humanity and imagination are the key ingredients, and then you're pretty sure to fail. True or not, this was a pure manifestation of ourselves, an ideal expression of who we were. We were putting our life experience into a living, breathing restaurant.

We called the number on the For Rent sign and met with this guy Hassan, who was like the sultan of Albanian-Muslim restaurant slumlords in New York—he wore tracksuits and had a fucking scimitar hanging on his wall, and this is where we learned another important lesson in the New York restaurant business: Every restaurant opens based on a real-estate deal. Eventually we'd open places just because we could get the location, before we even had a concept. When it comes to you, you don't say no. Like George Costanza and parking spaces. You see it, you take it, because it's not apt to happen again. Not only did we get the lease, but we were able to sneak in this option-to-buy-the-building clause, because Hassan thought we were just a couple of mooks, doomed to fail, who were never going to have the money to close the deal, so he put it in there at a fixed price. A few years later, we bought it. He should have taken us more seriously—by putting in that option, he had left a few million dollars on the table.

When we first walked into the building it was still the old Coach House—creepy cool in that spooky Dickensian kind of way, where nothing has been touched for years, and it looked as if the Ghosts of Christmas Past were having a party. The tables were still set with glasses and silverware when we walked in—there was everything except the food. The cast-iron pans that they'd used to make their famous corn sticks were hanging on the wall ready for another big night. There were brass chandeliers, red banquettes, an old-school cash-register stand with toothpicks and mints, and a clunky six-line telephone. The number was SPring 7-0303. Still is. Classic New York.

This was like stepping back in time with Leon Lianides, the legendary owner of the Coach House and a charter member of the Restaurant Man Hall of Fame. He was like a mythical figure in New York restaurants—he had opened in the 1940s, and James Beard himself was one of his biggest fans. He had fallen ill and retired, and when the business started coming apart, he got rid of the restaurant. But there was still money in the register, and in the locker room there were all these white jackets hung up ready for the next shift— they employed only black waiters, and they all wore white with black bow ties. It was like *that*.

We didn't have a huge budget, but we decided to gut the joint, put in a new kitchen, and give it our take on a very hallowed space. Once upon a time, this had been the Wanamaker carriage house, before it was a restaurant. When we tore up the floorboards, there was hay and horse shit under there.

We did what we considered a respectful and modest but elegant restoration, cleaning it up to what we thought it could be without losing what it had been. We built a grand bar, which the Coach House never had. We wanted it to be an eating bar, which was going to be a big part of Babbo. In retrospect Babbo pretty much launched the trend of eating bars in good restaurants—you see that everywhere now.

As we got into it, the conflict of Restaurant Man—putting art before commerce—became a little bit scary, never mind the concept itself, this crazy idea to reimagine Italian food.

It's not that I didn't believe in Mario, but I was kind of caught in the middle. I was brought up to do traditional Italian food, and my mother was always telling me to be careful, don't let this guy go too crazy. Stick to what you know. Make sure the dishes are authentic. And Mario was cooking all this shit that he was just kind of coming up with out of nowhere.

I knew he was a good cook and a real personality, but we'd never worked together. We had very different ways and styles of looking at things. He was coming up with these Beef Cheek Ravioli and the Calamari Sicilian Lifeguard Style. There was no fucking Sicilian lifeguard—he was just like, "Hey, how do you suppose a Sicilian lifeguard would make calamari?" And then he did it. I didn't quite know what to make of it all. I was panicked, because right in that moment of pressure and being out in the public eye, I was kind of reverting to what I knew, which was really classic, traditional food. Mario was spinning that food and that tradition into something new. He was right, of course, and it launched our complete evolution of ideas. We never accepted anything just because that's the way it was done. Everything from serving wine in quartinos to our dining-room presentation—French service, crumbing tables with spoons, and Led Zeppelin roaring on the stereo.

The quartino is one of those things that I took with me from Italy. My grandfather was a famous drinker—they would call him "Quarticci" because he would go down to the osteria and order quartos of wine all day long. But the philosophy here is to combine the circumstance and service of wine by the bottle with the attractive price and consumption of wine by the glass—and it was revolutionary.

With the glass of wine, the problem is always how much wine do you put in? Is there too much wine? Too little wine? Should I have another glass . . . ? A quartino is a third of the bottle. It's a fixed amount of wine, and it comes in a separate vessel—a mini-decanter—so you can manipulate how much wine you want in your glass at any time, and it gives you the opportunity to try a couple different things, maybe move from white to red, without a big commitment. It's the pomp and circumstance of wine-by-the-bottle service in wine-by-the-glass consumption. It's the best of both worlds. Now you see it everywhere. We do it in all our restaurants except Del Posto.

At Babbo each dish grew out of a conversation, trying to put something forth that was new and different. It was a combination of culinary adventurism and the dining-room experience with respect for the classic but with an eye toward innovation.

And it was about eating locally, whether produce or fish or meat. An Italian chef in Venice would never cook with shrimp from the Gulf of Naples. It was taking that sensibility and applying it to New York, the United States, the Hudson Valley region. Using the great techniques and condiments of Italy but with the bounty of local agriculture and the focus on locality. We were the first to do it in a very Italian way. Waste not, want not. Living a sustainable lifestyle seems to be such an of-the-moment idea, but it's really not—it's a tradition of people who have had to struggle in life for food or for

sustenance. That's the way people lived. Just talk to my g
mother. She's been living sustainably since 1921.

The menu is the document that drives the business, that brings
home the spirit of the restaurant. It is the most important document
in our lives.

Caesar salad, salmon, and tiramisù are like the paradigm of
menu planning—they're in the DNA of most people who are going
to go into a fine-dining experience. Not very imaginative, but Americans are just hardwired that way, and every time you deviate from
that, you are moving them out of their comfort zone. You are asking
them to indulge *your* whim. And in the bigger picture, that's what
every menu is about. It creates a structure for the meal, on your
terms. It's like the operator's manual for a good time, so even if you
are one of the jabronis who just wants to have the same old thing,
you can read it and be inspired to taste and experience foods outside your world, which is the only way we succeed.

The menu is the Rosetta stone of the restaurant. It is Restaurant
Man's Constitution, Declaration of Independence, and Magna Fucking Carta. It says so much. It tells you the personality of the people
who created it and will give you the first clue that the restaurant
you're about to eat in sucks—if there are misspellings on the menu,
how much do you think the people who created it really care? It's
an important document and should be created with respect. If the
menu looks bad and has mistakes on it, get the fuck out. The menu
should be part of the entertainment, part of the dining experience.
It's kind of like reading the *Playbill* when you go to the theater. It
should be an alluring and engaging document. Does it have burn
marks on it from the candle? If you ever get a greasy menu with food
stains on it, it's time to run like hell.

The menu also clearly states your financial commitment—as a

customer, you look at a menu that has twelve- to twenty-five-dollar apps and twenty-two- to thirty-two-dollar entrées, and depending on what you drink, you basically know you're in for a meal that will run from fifty to seventy-five dollars, and you need to be comfortable with that.

I think a lot of people overlook the importance of the menu as a marketing tool and a way of communicating to the customer what the ambition of their restaurant is. Not only the typeface and the design, but what is it printed on? Is it cheap-looking? Is it the right kind of paper for that restaurant? Is it in a nice leather binder . . . or fucking *pleather*?

The greatest menu of all time was the Sparks Steak House menu, which we have interpreted and knocked off pretty successfully at Carnevino in Las Vegas. It was basically all the food—entrées, apps, steaks, salads—listed on the front page of a giant piece of cardboard about two feet tall and a foot and a half wide, a four-fold, and then three pages of wine. It was very straightforward, but it led you to believe that you needed to spend money. The Sparks menu was epic. I have one framed—I wish I had a signed one. It spoke of the power of the experience and was completely appropriate for the place. It reflected the personality of the boss, Pat Cetta, in a real way. He had a thousand wines on there. It was the greatest wine list in New York in its time, with incredible values and vintages. Pat taught me how to use wine to drive the business and that investing in the wine list and being thoughtful about it would bring a huge return—he was a mentor to me. He used to call me "lover" while he groped my date. "Hey, lover, let's have a bottle of something sweet," which was code for "let's slam a split of d'Yquem."

We made a miniature version of the Sparks menu when we opened Otto. We wanted to put the wine list in everyone's hands, because some people don't look at the wine list. It started at Becco when we invented the fifteen-dollar wine list—a hundred wines, all of them on the menu. Babbo has a separate wine list, which is part of the experience there, but at Otto and Carnevino the wine list is part of the menu document. When you're dedicating 25 percent of the printable real estate on your menu to food and 75 percent to wine, I think that sends a big statement to your customer.

At Babbo we started with a plastic insert menu when we first opened, the classic one with the green border and the little metal tabs at the end. We chose a piece of art on the front, and we printed new ones every day. But soon after we opened, we went all the way—Mario's father-in-law had founded Coach Leather and later sold it, but we still had the contact there, and they did a four-page, leather-bound Coach-branded menu for Babbo. People steal them all the time. If we catch you we'll put it on your check at full retail— that's a three-hundred-dollar souvenir, lover.

We have antipasti, primi, secondi, and then we have pasta tasting and the traditional tasting menu. The wine list is separate, and the dessert menu is separate as well.

Babbo's menu is only four pages, but it's overwhelming—there are twenty different pastas in there, a lot of stuff. There is nothing I hate more than a useless, lazy menu with only three appetizers and four entrées. That's not even a menu, that's bullshit. You're a fucking restaurant, cook something. I think part of being a dynamic and versatile restaurant is offering people options. That's what it's all about. Dining options. Otherwise don't even bother going to the restaurant to have dinner—just show up between service for family meal and take what you get.

When it comes to writing menus, Mario is like Kurt Vonnegut meets Einstein—he knows how to create the document that does it all. He knows how to write the words to sell the dish. He knows where creative meets informative meets slightly snarky but intelligent. He can put a menu together better than anybody else.

There hadn't been a menu quite like Babbo's before—it is very creative but also very easy to understand, and it opens the doors to infinite possibilities of putting together a three-course meal, from ethereal and conceptual combinations of white anchovies and a caprese salad that I promise you are the freshest things you've ever tasted in your time on earth to a powerful one-two punch of pasta and steak, cooked to a level of perfection that you probably didn't even know was possible. But again, Mario's genius is that he doesn't overcomplicate things. He is extremely black and white. And that's a very back-of-the-house state of mind—either it's cooked right or it's not. Good or bad. Smart or stupid. At the back of the house, when you're producing dishes and running labor, you live in that world, whereas in the front of the house you live in the world of the perception of the consumer, which is the abyss of gray between the black and white of the kitchen. It's two parallel universes that have to overlap seamlessly to create the perfect restaurant experience.

Mario is also delusionally optimistic. And I'm the opposite. I'm the Doubting Thomas of the relationship. He's always thinking about what will go right, and I'm always thinking about what could go wrong. Mario was sometimes more confident and brash, and I was slightly more conservative. That seesaw balance to the partnership continues to make it prosper.

It might seem that he's the artist and I'm the businessman, but actually in some ways I'm much more of the creative artist and he's much more of the nuts-and-bolts guy when it comes down to actually running the business. He's a creative chef, and very whimsical, but he's probably more dogmatically tied to the concept of margin and making money than even I am. Sometimes I'm willing to forgo a buck to try an idea.

What really distinguishes Mario is that as much as he's about the art and doing it for the love of it and doing it right, he won't do anything unless it makes money. There are a lot of chefs who are willing to forget about margins to create art, but Mario will not even sell food or craft concepts that elevate his own brand and his own artistry at the cost of the business. He has always been incredibly grounded by this focus on keeping good margins and generating profitability. He said to me when we first started, "I like you because you're a cheap fuck from way back." That was his mantra, too, a real Restaurant Man. You can bet he got along great with my old man.

So, sure, when we started, we said let's fuck it all and do what we want, we'll just follow our artistic inspiration. But as soon as we got into it and spent six hundred thousand dollars of our own money building it, that whole footloose-and-fancy-free thing went right out the fucking window. It had to. But fortunately, we understood early on that we were onto something so special, and even though you can bet your pants that we were looking at the margins—you know the math—we were also living in some pretty rarefied air when it came to creating the experience.

After all that conceptualizing, finding a name for the place was actually one of the most challenging tasks. We were very troubled— we were getting ready to open, and we still didn't have a name. When we started the place, we'd both just had our first kids, and Babbo is Tuscan slang for "Daddy." Somehow that's what came up, and it stuck. We figured it didn't mean a lot, but it sounded friendly and fun, and if you knew the Italian, better yet.

One night we were out on the stoop having our customary bottle of stoop wine and discussing the vast merits of our genius. If you live in New York and you don't have chairs outside, you sit on the stoop. It is the New York mini-amphitheater. Ten people can sit around talking to one another, and then there'll be someone on the sidewalk addressing the group—performing, really. There is a whole stoop dynamic. It's the urban conduit for socializing and communication. Where I grew up, it was all stoops—we played stoopball and had stoop barbecues, we had our meetings on stoops. We are a product of stoop culture, for sure. After Babbo opened, we still drank outside—we'd call in to the maître d' to bring us something white and fast, fast and cold, and we'd sit out on the stoop and drink. People would stop by and have a glass. Sometimes we'd have twenty people out on the stoop.

Some of the biggest decisions were made in the theater of the stoop. We did interviews, hired people, conceived of new restaurants, all out on the stoop. The one rule was, only positive things on the stoop. If we had to fire someone, we'd bring him over to the diner.

One night we're hanging out on the stoop and these two guys came walking down the street, headed toward some frat-boy bar on MacDougal Street. They were in their full Brooklyn guido regalia—pompadours, sweat suits and chains, Adidas high-tops untied. They looked up at the name on the awning, and one guy goes to the other, "Look, it's Babboo's!" And the other guy says to us, "Hey, Babboo!" They thought we were opening up some sort of Pakistani or vindaloo joint, some kind of hookah place. Now, that was a real moment of panic.

•

CHAPTER NINE

Babbo: Secondi

We have a stupid, insane tradition in the restaurant business that's known as "friends and family"—which means trying out the new place with tons of trial dinners and getting feedback from your so-called friends and family, to see how the people you supposedly know and trust respond. But it might as well be referred to as "enemies and detractors," because no matter how much you like these people or think you value their sagacity when it comes to your food, the second they start eating for free and offering opinions, you realize how much you'd rather just line them up in the street and shoot them in the fucking head.

They order inappropriately and they behave like animals because they're not paying. They make asses out of themselves because it is completely counterintuitive to everything that trying out a normal restaurant would be. Then they think they're going to tell you what's wrong with your restaurant after they're drunk and they've eaten all your food for free? And then you get the sotto voce—you know, they'll leave that night and tell you everything was great, and the next day you hear the gossip of what they really thought, because they didn't have the nerve to tell you to your face, even on the off chance that they were right.

I'm all about rehearsing on paying customers these days. Because the paying customer is the real customer. That's who's invested in the experience. When people don't pay, they don't act like customers. There is no fucking point—you might as well have them over for a dinner party at your house. Ask any musician: People on the guest list, and that includes critics (especially critics), never enjoy the show as much as someone who ponies up for a ticket. It's a fucking rule. After years of so many painful "friends and families," I want to slit my wrists and fucking bleed to death in the middle of their table. We've eliminated it. Now we try to open really quietly so not too many people know right away, a nice soft opening for paying customers.

In the beginning I think that some people were a little shocked by what we were trying to do at Babbo. We were always inspired by the response to our own restaurants—Becco and Po—but of course they were very different. Mine was in the Theater District and his was in the West Village, and combining those two aesthetics was part of our challenge. So Mario brought his people in, I brought in my crew and some others who worked with my mother and me, people I had learned from and trusted, and we had to reconcile these two styles of how we envisioned the food—The Traditional versus The Reinvented. They honestly weren't as far apart as it might sound, but they were stylistically diverse, and it made people crazy until they opened up to it. The beauty of Babbo, in the end, is that we were able to unify all our different influences and ideas into creating one product that was the Babbo menu and the Babbo dining experience. It was no longer a mess of ideas. It was one solid thing. Babbo. Babbo was the perfect intersection of uptown and downtown. It was a place where Upper East Side bluehairs would be comfortable to come down and have a dinner at 6:30 P.M. and musicians and artists from the Lower East Side could come in at 10:30. It was like the crossroads of New York society. When you can get different strata of New York life to collide in one environment—and truly, the restaurants in New York are our public spaces, are our living rooms, where we live our lives—that creates the magic.

The balance between Mario and me is key to the formula. I was working the front of the house, Mario was in the kitchen. And it was bringing the very best of both worlds together, to really take care of each person thoughtfully and completely and blow them all away. It was a one-two punch. Tag-team champs. And then the critics came and everything else happened, and it grew from there.

Mario, in terms of his public persona, is more flamboyant. He's definitely a little more gregarious and likes to run with the crowd a bit more. I've been more laid-back, and when I had time, I returned to Europe and eventually started making my own wine, which ate up a lot of my time. When I wasn't here, I was in Italy working on that, and that's what I really loved.

We heard a lot of noise when Babbo first opened about our chutzpah in putting out a menu that didn't seem to have one single Italian staple on it, no warhorses, no greatest hits—not to mention our taste in loud rock 'n' roll—but we stuck to what we believed in, and in fact about 70 percent of the menu has been solid since day one: We always have pig's feet, tripe, and *testa,* as well as barbecued squab, a pork chop that takes longer to eat than a Dave Matthews concert runs, and fresh branzino cooked with ingredients and flavors that my father had never even heard of, plus the famous two-minute Calamari Sicilian Lifeguard Style, and a mess of completely imaginative and sexy pastas including the pappardelle bolognese, which sounds simple enough but blows everyone's mind. You think you've had bolognese, and then you try Mario's and you just want to weep at the tragedy your life has been. The Mint Love Letters—ravioli with lamb sausage and mint—have become a signature dish, and you can bet they didn't even exist before Babbo. Plus, 30 percent of the menu gets changed continually, which is part of the organic nature of a great restaurant.

When we began, the wine list was relatively humble—about a hundred wines, with the price point kind of low. It's huge now, though. A multimillion-dollar inventory. But it started off as something quite simple. We had six hundred thousand bucks to do the whole restaurant start to finish and to open, which is a lot of money, but not considering that we opened what would be a three-star Italian restaurant.

Babbo is a pure partnership, but the wine program is all me. In the beginning I opened every bottle of wine there. When we started becoming successful, I started buying wine like crazy, and Mario was always 100 percent with the program. I remember telling him, "I'm buying wine like this restaurant is going to be open for fifty years. You down with that?" And he always was, and we really invested very heavily. Now we have an incredible cellar of aged wines, beautiful wines. Crazy stuff. Where some people try to pull money out of their restaurants, we always tried to put it back in with more inventory. We built the cellar, we invested in the building. It was always about investment, because Babbo always paid back in spades.

When we were ready, we had an opening party at Babbo with a lot of media attention. Alice Waters was there, a lot of the food critics came out—the Mimi Sheratons, the deans of the *New York Times,* the Village food intelligentsia. We had a lot of support right from the beginning.

Which is not to say that we didn't have our problems. We had our balls on the line from day one. We had invested all our money in this place and were sort of flying by the seat of our pants. I was fighting my instincts to count nickels and, at least for a moment, was putting art before commerce. And there were some moments spent doing what we call the Curly Shuffle, which is a glib way of saying we were trying to figure out whom to pay first, since we didn't have enough dough to pay everyone. The Curly Shuffle.

It's like this: You've just opened your restaurant. You're probably upside down a couple hundred thousand dollars to your contractor. You owe the last 20 percent to your kitchen supplier. He's holding paper on all the kitchen equipment, which means that he can come in and repo it any second. You're up and running. But if you don't have the cash flow, if you don't pay the liquor companies, they don't deliver. (If you don't pay your liquor bills in a thirty-day cycle, they have to report you to the State Liquor Authority, and then you can't buy any more liquor wholesale, so you cannot even think about playing games with them. In that case you have to buy wine every day at the corner liquor store to sell to your customers, which is illegal and expensive. At least we didn't have that problem, but I've seen it.)

You're taking in money every night, and you have these lists of people who need to get paid. Rule number one is, never bounce a payroll check. Because the minute you bounce one payroll check, the word is out. The rats smell a sinking ship, and they're scurrying in every direction. And then there's sales tax. You have to pay it, because you're personally liable for sales tax—you don't pay, you go to jail. But that's the easiest one not to pay because it's kind of like a self-control, good-guy honor system. Just pray you don't get audited.

And the bottom category is your food vendors. Fish guys are always first in line, probably because they run with the thinnest margins, so they're the most hard-edged about getting paid. Once *they* smell that the ship is sinking, word gets out. So the fish guy tells the meat guy, who tells the dried-goods guys, and so on . . .

Once word gets out that you're a bad credit risk, people are going to demand COD. Which means you have to stand at the door with your fucking checkbook. Some people won't even take checks, only cash. It's all about juggling. If you're out ninety or a hundred fifty days with your meat guy for fifty grand, he doesn't want to sell you meat anymore. You try to find another meat guy, but chances are he'll know you're out fifty grand to the other guy. Because everyone is sharing this information on the back end. So with the daily cash flow, you've got to cover what it takes to keep the restaurant open. You have to pay your rent. Got to pay utilities, or else they'll turn off the lights and gas on you. You can always negotiate with the landlord, but you can't run a restaurant in the dark without fire. So you prioritize what needs to be paid to stay open, because when you're open, you generate more cash flow every night to pay more bills for the next day. It's a little bit of a pyramid scheme sometimes.

The ideal thing is not to start at a two-hundred-thousand-dollar deficit with no money in your bank account. Ideally, you have operating capital and you can actually pay everyone. You want to be cash-flow-positive, or at least cash-flow-sustainable from day one. But you can run at a cash-flow loss. What you're doing by not paying your vendors is using them as a bank. You're buying that steak for ten dollars, selling it for thirty. But of that thirty you take in, ten of it has got to go to pay the cooks. Ten of it should go back to the guy who sold you the steak. But it's not. You're taking his ten dollars and you're paying it to the power company, because they're actually going to turn off your lights. The people who have the least leverage get paid last.

This is how it went in the early days at Becco, and again in the early days at Babbo. Most restaurants, when they open, this is the action—it's high finance gangster style. And it's all counterintuitive, because you open up and you need the money, but you're thinking,

Oh, my God, am I really ready to serve? I really should do twenty covers tonight and nail them so that the customers love it and take off into the world singing our praises. But if I do forty covers, I could double the revenue. But what's my risk-return on doing more covers than I should be doing and delivering a half-assed experience? And then they're going to tell their friends this sucked. But I make more money immediately. Ugh. You built this palace, you spent all this money, and you want to build a quality experience. So do you go for the immediate buck, allowing you to write a check to your fish vendor tomorrow morning or hold the line and do less business in order to perfect it and slowly grow the business over time, which is expensive? You probably have enough staff to do the forty covers, but you choose to do twenty, because you're investing in the experience of the restaurant. But someone has got to pay.

It crashes when the sheriff comes and padlocks your door. The landlord will go to court and get a warrant and seize the property, which means they'll put a big yellow SEIZED sticker on the front door. That's one way. The second way is, you're treading along one night and the lights go out. They padlock your meter. They come with a wrench, turn the switch on the meter off, put a padlock on it, and you're done. Out of business. Third is, you bounce payroll checks. You show up to your restaurant one day and no one comes to work. We've never gotten to that point, but I've seen it lots of times, and when it happens, you are fucked. There is no coming back from the dead. Once you see the SEIZED sticker on the door, or once the third busboy from the restaurant down the street comes looking for a job, you know the jig is up. The classic sign is CLOSED FOR RENOVATIONS. "Closed for Renovations" equals out of business.

No downtown restaurants with punks like us calling the shots ever got three stars.

No stars actually means "satisfactory"—the idea is that it's enough that you're getting reviewed. One star means "good," which is actually a lot better than good anyplace outside New York. Two stars are "very good," which would be like a miracle anywhere else in the civilized world. Three stars are "excellent." Three stars qualifies you as a destination. People can plan a vacation around a reservation at a three-star restaurant. Four stars is fuck you—you have to be so incredibly fucking good to get four stars that it's practically an abstract concept. Ever read Stephen Hawking's books? Four stars is like an imaginary number. It's like a black hole, or an event horizon, or traveling sideways in time—it is impossible for any normal person to understand, although once you are confronted with it, it is a real holy-shit moment. You grab your balls, because you can't even believe it exists. Four stars is an epiphany.

Felidia was a three-star restaurant. San Domenico was a three-star restaurant. Those were the two old-school three-star restaurants. So to have a young, downtown, maverick three-star Italian restaurant was a game changer. I don't think it was something that we ever really came out of the gate to pursue—Babbo was its own organic evolution that started with very moderate ambitions. We kind of responded and fed on the fuel of the city and the energy that came through the door, and that fed our passion and, to a certain extent, our egos. And then the sky was the limit. Reviews started rolling in. This was before the days of the blogs and the Internet, when it was all about the print media, and it was untouchable. We were bulletproof.

Everyone loved Babbo. It became the new standard, certainly for Italian food—the interpretation of the experience, the service, the hipness, the music, the look. It became the standard for all Italian restaurants that came afterward, and the critics were the ones who put it on the map. Getting three stars from Ruth Reichl in the *New*

York Times was the defining moment in our careers. That made Mario and me. Along with the four-star review that Del Posto got twelve years later, which really made me dizzy, it is the most important thing that ever happened to me professionally.

One of the few issues Mario and I would disagree about is comps—who eats for free. Restaurant Man hates comps, but grew up in a world where it was considered a necessary evil. We were supposed to carry old-school, free-loading critics, and Mario just wouldn't. He was adamant and obstinate about that. I was of the old school, the way my parents brought me up—the restaurateur was still kind of a second-class citizen, and the customers were the aristocracy, and the only thing above customers were critics. And critics didn't pay for food, because they paid you back when they wrote about how wonderful your restaurant was. They were golden.

Then along comes Mario with a little bit of "Fuck the critics. Like everyone else, they should pay." That was an eye-opening experience for me. I came around to it, because what it comes down to—and I knew it all along, of course, from the "friends and family" fiascos we suffered through—is that if you give it away, you devalue it in the eye of the person who is supposed to be evaluating it. So by saying to you, Mr. Critic, that you don't have to pay for this great experience—even though it's the best one I can create for you in your entire career of food and wine—that somehow makes it worth less, even in the eyes of someone who's supposed to know better. Now I'm with Mario. Everyone pays.

When Ruth took the helm of the *New York Times* restaurant reviews, we figured that maybe we could get a good look—she was that California, slightly left-wing, liberal, open-minded, Italocentric gal who could open up to the concept of Babbo. And she loved it, hook, line, and sinker. She really believed, and she became a great advocate not only of the food and the experience but of what Babbo meant to the landscape of the time. And she always paid. The *New York Times* critics always pay, and tip, like real journalists, not some fucking schnorrers.

And it was a good time for us, because as restaurants were changing, reviewers were changing with them. You were losing the old-school dinosaur reviewers. But this of course invites the question, do restaurants mold reviewers or do reviewers mold the restaurants?

With wine the latter is definitely the case, when—and it's been said many times before—there's no single person in the world who has such a powerful and dominant effect over an entire industry as Robert Parker does in the wine industry. There's no other example of anything like that—the world makes wine for Robert Parker.

So do we open up restaurants for Sam Sifton, who was the *New York Times* food critic? Probably not. But when we see the type of person that Sam is, and certainly in the case of Del Posto—and with that restaurant we always had the ambition of scoring a four-star review—we definitely realized that he was the guy to give us that review, and we worked it. We laid it out there. Baited him, put the word out in the market to his friends. We played the game. That's how it gets done. You can't cheat. Either you've got it or you don't. But if you want a four-star review, you've got to go out and tell those people that you're a four-star restaurant. They may agree or disagree, but unless you have the ability to communicate your intentions to the marketplace and to the critics, you won't even be considered.

At Babbo we knew when Ruth was coming. We knew what she looked like—we had gotten the heads-up. She was trying to go incognito, but we knew some of her guests. Restaurant Man also trades in intelligence. So we planted a few of our friends next to her. That's a big thing, we always do that—you put a plant next to important critics, and they order everything on the menu and ooh and aah, and you do all your fancy table stuff for them while the critic looks on, because critics eat not only their own dinner but everyone's dinner around them. When Ruth was there, we controlled that room down to the bread crumb, from what song played when she walked into the room to Led Zeppelin with the linguini and Jimi Hendrix with the saffron panna cotta. It was curated to the micrometer, every detail of the experience.

Someone once accused us of being cynical when we micromanage like that, but you know what? That's our job, to dazzle people and to get reviewers on board. But you can't fake it—either it's there or it's not. You can enhance things. And sometimes, if you overdo it, you can fuck yourselves up. We've been busted acknowledging critics' presence. And at a certain point, when everyone knows you know who they are and they know who you are, it's just about respecting people's privacy and their anonymity, which can suddenly become the elephant in the room. You want to have fun and show off, but you have to pretend that it's just another day in Dodge.

If we did try to game the system, though, we always did it with a great amount of prudence—a restaurant can't change its stripes for one table or one night. What you are and the quality of the experience will ultimately come through. The truth is that the margin between our riding the controls and just letting the machine do its thing isn't much. Every table is different, but we are consistently good.

The Babbo building, 110 Waverly Place, is magical. Does that sound too hippie? I can handle it. Because, no shit, there's definitely a vibe, an energy there. People have been eating and drinking and having fun in this building for over a century—before it was the Coach House, it was a speakeasy.

I never foresaw the tremendous success we would have; it was just one of those amazing things. With Babbo it was always great—everything we did just seemed to take off. There were never really any negative reviews, any negative comments. I always tell everyone, "You only get one Babbo in your life." Yeah, if you're lucky. Babbo always seemed to be greater than us. There seemed to be a positive energy that affected the customers, the neighbors—everyone.

We don't have any real competitors. I think we rolled into a lucky position where we stand alone, and we don't feel threatened. In New York we're fortunate, because there are enough customers who enjoy good restaurants, so we don't have to recruit customers as much as we trade them. People who go to Nobu probably come to Babbo as well. And every great Italian restaurant in New York is just one more reason for people to get out and eat Italian every night. If they eat out more, chances are we're getting a good piece of that business.

There are a lot of people trying to be Babbo, but there is only one. We've been ripped off consistently—there are entire restaurant groups that have been born out of former Babbo sous-chefs, wine directors, or whatever. Jay McInerney said in the *Wall Street Journal* that we kind of gave birth to a whole category of restaurants. Ultimately, that's the best compliment. That's the proliferation of our species.

Babbo let me move away from Becco. Becco was mainstream—we were servicing tourists and Europeans and lots of people who loved the food but didn't know who was behind it or, really, didn't care. Well, sure it mattered to some people, and that was great, but at Babbo it was all about who we were. That was very powerful and very addictive, the fact that we were expected to be there and that people actually cared we were there, curating their experience. And the fact that we were there brought people who were important in the world. It was about getting to smoke Marlboro Reds with Keith

Richards at the bar or hanging out with Jimmy Page and Chris Robinson, you name it. It was one great night after another. Babbo was definitely where people came for a late night—musicians, celebrities, authors, people we really admired—and somehow, from an artistic perspective, from their perspective, we were their equal. That was very potent and enthralling. This was the vanguard—when restaurant people became more empowered and the restaurateur became as important as the customer. We were no longer the servants. We were the artists.

●

CHAPTER TEN

Heroes and Villains

Elaine Kaufman died today. She was the essence of the front-of-the-house person. The classic restaurant owner. But what was she, really? Was she a restaurateur? Was she just a host? Was she Restaurant Woman? What was Elaine Kaufman?

People loved her, and it got me to thinking. Where could you go to a restaurant and find a front-of-the-house guy who still owns the place? The classic guys were Sirio Maccioni at Le Cirque and Ken Aretsky at Patroon, Laurence Kretchmer and Bobby Flay, who of course is also a superstar chef. And Drew, of course.

But all these people, me included, are culinary obsessives, and Elaine wasn't. She was really kind of a dinosaur, in the sense that she ran a restaurant that not only wasn't chef-driven, it was hardly food-driven. You wouldn't go there to eat; the food was notoriously bad. It was like *Jurassic Park* over there—it was all about a time when dinosaurs roamed New York.

She's famous for telling people who asked, "Where's the bathroom?" to "Make a left at Woody Allen," but it wasn't really a celebrity hangout, at least not as we remember it today. It was where New York's literary elite met middle-of-the-road avant-garde filmmakers—George Plimpton and Mike Nichols having dinner in the same room at different tables, that was the classic scene at

Elaine's. But that era is dead. No young person ever went there in the last twenty years.

She was a genius at running the front of the house, though. She was the star of the show, and she had to have a big enough personality so that you would actually go to a restaurant where the food didn't matter. All these people liked to eat well, and a lot of them started coming down to Babbo. So why would they still go there if the food was bad? There must have been some kind of powerful charisma for her to be able to draw that kind of room, to have those people in her place. She was an odd breed of Restaurant Superstar who had nothing to do with the kitchen, and I was kind of in awe of that.

You admire a lot of people for different things. Some people you admire for improving the quality of the business, the Danny Meyers of the world. He basically crafted and inserted enlightened hospitality into our industry.

In the seventies and eighties, in a plastic world of ass-licking *"Oui, madame"*s and patronizing double air kissers, he had the idea that instead of placating customers and treating them like morons, they should actually be treated like intellectual, thinking, sophisticated consumers who were on an equal playing field with the restaurateur. For a long time in New York fine dining, even though the customers had the money, they were considered to be stupid and not to know what the fuck they were talking about.

Danny has also been a great leader of evolved restaurateuring. His Union Square Café was an important restaurant for New York, really the first of its kind—market-driven, local, and sustainable in its concept. He pioneered a very progressive American wine program and was extremely customer-friendly. There is little doubt why it was the most popular restaurant in New York for years running.

He is also directly responsible for the death of the six-day work-week in restaurants. It's a disaster that he'll take to his grave.

Until Danny came along, everyone in the restaurant business worked six days a week. It had always been a six-day week. One day off, and that was it, and everyone was happy. He single-handedly spread this cancer of a five-day workweek through our industry

I think he did it because he truly believes in the quality of life of restaurant workers and employees—as do I. We always try to make sure that our employees are happy, for many reasons, but not least of all because it is in our own self-interest. But ensuring their happiness doesn't always mean giving them a birthday card and telling them how great they are and what a great team we are. It means seeing to it that they make enough money, that they're treated respectfully, and that what they bring to the workplace is acknowledged. A professional environment where quid pro quo rules is the kind of environment restaurant workers are looking for. I think it's very much give-and-take. You work this many hours, this is how much money you make. I treat you like the talented server you are, you bring that talent and intellect into dealing with my customers. I don't make you work when I don't need you. I don't spread the pool too thin by putting too many servers on. I respect your economic value. It's a very, very give-and-take relationship.

But just because you work six days instead of five, that doesn't mean you don't have a great quality of life. Classically, you worked five doubles, Saturday dinner, and got Sunday off. Think about that. Come to work, lunch, you get a break, between lunch and dinner you go out to OTB, read the sports page, have a quick game of dice in the locker room, eat a family meal, pull three chairs together, take a half-hour nap, back to work. Work the night shift. Everyone worked a double and a Saturday night—waiters, cooks, everyone. Normal weekends were not the legacy of our business. Our business was a six-day-a-week business. That's what people worked. Danny, along with various pieces of legislation, basically sealed the coffin on that.

There are a few other people I think are worth mentioning as restaurateurs in the classic sense, real Restaurant Men, but much different from Danny or Drew or myself. Steve Hanson is King of the One-Star Restaurants. Basically, he's about knocking off ideas—Ruby Foo's, Dos Caminos, Prime House, Atlantic Grill. They're big, shiny, solid restaurants, created and inspired solely to make money. He's a total numbers guy—a classic cheap fuck like the best of us. He's been a great guy in our business for creating a model of how restaurants can operate in the city and make some real dough, but I think the net result is that the restaurants are a little bit void and soulless.

Andrew Silverman was my predecessor as one of the original Restaurant Men in New York City, a real old-school operator, down at the fish market every day buying junk fish. He's just a hard-driving motherfucker of a restaurateur. His restaurants are City Crab and City Lobster, and he used to have Steak Frites. Everyone in the business knows him, because he's such a take-no-prisoners, fuck-you kind of guy. He's another one-star wonder—his restaurants are like food factories without culinary aspirations. A little bit designy, a little bit trendy, priced right for that Gen X crowd and for tourists, for young professionals, people who don't have a huge budget but want to get a fancy dinner and feel like they're having a big night out.

Truthfully, the one-star restaurant is a good concept, but it's just not what I do. Silverman and Hanson are great Restaurant Men in that they're about making money and controlling costs and delivering margin, without fail. There's nothing wrong with their places. I just can't imagine the experience ever being personal.

And then you have a withering douchebag like Pino Luongo.

For five minutes about a thousand years ago, he was able to convince New York that he was some kind of Tuscan cook, but frankly, I think he was always full of shit.

He came up in the 1990s with Coco Pazzo in Manhattan, and then later he opened up in the Hamptons. He was partners with probably the biggest asshole chef I've ever met in my whole life, a little, short-dicked Napoleonic fuck. He might be dead by now—I have no idea.

I remember going up to Pino's office in the 1990s, hoping to get some guidance because I wanted to open my second and third restaurants, and he just looked down the end of a big cigar and spit at me, "Kid, you don't know what you're doing." He dismissed me as some kind of meaningless wannabe hack.

Pino's downfall was the typical mega-asshole mistake of believing that because some important people in New York ate at his restaurant, he was as smart and powerful as they were. He committed the ultimate sin of buying into his own press, which everyone in the business knows—and Pino proved it—is a one-way ticket to irrelevance. Now he's just a sad and bitter clown. If he weren't such a prick, it might be tragic.

The best thing I can say about him is that he's a good lesson in exactly what not to do in this business. Over the years so many people ride their egos right to the top and then ride them right to the bottom again. Once your ego is making decisions, it's over. You have to step gingerly on the heads you use to climb to the top, because you're going to step on the same heads when you stumble down.

There are other storied Restaurant Men who are also facing oblivion. Tony May no longer has San Domenico, which was for many years one of the premier Italian restaurants in the country. Now he has a trying-to-be-trendy room called SD26 with his lovely and talented daughter, Marisa. Even if the food is good, it's no place for a seventy-four-year-old man smoking a cigar, seating people. Tony—you're a great Restaurant Man, but enough is enough. Take your wife to Positano. Get in some golf. Do some fucking thing. Please.

These are the people who have had a hard time making the leap across generations, guys like Sirio at Le Cirque. In 1987 he was on top of the world. They called him the "Ringmaster." I really don't dislike the guy—although he always treated me like a piece of shit, I still have a world of respect for him. But how are you ever going to transform something like Le Cirque? How can you even think about bringing that business into the future? When I think of who ate there, it's Barbara Walters, Walter Cronkite, Nixon, and Kissinger—his customers are all dead or dying. Le Cirque never appealed to a younger audience, it never evolved to accommodate the next generation of restaurant-goers. It was always dominated by Sirio, and he never let his kids perform in the center ring.

My experience was different, because my mother was willing to let go. When I first opened Becco, she was there to catch me when I fell, but certainly when I soared a little bit, she didn't try to clip my wings. I'll always respect her for that ability to really prop someone up. She wasn't in some cheap competition with the world to prove how powerful she is. I'm certainly looking down the pike at my own reality, and I hope that includes passing these restaurants on to my kids, who will, I also hope, have their own vision as well. I think a lot of the old guard are afraid of losing their power, that after being the Ringmaster there is only nothingness. But that is a sad truth that manifests itself over and over again in our business. For Restaurant Man there is sometimes no exit strategy.

Drew always told me, "When you have the demand of New York, you become the gatekeeper. Then you decide how you decorate the room." There are very few restaurants that achieve that stature, but when yours does, that's a very powerful thing. You're deciding when the captains of finance sit next to the titans of media and who are dashed and dotted by the creative elite. That's a pretty influential position to be in. We're in the New York business—what we do is totally ingrained in the socioeconomic fabric that is New York. Elaine understood that.

We achieved that at Babbo, and perhaps later at Del Posto, but Babbo really is the place, because it's got only eighty seats and it's not superexpensive—it's sort of elitist and populist at the same time. Elitist because it's tough to get in without a reservation months in advance unless you know somebody and populist because it's not prohibitively pricey. Fifteen years after we opened, Babbo—along with Nobu—is the toughest table in town.

When it comes to dressing the room, we are very hands-on. We block out the prime-time tables. Mario and I decide who gets what at what time, and that's how the mix is built. There's no master plan—the rules are that we reward people who are good to the restaurant. People who appreciate the experience add to the room and add to the environment. There are a lot of famous, cool people who are total assholes and are not restaurant-centric. They don't get in.

Some people might find that haughty or snobby or whatever, but it really isn't. It's about adding to your own good fortune. Successful people want to be surrounded by other successful people in other industries. It adds to their experience and stature in society. So when we decorate a room that way, we're increasing their pleasure and therefore increasing our success. We are definitely facilitators— we weave a certain part of the fabric that is finance, art, creativity, power—everything that New York is.

But at Babbo, once you are seated, in no way are we preferential to celebrities or VIPs. Everyone gets the same experience in terms of hospitality and food. We're egalitarian, and that's a big part of it, because we know that no matter who you are, when you come to Babbo you want to have an eclectic mix of cool people around you. We're creating a better experience for every customer by creating the right vibe. We want people who appreciate the art of the restaurant, the food and experience, who give something back to you—and I don't mean that they just spend a lot and tip large and that's it. We give them something personal, and they give something personal back. Everything is about a give-and-take, even if it's based on a business transaction. So what I'm doing is asking the paying customers to open themselves up to the experience and become a part of the environment. To interact with the maître d'. To engage the waiter, to give feedback, to talk about the food and wine. To talk about their expectations of the menu. It's true—I am asking you to do something. If you're going to enjoy the experience fully, you have to be willing to contribute, to become involved in the experience on an intimate level. That's what creates the magic. If not, you're a voyeur and you can go somewhere else. You see a picture on the menu, you point at it, they bring it to you, you eat, and then you leave.

The old school are the people who think that restaurants are there to serve them, so everyone who works in the restaurant is beneath them. Those people are assholes, and we keep them the fuck away.

Generally, the bigger your ego, the worse your chances of being a good customer. Famous people who are ultimately insecure feel threatened by what we're asking, and they are never going to get the best of what we do. Fashionistas suck. A lot of people I've met in the fashion business don't really give a shit about what we do. Besides, they never eat anyway. With the fashion people, it's never about what we do; it's all about them and who they're with, and our restaurants are not that kind of restaurant. If you're not going to engage with the food, the experience, the hospitality, and the wine, if you're just going to sit there being "fabulous," then maybe you're better off someplace else.

When you go to a restaurant that's powerful, compelling, and moving but you're an ego-tripping rock star and you feel that your table is going to compete with the restaurant—like, who's going to be more important, me or the restaurant?—that's when it goes bad. You should have the generosity and freedom of spirit to lend your celebrity and yourself to the experience, because the whole is greater than the sum of its parts. The people who are so insecure about their own celebrity or importance and try to compete with the power of the restaurant or the room, those are the losers.

Some people come in thinking that they're going to crack some code; they think we're trying to trip them up. They feel as if the restaurant is trying to get something over on them—trying to get them to spend more on a special or on some bottle of wine the boss is trying to offload—as if we were in an adverse relationship of some kind. If you feel that way, then you are going to the wrong restaurant. We didn't make our reputation by ripping people off; we made it by delivering something truly exceptional. You already know coming through the door what it's going to cost, so why would you fight that? The good customers are trusting. They embrace the concept, embrace the staff, interact in a personal way, allow the people in charge to really create the best experience for them. If you're not letting them do that, then you're just a monkey wrench in the works.

The essence of hospitality, at Babbo or Del Posto, would be like the experience you'd have if you were eating at my house. I'm going to give you tableside service. I work hard at being the consummate host, and in a very real way we always try to re-create that experience. What we do is marry what the customer wants with what the restaurant can give. When those two things match up, there's magic. When they don't . . . well, that's a problem.

The rule at Babbo is, we'll let you take anything off a dish but we won't let you add things in, because it's not your job to write the menu. It's ours. At Del Posto we have much more liberty to facilitate those kinds of requests, because it's more expensive and is a different kind of experience—but again, the good customers, they let go. A guy like Bono is one of the biggest stars on the planet, and he doesn't feel challenged by the room or the restaurant. I have heard him gush to a waiter, "I love that wine you chose for me. Thank you." He comes up to the chef to say thank you for creating the food and how much he loved it. He is in awe of the restaurant. He's not about being *served,* he's about being *interactive,* and he has no problem appreciating someone else's expertise or some effort that's so small compared to whatever his mega-importance in the world may or may not be. I've heard Bill Clinton hold court at his table with waiters and line cooks to discuss the lamb chops. Those moments of communication are brilliant.

Clinton is always a great customer. He's always wanted to be a wine guy, and he asked a lot of questions. I tried to explain to him about the wine I make in Friuli, in northeastern Italy, but he had no idea what I was talking about. Then it dawned on me that right next to the winery, twenty clicks down the road, is Aviano Air Base. Once I mentioned that, he knew exactly where it was—he had been there many times, of course—and now he was enthusiastically telling me things about Italy and insane details of NATO policy that I could not possibly understand. No matter, he always drank whatever I recommended—always my own wine, and he loved it.

President Clinton would stop traffic when he got up from the table to go to the restroom, and he would literally go to every other table and say hi to everyone. He'd work the whole room, then go outside on the street and work the line. He was always working. Bill's got giant hands, very warm and soft as marshmallows. When he shakes your hand, you get the feeling that you're floating in amniotic fluid. It's hard not to trust him.

He used to come into Babbo pretty often. He would roll with these heavy finance guys. They liked to whoop it up, a lot of wine and a lot of talk. We got to know him a little, and the people who work with him at the Clinton Foundation, which is based in Harlem. We believe in Bill and his charities—we've done events for them and have always contributed. One year we donated a barrel of wine—that's 225 liters, which is three hundred bottles, or thirty cases of wine—but we bottled it into twelve massive eighteen-liter bottles, each with original art, hand-painted right on the bottle and signed by Bono. Someone paid half a million bucks for the whole shebang.

One night he came in with Bob Kerrey and I think another man and a woman, and we sat them at Table One, which is the four-top in the front left corner as you come in. This was in 2001, and they had come from a St. John's basketball game at Madison Square Garden. He always had a few Secret Service guys with him, but not as many as you'd think, and they did a good job of staying out of the way. I kept thinking, *Boy, that's Mission Impossible*—keeping an eye on Bill Clinton must be like herding cats.

Now, if you recall, Bob Kerrey, back in 1991, when he was still a U.S. senator, sabotaged his run for president by telling Bill Clinton a lesbian joke that was picked up by a TV camera. (At the time Bill waffled and refused to say if he'd laughed or not.) That gaffe pretty much cost Kerrey the election and any chance for higher office.

The tables in Babbo are tight. At the table next to Bill and his party were four very sharp women who saw them come in and just hunkered down. I think one of the girls was from *Vanity Fair*, and she was with her friends, who all had the unmistakably hungry look of gossip columnists and publicists, and they were not moving, not a fucking inch—never mind that they had already finished dessert and had already called for the check.

At Clinton's table it was like guys' golf-course talk, lots of back-slapping and drinking. The ex-president is always funny, but he appears to have a hard time with any sort of self-governance. Like, it seems that he is always trying to watch his weight, but when it's time to order, he goes nuts with the menu.

These guys, wherever they show up, are treated as if they're on a private jet. Wherever they are, they behave like they are the only people in the room. Sometimes that doesn't quite work out for them. The women sitting at the other table across from them were tuned in and turned on, and they weren't moving.

At a certain point, I told President Clinton, politely, that they might want to dial it down—there was a table of plugged-in celebrity-journalist types sitting next to them. Discretion may turn out to be the better part of valor after all. He was cordial and polite, as always, and kept on telling the jokes.

And I wasn't the only one telling them to cool it—the woman at their table, who I was later told was a former White House counsel, was also telling him to shut the fuck up.

The whole Monica Lewinsky thing was still very much in the air. Try as he could, Clinton could not separate himself from his reputation as a sleaze. Lately he'd been making a huge public effort to behave, but what with his wife making a go at a career as senator, you'd think he would have been a little concerned about getting busted telling dirty jokes in a restaurant. But there is definitely an air of Greater-Than-Thou-ness about Clinton—in the sense that after all he's been through, he's still a total rock star. Shit doesn't stick to him; he's like the Teflon Don. Maybe he kind of cares about what people think, but he doesn't *really* care, because he's Bill Clinton.

At the moment the joke that got him in hot water didn't seem like such a big deal—in fact, he was just repeating the same bad gag that Kerrey had told him years before. You could even say that at this juncture it had historical significance.

And, truthfully, not only isn't it all that offensive, but the butt of the joke wasn't even lesbians-at-large—rather, it was Jerry Brown, the ex-hippie former and now present governor of California. The joke was about Brown going into a bar and approaching a couple of lesbians. For those of you who can handle it, the punch line went something like this: "I like to eat pussy. Does that make me a lesbian, too?"

I guess that's what passes for humor in the locker rooms of liberal politicians.

The next day the papers and the Internet were howling. That gag had sunk Kerrey in the '92 Democratic primary, and now, nine years later, they still hadn't learned their lesson! Oh, the humiliation! One Web site wondered if Clinton and Kerrey were going to face a lesbian firing squad—what they called a "Militia Etheridge."

A few others who didn't think it was so funny wondered just how many times he was going to embarrass Hillary before she finally tossed him out.

We make such an effort to keep things chummy at Babbo, and yet President Clinton got busted for telling a dirty joke, no easy feat. Even more embarrassing, Bob Kerrey got screwed for the same joke for the second time. For him it was double jeopardy. To me it was always amazing how Bill Clinton, a brilliant lawyer in a previous life, could ever let something like that happen.

●

CHAPTER ELEVEN

Sour Grapes

N o bottle of wine costs more than five dollars to make. Understand this and you are well on your way to cutting through the bullshit of the wine world.

Wine is a commodity item, even though it has less inherent value than most things you would buy or trade. The price is driven purely by supply and demand, mystique and marketing, and ratings.

Grapes are basically 90 percent sugar and water, plus some dry extract, the pits and skins. What distinguishes wine from grape juice is a naturally occurring phenomenon, the wonderful process of alcoholic fermentation. Single-cell yeasts are the heroes of this story—their whole life function is to transform sugar into alcohol. Can you imagine? That is some noble shit.

You may think that survival is an intuitive, instinctive reaction that exists solely among animals, but even plants struggle to exist. It's a reproductive imperative, and grapevines, as all living things do, put every ounce of vigor they have into reproducing themselves—the fruit is essentially the vine's attempt to propagate its species. It takes a lot of passion to want to exist in the future. You have to respect that.

The phenomenon of fruit fermenting into alcohol is something that happened before man had the bright idea to control it and have a party with the results—it really is God's way. Beer is like cooking—it needs a recipe and a kitchen—but wine, it could use a little nudge, of course, but it's going to happen. It was always there.

Wine is an agricultural product, not so different from orange juice or olive oil. A vine left to its own devices, a mature fifteen-year-old vine, will produce between ten and thirty pounds of grapes a year, and it takes about a pound and a half or two pounds of grapes to make a bottle of wine.

So if each vine has the potential to produce fifteen bottles of wine, what is the true cost of a bottle?

When you look at the material needed to construct a bottle of wine, no matter where it is in the world, you will find that it does not cost more than about a third of what it costs to go to a movie in New York City. Then why should glorified grape juice be so expensive? The first thing that factors into it is the cost of the land. Real estate and rent. You've got your Rodeo Drive rent—maybe an address in Bordeaux—and you've got your ghetto rents—maybe a region in South America that hasn't caught on quite yet as a producer of great wine or a patch of wind-strewn, high-plains desert in eastern Washington State, formerly home to a warren of meth labs, that all of a sudden gives life to Cabernet Sauvignon, Merlot, and Cabernet Franc that make you think Left Bank or Right. But the act of pressing and turning grapes into wine, and the fermentation process, is inexpensive. There's really no cost involved with that. Barrels can be expensive—a single new standard-size oak barrel that you would see in Californian or French wineries costs almost a thousand dollars. Two hundred and twenty-five liters go into a barrel, basically three hundred bottles of wine. If you were to use a barrel only once, you would be talking about three bucks per 750 milliliters for that toasty wood-juice goodness, but barrels are often used many times, so the cost can be much less than that.

And then there is the grape market, which sets the value of wine grapes. Today there are not many grapes in Italy that cost more than two dollars a pound, and in fact there are plenty of quality grapes that cost less than a buck per, depending on where they're from and the relative quality of the vintage, which can be based on any number of things no one can control, like a sudden hailstorm. Right now the global market for grapes is as low as it's ever been, because of both increased production to the point of overproduction and the global financial markets. In California they trade in tons—five hundred dollars a ton, one thousand dollars a ton, but there are very few scenarios where the pound and a half or two pounds of grapes that go into a bottle of wine cost anywhere near five dollars. If you take out the cost of capital, what's left is the time that you're holding the wine. So you are basically a wine bank, and that has value, too; it's capital over time. But still, the real cost of making any single bottle of wine, not counting the value of the land you grow it on, will rarely exceed five dollars. What drives wine prices is the perceived supply and demand—scarcity and rarity that are, for the most part, fabricated by the industry. The wine industry has succeeded in creating a delusional commodity market where factual overproduction is subjugated by contrived demand.

Managing the perception of supply is one of the dirty secrets of the business. Look at Dom Pérignon—they'd like you to think it's somehow rarefied, somehow limited in terms of production. The most important thing Dom Pérignon has to do to preserve the price point is to create an illusion of limited production for a brand that exists in extreme abundance. You can get it anywhere—down the street, at an airport, in the world's crappiest nightclub. You can buy it by the case at Costco. They make around six million bottles a year of Dom Pérignon. *Six million bottles.* That's heavy industry.

Wine is not like other luxury items. For instance, a Mercedes-Benz is definitely better than a Toyota. That's not subjective. Close the doors of one, it goes *pffft*. It's practically orgasmic. The other goes *chonk!* It's like having the door to your jail cell slammed shut. One is so much better that you can actually hear it, smell it when you climb in, never mind when you start it up and go wheeling down the road and can really feel it. Quality tells, every time. But is a bottle of Dom Pérignon that costs a hundred and fifty dollars three times as good as a fifty-dollar bottle of Bollinger NV? Do you think most people could tell the difference or would prefer one so much over the other that they would spend three times as much if these wines came in bottles without labels? To what extent is the myth of the brand informing your taste? The connection between quality and price point in wine is an illusion. A Mercedes-Benz might cost five times as much as a Toyota, but it is tangibly, significantly better. I don't think that paradigm works with wine.

Which isn't to say that a hundred-dollar bottle of wine isn't going to be better than a twenty-dollar bottle—you are paying for the terroir and for the experience and reputation and talent of the winemaker, which has real value—but five times better? I don't even know how to measure that. This is the great truism of the wine business: What is the baseline? This bottle is worth twice as much as that, but what is that, really? It's more like art than like cars—the subjectivity is what drives its price, but the quantitative costs quickly dissociate themselves from the price when the product reaches the consumer.

Of course industrial, mass-produced wine is going to cost less, or wine that doesn't have centuries behind it, or a heralded family name—but at the most basic level, in the wholesale world, wines are priced on the illusion of rarity of the product. The myth of scarcity has proliferated through all strata of the wine industry. The golden rule in winemaking is, *You always want to make six bottles short of*

Whole lotta love: with my first guitar, circa 1973.

RIGHT: My dad, Felice Bastianich, the original Restaurant Man.

With my mom, Lidia. Years later, we'd take the act on the road and open up Becco.

Ground Zero: Buonavia, my parents' first restaurant, on Queens Boulevard, complete with the family station wagon parked outside.

Inside Buonavia, in all its plush red-velvet glory— the same color as the sauce.

My twelfth birthday, with my grandmother and Felice overseeing the proceedings.

On an early Italian boondoggle with my folks. Note the Stones patch on one of the first versions of my ubiquitous denim jacket.

The Fordham Prep photo lab, stoner central back in my senior year.

A mid-1980s family portrait. From left to right: me; my sister, Tanya; Lidia; and Felice. I'm rocking my Brooks Brothers best.

Bonfire of the vanities: on Wall Street, sporting my first Gieves and Hawkes pin-striped suit and my gold-and-steel Rolex Submariner.

Restaurant Man 2.0, bringing the message to the masses: I love doing the *Today* show.

Bringing Italian to L.A.—NYC style!

The results of the Great Roman Boondoggle.

Joe and Mario do the burbs.

Del Posto: from delusional to four fucking stars.

You only get one Babbo in a lifetime.

The nightly dance at Babbo—midservice.

Carnevino, Las Vegas. Giving the people what they want.

The birth of crudo.

At dinner with the pope. I still can't believe I spilled my wine on him.

Plotting Eataly with managing partner Alex Saper.

The high-camp ribbon cutting at the opening of Eataly, with (from left to right) my niece Julia, managing partner Alex Saper, Mario, Lidia, Mayor Michael Bloomberg, Eataly founder Oscar Farinetti, me, and managing partner Adam Saper. One of the best days of my professional life.

RIGHT: An afternoon at Babbo before service.

Even Restaurant Man has to recharge: a quick nap in the office.

what your distributor asks you for. As soon as you make more than the market wants from you, you're immediately depressing the value of your brand, globally. And that's the wine business. It's always, "I can allocate you twelve bottles. If I look around, maybe I can find you another twelve. . . . But it's going to cost you."

It used to be that great wine producers would try to wield power through the perceived scarcity of their product: "This is your allocation, you get twenty-four bottles, period. You should be thankful. You should thank your lucky fucking stars that I'm going to give you that. Forget about what it even costs." There was always that attitude in the industry.

If you shop hard and really take your time and look, you can find a decent bottle of fifteen-dollar wine. People make a living doing that, selecting quality wines for every budget. That's what being a wine professional, a sommelier, a wine critic, is about. Being able to discern quality for consumers and then putting it into their hands without putting *them* into the poorhouse.

Robert Parker is the emperor of wine. Is there anyone else who can even come close, any restaurant critics who can drive menus and concepts, or movie critics who can dictate next year's releases the way the world makes wine for Robert Parker? Robert Parker is a very smart guy, also an incredibly nice guy, especially for someone with so much power in an industry lousy with snobs. He was the first one to popularize this qualitative approach to wine criticism with the 100-point rating system. He's certainly not infallible, and his palate has a very particular bent to it, but a lot of people happen to like it. He's helped create a world where the value of wine is driven by the critics. Obviously, when a wine gets a big Parker score or *Wine Spectator* score, there's more demand for it, which drives up the price, right up to the point that the market will bear. Parker is slowly handing over the reins to Antonio Galloni, the perfect successor, who will evolve the *Wine Advocate,* navigating the ship to a more old world heading.

Part of this has to do with a lack of education—people don't trust themselves or their instincts when it comes to wine. Quite frankly, being a wine consumer and having the confidence to judge a wine and to determine what you like and what you don't like, and then to articulate it, is a skill set that a lot of people who genuinely enjoy wine will never have. So, because of their own insecurity, they feel that they need to be led—that they need the *Spectator* or Parker to score everything. I always try to encourage people not to worry so much. It isn't that different from how we feel about the experience we create in our restaurants—you have to open up and let it come to you. What's the worst that could happen? You drink a bottle of wine that you don't fall in love with? You can fuck a lot of broads before you buy a diamond ring.

We've all heard a lot of so-called wine experts say that the best bottle of wine is simply the one you like—and I'm calling bullshit on that kind of irresponsible, passive, facile, lazy advice right here. There is a quantitative aspect to wine, a very real way to measure and discuss it, and that's why wine professionals exist. A lot of people like shit wine because they're chumps, but it's my job to protect those who should know better and who will benefit from my knowledge, protect them from consuming bad juice. This is very real to me. I take this very seriously.

The entry-level directive to the wine experience is the dichotomy between letting your palate guide you *and* letting people who know better help your journey. That's how you rise to the level of a knowledgeable wine drinker. You should expose yourself to good wines in curated, professional dining experiences in good restaurants and tastings at good wine shops.

One thing I can't stand is when people drink wine inappropriately or blindly or, worse, knowing that it's going to suck and then not even noticing when it actually does. The wine in a curry joint is never going to be any good. Drink beer in Indian restaurants, and don't order fucking Pinot Grigio at a fucking sushi bar. It is bad for you, and it is bad for the world. It is a sin against the gods of wine. Don't be fucking stupid and tempt them to punish you.

That being said, drinking wine is not supposed to be a brain-teaser. It's fun to get into the depth of it, and some wines will actually have the profundity to let you do that, but you should never be intimidated by them. Do you like it or don't you? Is it better than the bottle of plonk your brother-in-law brought over? Is it adding value to your dinner, to your day, to your evening?

I like going to the opera, but I know a lot of people who don't go because they have the idea that they won't understand it. They think it's like doing homework, which is bullshit. It was created to bring pleasure to you, not to stress you out. More people I know like to listen to Led Zeppelin than to opera. That's cool, I love Zep. My question now is, how far do you want to take it? I can *hear* their terroir—the Mississippi Delta or the California coast or Northern Africa. Maybe someone else just hears some loud guitars and a giant fucking beat. The point is, you don't have to know that "Whole Lotta Love" was swiped from Willie Dixon, or that "When the Levee Breaks" is an old Delta blues that was recorded in a former Victorian poorhouse, or that the guitar on "Kashmir" is tuned DADGAD, but if you get that far, that's the next level. I love geeking out like that. But it doesn't mean you can't just respond viscerally to "Misty Mountain Hop" or the joys of a glass of Burgundy without having some music nerd like me argue the relative merits of *Zep II* versus *Zep IV,* or a know-it-all oenophile timing the finish on a sip of a big red with a stopwatch—and that's no joke, I have actually seen it. Don't sweat it, just enjoy. But be leery of the overly pushy waiter with an agenda, trying to sell you a bottle of wine. Waiters are often incentivized to sell "target" wines and are sometimes rewarded by the house for selling bottles with the greatest margin.

Find someone, anyone, who loves wine, to help you. Wine is a true love, and you shouldn't be shortchanging the experience to make an extra buck or to save a buck. If I were spending money in a restaurant, I'd want to know: Who chose this wine? Who buys it? Who wrote the list? And if the sommelier can't answer the question, fuck 'em. Game over. As restaurateurs and wine professionals, I think that our job is as much to be consumer advocates as it is to be wine experts. We have to discern quality for people and present alternatives that fit their needs as diners and wine consumers. Mario and I have made a reputation and a living by never dumping inventory on customers, because the people who sell wines in our restaurants truly love wine, and anyway, whatever we have in the cellar, we're going to sell it. We don't have to push. In our places, as much as we'll try to sell you up to something really incredible, you'll get downsold to a great value as well.

One thing I'm good at is remembering wines—I can taste them blind and usually identify them. Wines in my mind are collected like books in a reference library. I have my own abstract way of keeping all these sensations—the smell, the taste, the feel—of all these wines stacked up in my brain. I learned in my early days at Becco, and in Italy and at Felidia before that. Back then there were times when I would taste fifty wines a day. And not only taste them but academically, categorically, methodically analyze fifty, sixty, seventy wines a day and file all this stuff in my head.

It's like a form of savantism. I'm a librarian of olfactory impact. When I smell wine, it talks to me. Takes me to another place. It makes me either happy or sad. Or angry. Immediately the olfactory quality of a wine elicits emotion in me more than anything else in the world. Putting my nose into that first glass of wine before dinner or after a day or even in the morning—whenever it is, it brings me to places, which to me is more easily relatable than trying to deconstruct it in terms of other flavors. Sure, I might describe something as earthy or big or musty or having notes of cranberry or whatever, but I'm more likely to peg it right out of the gate as Burgundy or Barolo—this is from Piemonte, this is from Sicily, this is New World garbage.

Some of the best tastings I've ever had were in the mornings. One of the greatest mentors of my life was Josh Greene of *Wine & Spirits* magazine. We used to start a tasting at eight in the morning and go through a hundred twenty wines before lunch. Not drinking, just spitting. Once you've gone through six, eight, ten wines and you're not spitting, you're not tasting it, you're drinking it.

Tasting the first wine in the morning is like seeing the first pretty girl of the day—the impact is clear, the impression is vivid, there is little ambiguity. Beauty is apparent, and it lingers. But with every wine tasted after the first one, it's the same as with every girl you see on the street—you're more likely to observe a ripple or a wrinkle, a blemish, poor posture. As you taste through a massive quantity of wines, what once was crystal clear becomes a blur of sensations, tactile and olfactory, from sublime to disgusting, but, mostly, simply good and bad. But even after a twelve-hour day when you're sweating it out on the F train trying to get back to Queens and you see a beautiful woman, it's like seeing the sun rise all over again.

At least that's the tendency. Being a focused taster means that even drowning in this abstract miasma of taste, you're able to tell one wine from another, you can zoom in on details most civilians will never savvy, like how paint drops in a gorgeous splatter painting can either stand out from the background or compete and combine to make the whole picture.

For me, I have a mental index card for each wine, and they all go into these metal file boxes I have in my head, and there are a lot of them. Some are schoolhouse green, or rusty red, or gunmetal gray, chipped and stained, and each one represents a topology of wine. And on each card are my impressions—they're like snapshots of smells and flavors. Of impact. A taste of wine is one moment frozen. And I file it. The real skill is that when I'm tasting a new wine, I can riffle through the tens of thousands of these sensations and cross-reference the new experience with the old. It's about cataloging sensory experience.

My palate has evolved, naturally, over the years. As a serious wine drinker, you kind of start off big and bold, maybe some juicy California crap. Then soon enough you're not pounding juice, you're drinking wine from well-defined terroirs like Bordeaux and Barbaresco. Now you're hopscotching around the world looking for fruit, acid, and funk in the mountains of Priorat or the valleys of the Loire. And in all the wine journeys I have ever seen people embark on, they invariably end up drinking vintage Champagne and perfectly aged Burgundy.

New World wines will never catch up to the great wines of Old World Europe. It's like going to a classical liberal-arts college versus going to vocational school. It's the difference between Princeton and the Apex Technical School. It's the difference of generations, and experience, and understanding. It is the difference between Sophia Loren and Pam Anderson. Of course there are quality, delicious wines from California, but in the global wine scene they are the new kids on the block.

Vintage Barolo is like smack for a wine junkie—it has a timelessness and a complexity and an otherworldliness to experience that isn't so obvious. I think the progression as a wine drinker is that you go from needing to be smashed in the head with a two-by-four—something frighteningly fruity, big, and aggressive—to a higher realm of finesse where the pleasures are almost—almost—out of reach and the sensation is almost fleeting. Trying to grab onto it, that's where you get your high. That's where you get your thrills. The wine brings you up to its level. You never drag it down to yours.

By the Becco days, I was becoming a little more savvy about wine importation and distribution, about who was making what money and how I might get in on the action. Babbo wasn't open yet—we were still just talking about it—but Becco was moving boatloads of wine, and that was the real spark to understanding how the economics of wine work, what the true cost of wine was, and who was driving the cost. The idea to get into the wine business at first was powered by one of Restaurant Man's favorite maxims: Eliminate the middleman and widen the margin.

When I was in Italy after my time on Wall Street, my mother's friend Bruno set me up on my first big wine trip. He had a buddy named Valter Scarbolo who made wine in a town called Lauzacco. We drove there one night, went down into his restaurant in the basement around five o'clock, and resurfaced at about eight o'clock the next morning. We probably drank twenty bottles of wine and became fast friends. Every day we would wind up drinking Tocai Friulano made by a local farmer, out of these thick, chewed-up glasses. The wine was kind of a golden brown in color, which was simply due to lack of attention on the winemaker's part—there was some skin still left on the grapes when they'd begun to ferment. Skin is the only thing that gives color to a red wine—the pulp inside red grapes is white, it's not colored. But this wine had such great richness; it was really waxy on the palate, almost thick and viscous, served chilled, but never too cold, and with a slice of prosciutto San Daniele it would give you an incredible sensation, like separating honey and beeswax right on your palate—the wax would remain between your teeth, and the honey would dribble down the back of your throat and warm your whole body.

Trying to parse the richness and complexity and soulfulness of a white wine made like that, so down-to-earth, inspired me. It felt like the source of life of the people there. It really made you feel part of the place. It's one of those things—that wine is so inexorably linked to that place that they're one and the same. I always think about James Joyce. I like to think that *Ulysses* and *Dubliners* and *Portrait of the Artist as a Young Man* were fueled by Tocai Friulano. When he lived in Trieste and wrote those books, he must have drunk bottles of it in the Piazza Unità, gazing out on the Adriatic.

I love all kinds of wine, but that's where I became a committed white wine drinker, and now I always say that if you're going to drink wine every day of your life, and I mean a lot of it, you have to drink white wine. It's more conducive to bodily and mental health than red wine is. There is a lot of shit in red wine, all that dry extract, which is what gives it the color and feel, whereas white wine is just like gently flavored water with a dash of alcohol and some acidity.

Eventually I started to buy Valter's wines and serve them at Becco and Felidia. And then Bruno came up with the idea that I should make some wine of my own.

I bought the first winery in '96. It was effectively a historical estate, the Belvedere Vineyards, which were part of the Zamò and Palazzolo estate in the town of Buttrio, the DOC of Colli Orientali del Friuli, in the region of Friuli–Venezia Giulia, in northeastern Italy. I knew that that area had the unique combination of climate and terroir to create the most powerful, long-lived white wines in Italy.

The deal happened the same way it always does in the Old World: The farmer told the priest, who told the bartender, who told the town drunk, and eventually someone whispered in my ear that this vineyard *might* be available. Of course, in that part of the world nothing is officially for sale, because no one ever wants to be seen as needing to sell something, but of course we got to talking, and when we were done haggling, he didn't sell *me* the vineyard, I had made *him* an offer he couldn't refuse. Or at least that's what he would tell his friends. The first vintage was '98, the year Babbo opened. Few things in my life have made me prouder.

A lot of people thought that if I went into producing wine, I would just have someone else make some shit for me and slap a label on it, then import it, right? That is still, unfortunately, sometimes the perception. And it couldn't be further from the truth—we own every vineyard, and we grow every grape used to make these wines. They are completely a product of passion and an extremely intimate expression of who I am.

We make Friulano, Vespa Rosso, and Calabrone, which is a blended red wine and pretty much our premier red, retailing for eighty or ninety bucks a bottle. It is very extracted, very concentrated, extremely dense and rich. Our Rosato is very easy to drink, I know people who say it is our best stuff—you can drink it with pizza or crudo, you can have it with dinner at Babbo or take it on a picnic. And we make Tocai Plus, which is kind of like our kinky, bisexual wine—it's almost like a white Amarone, but there is something a little bit ambiguous about it that really turns people on. Our flagship wine is the Vespa Bianco, which is a blended white wine and the signature wine of the winery. It costs something like forty bucks in the store, pretty reasonable for a great bottle of wine, and in my opinion probably the best white wine made in Italy.

I started out selling the Bastianich wines in our restaurants and then making the rounds, knocking on doors, getting people to taste them and telling them my story. Robert Chadderdon started importing some, which gave me a lot of credibility, even if he is a pretentious bully.

Back when I was working at Felidia, I saw that some of the great Barolos had a sticker on their bottles, IMPORTED BY ROBERT CHADDERDON SELECTIONS, with his signature on it. The way he branded his bottles, the "imported by" sticker became more important than the label itself.

This guy was all about quality. And all the wines he imported and distributed were excellent. Eventually I was buying wine for Felidia from him. And I got to meet him, and when I opened Becco, I started to order wine from him. But first he had to test me. I had to audition for him to convince him that I was worthy of his time and of buying his product. It was kind of crazy—he ran this two-person show, he and his assistant, Mary Ann. She was like a throwback to the secretaries of the sixties, real *Man in the Gray Flannel Suit* stuff. There were no salespeople or any other staff.

She was the keeper of the gate for their office in Rockefeller Center. The whole scene was ridiculously pompous—Bob was very buttoned up, very Waspy. He actually wore field jackets with khaki pants, working the lord-of-the-manor, landed-gentry look. It made me want to club him over the head with a pith helmet.

He had a waiting room with brass lamps and portraits of dogs, plus nautical-themed relics on the wall. Mahogany paneling with hunter green glen-plaid cushions. You feel like you're going to the reading of a will at an attorney's office in Stuck Up, Connecticut. In his office he had two guest chairs with a giant globe between them, and he sat at an enormous desk with bottles of whiskey literally from centuries ago, half tasted, and he'd interview you while peering over them. He would put out two wines, blind. Give you a white and a red, or maybe two reds, and ask you to taste them, without telling you anything, always projecting this greater-than-thou attitude, as if you were lucky to be in the presence of this Master of the Wine Universe. He would make you fax over your wine list and your menu. Maybe, if you were lucky, come and check out your restaurant. And *then* he would tell you what wines *he would give you,* which wines *he would allow you to have.* So it wasn't even like you actually ordered any wines for yourself. He would pick the wines out of his portfolio that he thought were appropriate and just send them to you. He might send fifteen thousand dollars' worth of wine or a thousand dollars' worth. You had no idea. And you still had to pay for it within the time allotted.

The second order he sent me was a ten-case lot of oxidized Soave, which was completely defective. It was totally rank shit. That was our first battle, because I refused. I couldn't sell it. I didn't want to get stuck with it, and he was pressing on thirty-day terms. That really drew the line in the sand. Somehow we got through the Soave incident—I think he credited me for some of it or gave me a couple cases of something else. It wasn't easy. I ended up pouring it down the drain, but I chalked it up as an investment in our relationship, and I even wound up getting to taste with him a little bit, and went to Europe with him. He is a great taster, but also the best wine spitter I've ever seen. He would sit at his desk, sip wine, and the bucket could be either across the room or right next to him, and without even turning his head he would go *sprffffft!*—right into the fucking bucket. Which is a real skill. In the professional wine world, in cellar tasting environments, a good spit puts you in the big leagues— velocity, location, quality, flow, and linearity, it all counts. Someday I'm going to make up a scorecard and have a legit spitting contest.

When I was buying the first vineyard, I actually brought him with me. We went through tasting older vintages and looked at the terroir, and he gave me his opinions. As much as the guy was an arrogant douchebag, he is one of the most intuitive wine tasters I've ever known. He is certainly one of the best out there, palatewise. Very classical, very Old World. Almost to a fault. He kept this

Eurocentric worldview—he would never deal with California wines. It worked for him until pretty recently. From what I hear, a lot of people don't buy from him anymore. He is not very well liked by today's hotshot sommies; in fact, people hate him because he goes against the grain of everything wine is supposed to be if you have a healthy attitude toward tasting, which is communicative, educational, all about sharing information. He made it supersnobbified. It was always, "It's a privilege for you to buy wine from me." He's snubbed and alienated a whole generation of wine buyers and wine professionals. To many of the most important buyers in this country, he's an artifact. He lived in a very old model of intimidation, fearmongering, preying on the insecurity and apparent stupidity of everyone around him. Kind of like a schoolyard bully, of the old Euro guard. But you could never question the provenance of the wines. I still say he is a pretentious tool, but you could never knock his taste.

The truth is, wine makes no fiscal sense. I will never earn a dime in my lifetime producing wine. It's a very expensive business. But for me, and I think for most people, wine is really about passion. I've spent a lot of the money that I've made in my life investing in and pursuing my passion for wine.

Having your name on a bottle that people are drinking from is a heavy responsibility. Wine is not like food. It's not like opening a new restaurant. A bottle of wine is like a piece of music or a book— you can take it anywhere in the world with you. You can open it anywhere on this planet and enjoy that piece of my art in that moment. I used to put my cell-phone number on the wine bottles in the early days: *"Call Joe when you drink."* People would call me from China, from India, from all these places in the world that you couldn't possibly have imagined reaching with your message. "Hey, dude, I'm drinking your wine, we love it. Thanks!" I loved it. I used to stay on the phone and talk to them. It was a real connection. The circle was being completed. I always say that drinking a glass of my wine is like getting to know me a little.

Because I had the ability to move a lot of wine in our restaurants, I was less concerned with what the market thought of the wines. I just made ones that I liked, according to the styles that I liked, which is a wide range but didn't always jibe with whatever was trending or popular and can be somewhat heartbreaking if the people don't catch up with you or come around. But you can't chase trends in the wine market. You have to have a vision, you have to believe, and ultimately the market has to come around to you or you have to find your consumer. It's not like running a restaurant, where you can play with the menu, think up new specials, invent shit on the fly because one night you're stoned in the kitchen and come up with an idea for sea urchin, jalapeños, and black pasta served cold.

Say today we decide that Petite Sirah is the new wine trend, or will be, but we don't have any Petite Sirah growing. We have to plant it. The first thing we have to do is tear up the old vineyard. We have to wait a year for the earth to settle. We have to plant a new vineyard. Three years to get 10 percent production. So we're already at five years. In seven years we're at 50 percent production. In ten years we have moderate production to produce a wine that may need to sit for another year or two until it gets to the market. That means our decision today will reap its first viably economic fruit twelve years from now. You can't do it. You can't anticipate where the wine world's taste is going to be. Who could know that with the global economic meltdown that we would have a complete back-lash against oaked wines? That no one would want to drink extracted wines, sweet wines, or any of these buttery Chardonnays? Suddenly there was some odd mandate for moderation and austerity, projected onto the palate! They weren't connected per se—the economy and the shift in taste—it just kind of all happened at the same time, but now you had a lot of crap on your hands that no one wanted, and no one had the dough to buy it even if they did. Suddenly everyone wanted wines that were real, that had a history, that came from a specific terroir, and for me that was great, because that's what I'd been saying all along, that wine should be connected to a real place, that the best wines could transport you. Unfortunately, it required a total financial collapse for the world to catch up to me, but I'll take it.

Obviously, the economy is a driving force in how people are personally changing their consumption—that sensibility of excess and just piling shit on top of shit to make something better is gone. And now everyone wants to eat and drink things that are sourced locally, or in a place that's at least identifiable. Just the idea that what we are drinking actually has a real source is often enough—a place you could go and breathe and eat and be inspired, like a vineyard in Italy, not a fucking wine factory that looks and smells like a petroleum-processing plant in Elizabeth fucking New Jersey.

I like to drink my own wines; they make me happy. Because I made them. Because I own the land they come from. I realize that is somewhat narcissistic bordering on pure solipsism, but so what? The wine I make is a very personal extension of me. And I never get tired of drinking it. I'm always the champion of this bottle and the next bottle—you can pin an entire generation of hangovers on me. But it comes from a genuine desire to share. You can't blame me for that.

I'm so drawn to wine because it's about identity. It's about who we are, who I am. It's about where I come from. Wine is one of the only things in the world that transcends our own humanity. I'm propagating a war-torn family legacy. With my wine I'm bringing my kids back to postwar Europe from which their ancestors had to flee and become refugees because Europe was being destroyed. Drinking my wine is like bringing them back to 1921, to the land where they come from. Maybe when they are forty or fifty years old, the wineries will all have been paid for and they'll be looking back while sitting on their porch in Tuscany, having a glass of my juice, watching their children running around the vineyard, and they'll say, "Look at my dad. What a great, smart guy he was. He left me this winery and paid for it for me. Now I can do whatever the fuck I want with it." That may be the point where I'll either roll over in my grave or come rising up like Joe the Zombie and join them for a bottle.

Wine is a bigger topic than we are—one life in wine is not enough to truly live the life of wine. In a world of ultimate immediacy, where we control and dictate and captain our ships and direct every movement, wine is only something we participate in, because ultimately the process of wine is the natural cycle of life and Mother Nature and nature in general. You can't control that; you can only take part in it for a finite amount of time. By the time you get to make wine, if you're a serious winemaker or a wine entrepreneur, you're already an adult. You really don't get to do it before you're twenty-five or thirty. Say you have a long career and you're able to keep making wine until you're seventy. That's forty vintages. Let's say ten of them are fucked up and unharvestable or for some reason cannot be used to make wine, which is very normal. That leaves thirty. So in a lifetime of wine, you have thirty opportunities to express yourself and your passion. Think about that. Thirty chances in a lifetime. And then you go away. You return to the earth, and maybe, if you're lucky, your kids will carry on your legacy.

From a cultural perspective as someone who has this history in Italy, and from a personal perspective, being a father, it's the only thing I can leave my kids that will speak of me and my story. It's the only thing that will transcend my humanity and leave my legacy to them. That's what's really appealing to me about wine. It's kind of at the core of who we are as a people, because it allows us to live in multiple generations and centuries. It allows us to participate in something that is bigger than our eighty or ninety years on this earth.

•

CHAPTER TWELVE

Romulus, Remus, and Me

Mario and I were flying high. We always were; it was our nature. More accurately, I think we had a knack for keeping our feet on the ground while our heads were in orbit, which is why Babbo worked. We found the right formula of Hard-Ass Restaurant Man versus Starry-Eyed Artist to achieve what had been initially some pretty far-out concepts. Mostly, though, ridiculously hard work paid for us to have ridiculously good times.

After Babbo was up and running, we had a little more time to enjoy the rewards of our success, so naturally we pointed the ship back to the motherland. We'd tell our wives that we needed to go to Italy, that it was very important for the sake of our future in the food and wine world—which wasn't so far from the truth, actually—and then we'd go on these boondoggle R&D trips, eating and drinking everything in sight.

We took on Rome as though we wanted to live like fucking gladiators. Full-contact eating and drinking. One of my favorite dinners was at Checchino, a restaurant built into a grotto in the walls of Testaccio, which once upon a time was like the Hunts Point of Rome, where all the butchers were. We had rigatoni con la pajata, one of the legendary dishes of Rome—we went to Rome pretty much just to find it—intestines of suckling veal, cooked while they still have their mothers' milk in them. They're braised in tomato sauce with rigatoni, and the milk from the intestines curdles into a ricotta.

I get that there are people who are kind of skeeved by the idea of braised baby-cow intestines with milk curdling inside them. This is nothing new. This is the food of the gods, and my message to people who are grossed out is simple: Don't go to Rome, and don't eat it. I really am not into any dare eating or stunt eating—I think Anthony Bourdain is out of his mind with the insects and the still-beating heart of the cobra and all that, but if something is sensible, within the culture, I'll eat it. Sometimes I get a little freaked out by it, but I'm no cheeky-smeeky eater. The one thing that really bugs me, though, about Mario is that he likes to suck on chicken knuckles, the fucking white, gelatinous part of chickens at the end of the bones. He likes to chomp on them as if they were a Twix bar. That is so fucking gross to me. He sucks on chicken bones like they're candy and loves to eat chicken feet. Boiled chicken feet. That's where I draw the line. But I have an issue with poultry. It goes back to being a kid and being practically waterboarded with bloody chicken juice in the back of my father's truck.

Anyway, at Checchino I think we started off with some cow's feet—all the parts of the hoof were boiled out and put into a gelatin mold and served with celery and wine vinegar—and then the rigatoni con la pajata. And then the abbacchio alla romana, which is a baby lamb smeared with smelly anchovies, roasted, deglazed with red wine vinegar, and served with fried artichokes. I think that night we drank an entire case of wine, which happened more often than you could imagine. The only problem was that the next day we had an early cooking class.

It was me, Mario, Mark Ladner, and Zach Allen, a great chef who also happens to be a narcoleptic. We were going to hire him to work at our new place, which would become Lupa. I remember interviewing him in New York before the trip. We were all sitting at a table, and Mark says to Mario, "This is Zach Allen. He worked for the Caballero. He's a good guy. I can vouch for him." Mario said, "All right. We're going to pay him two hundred and twenty dollars a week," basically what a dishwasher makes, and everyone looked around, waiting for a response, and Zach was fast asleep. Mario hired him on the spot—Mario's only regret was that he probably could have gotten him for twenty bucks less. Now Zach oversees all our West Coast operations and our new businesses in Asia.

The next morning in Rome, we were completely hungover. After dinner we were doing shots of grappa, and now we were suffering for that as well, a complete fucking mess. We were finally sort of getting it together to hit the road when we realized we were missing someone: Zach had fallen asleep with his face on the night table next to his bed, and he was now stuck to it. We had to slowly moisten sponges with some leftover grappa and work on him like a bunch of drunk EMTs to melt whatever adhesive combination of saliva and sweat and random Roman gunk had glued his face to the nightstand, without ripping his skin off.

Afflicted by the most blistering hangovers since Julius Caesar's coronation party, we had to drive out of Rome without directions, before GPS, to Castelli Romani in order to meet Paola di Mauro. They call her the emperor of Roman cuisine. She was seventy years old at the time. Her kitchen was her own coliseum of Italian cooking. She was going to cook with us and impart this great wisdom to us, and all we could do was pull over every ten minutes to puke.

I'm a good boy and, like my mama taught me, insisted that we had to buy flowers for Paola. So we're driving around Rome trying to buy flowers. But it's Sunday morning, and of course nothing is open. Finally I stole some flowers from a church cemetery.

Paola made zuppa romana with these crazy beans, cicerchia,

that are very typically Roman, and Romanesco broccoli. It was quite
a day. After paying her a compliment on the healing properties of
her cooking, I excused myself, yacked it all up, and steeled myself
for the next course.

Maybe there was a moment when I thought, *Holy shit, am
I becoming my parents, trucking across Italy on some quasi-educational
eating binge?* But that idea vanished pretty quickly. It was more like
we were becoming Romans. Our meals were epic, the wine consumption historic. Mostly we'd been eating in Rome's great tratto-
rias. In Italy there are different levels of restaurants. The simplest
one is a *frasca,* which could be a roadside kiosk that might sell fruit
and vegetables as well as one or two dishes, where workmen might
come and eat a lunch, maybe buy some pig bones and a slice of
cheese and a case of peaches to take home. Then there's the *osteria,*
which is slightly above that. Those will have a table or two and a
real menu. The *trattoria* is slightly more defined—a few more
courses, more of the restaurant experience. In the osteria you might
have some prosciutto, a bowl of soup, a plate of pasta, very casual
service. In the trattoria you have antipasti, primi, secondi—it's
more proper, but nothing like the *ristorante,* with white tablecloths,
antipasti, primi, secondi, dolce—more of the tropes of classical dining. And contrary to what the world might believe, there is no such
thing as an Italian bistro. It's a chafing concept, and yet there are a
lot of places trying to be that in the West Village. Italian fucking
bistros. Please. It upsets me.

The distinction really hit us on this trip: Babbo is a ristorante.
What we needed to do is bring a real Roman trattoria to New York.
It was one degree closer to street level—no deconstructed osso
bucco, no getting inside the heads of stoned lifeguards to figure out
how they would cook their squid. This meant pastas that you would
actually eat in Rome before a couple of lunatics reimagined them.

·   ·   ·

Rome is where the great commerce of food came from—long before Chicago, Rome was the greatest butcher in the world. The nobility in the surrounding countryside ate the prime cuts of meat, the people who lived in the city ate the secondary and tertiary cuts, and by the time you got to the ghetto, you were eating the innards, but that poor meat—things like stomach, lungs, and spleen—was truly the people's cuisine of Rome.

So while the nobility got the best cuts of steak, the rest would go on to the slaughterhouses to feed the populace, and the Tiber River would run red with the blood from the abattoirs. There was a bend in the river that was piled high with the carcasses of animals thrown into the water after they were harvested of all their meat.

The real charm of Roman food culture is just how basic and accessible it is to everyone. There's a magic about *not* eating in a grand ristorante—eating in the simplest trattoria in a winding alley of Trastevere can be even more incredible. The street experience was what we decided to bring to Greenwich Village.

Jason Denton, who was one of the first waiters at Po, wanted to do a restaurant with us, and together we came up with the idea of Lupa—Lupa is the she-wolf who famously nursed Romulus and Remus in the Seven Hills of Rome. Mario and I like to take these concepts as far as we can, but Jason had a big part in the success of Lupa. He is a great Restaurant Man.

Thompson Street, where we built Lupa, might not be a winding alley, but it has a nice vibe. It wasn't the ritzy part of the West Village, more like a no-man's-land between SoHo and Greenwich Village, just north of Houston Street. The space was a little bit industrial, in a tenement building, a restaurant laid out like a railroad flat with an air shaft dividing the space, with a room in the back, and another in the front. It was a very inexpensive renovation.

We used reclaimed wood, and we brought the Croatian sociopath Davor back to build it for us. We made these giant arches behind the bar and through the dining room out of rescued brick and again it was done on a very limited budget. By that point we were shipping stuff from Europe to our restaurants in giant containers, which gave us a great opportunity. We just threw anything we found on our trips onto the boat: antique tables, shoes, cowbells, you fucking name it. A lot of junk that became props for Lupa. I think people celebrated Lupa in its simplicity and its purity because it was cheap and really good. When we opened, pastas were nine to fourteen bucks and no lunch there was over twenty. It had a great vibe.

Babbo was a ristorante that interpreted this intellectual idea of Italian food—it was more of an artistic creation. We indulged in some highly conceptual menu planning. Lupa was a more literal translation of a kind of restaurant in a specific city in Italy. It was about chickpeas and tripe; bavette; cacio e pepe, the signature pasta dish of Rome; coda alla vaccinara, braised oxtail, butcher style. They've been cooking oxtail as long as they've been knocking off their heads in Testaccio, and there's nothing intellectual or interpretive about that. It was very literal, and very deliberately and specifically about understanding the attention to detail in all these incredible, iconic Roman dishes. In New York now, there's a wash of microregional, stylistically city-focused restaurants, but Lupa may have been the first, maybe the first restaurant that wasn't northern or southern Italian.

Lupa wasn't trying to be Rome in New York—we were still sourcing locally but thinking about bringing that true Roman feel to an urban, slightly gritty, nuts-and-bolts trattoria in mid-nineties Manhattan. That simplicity, that real translation of flavor, was really important at Lupa.

We didn't know we would be successful before we opened—no one had tried this before. Mark Ladner spent a lot of time with us in Italy and became the opening chef and a partner at Lupa. That's when we really started to see the brilliance of Mark, who to this day I think is one of the great cooks in New York, maybe in the world. Amazing that an American kid who grew up in Providence, Rhode Island, could capture and grow on the experience of food made by housewives in this urban environment of Rome and interpret that into a New York dining experience.

All the wines at Lupa are from central Italy, from the Mezzogiorno, a lot of Lazio, Campania, southern Tuscany, Abruzzo. The wine list was very much focused on everyday wines. No Barolos, no Barbarescos. Really easy, breezy simple wines. We knew the food. The dishes were researched. The ingredients were right. The lingo was right. We nailed the details and really delved into all the things we consider part of the authentic Roman experience.

For example, Roman restaurants are filled with these *amari*—which literally means "bitters." Fernet-Branca being the classic. When we were terrorizing Rome, we started each day with a shot of Fernet—it helped settle the hangover.

No one really drank *amaro* here in the States, but in Rome, after lunch, you would always be offered one. Essentially they are *digestivi*, born in pharmacies. They're very medicinal, with an alcohol base, and each town has its own style. Our thought for Lupa was that the whole back bar would be full of these *amari* we'd collected, bottle by bottle, all over Italy, that no one had ever seen before. Now *amaro* is in every restaurant in the whole world, but it was really Lupa that brought it to New York, and it grew from there.

Lupa was never seriously reviewed. We wanted it to be more populist. It was small. It was in a tenement. There was nothing fancy-pants about it. Eric Asimov wrote about it in the "$25 and Under" column in the *New York Times*, but that was it, and that was enough. Honestly, we weren't soliciting reviews. What for? If we got one star, it would suck. Certainly it's not a three-star restaurant. If it got two stars, that would be great, but it wouldn't change anything. The place kind of defies categorization in its own way.

And then, just as I was finishing writing this book and getting it ready to go to the publisher, Asimov, who was now sitting in as the *New York Times* food critic—in the wake of Sam Sifton, who had gone on to become the national editor, and while the restaurant world eagerly waited for the more enlightened musings of Pete Wells—came in to give Lupa another look, and he hit us with a flat one-star review.

Frankly, I was disappointed and hurt when I saw his review. I thought that of all our restaurants, Lupa was the most bulletproof. The concept was pioneering, and it's still relevant—the food remains true to its original vision: simply delicious. The entire message is crystal clear, and the prices are still extremely fair. Lupa has become a benchmark in our industry, so I was taken aback by his inability to translate its spirit and importance. It was a major disappointment for the entire Lupa staff, as well as to Mario and me.

He centered the review on the ebbs and flows of a busy restaurant—he was jostled while waiting for a prime-time table that he didn't have a reservation for. He also wrote, "At off-hours—a late night, a midafternoon—Lupa continues to be delightful, satisfying and attentive." What I get out of this is that the unequivocal success of a restaurant is now a liability? He had some quibbles, but he also praised the pasta to the sky, along with the salumi, another house specialty. But overall I think he missed the point, the simplicity of what a Roman trattoria should be. You know my philosophy: I'd rather be warm for twelve years than be hot for six months, and Lupa's long-term popularity is a testament to the meritocracy of the New York dining world, where people will continue to vote with their feet. But one star is just a complete letdown for Mario and me and all the people who work at Lupa eighty hours a week to create this experience. I feel bad for the Lupa crew, I am sorry they weren't honored with a better *New York Times* review, but the restaurant has been as good as it's ever been, and we are not going to change a thing.

Stars matter for certain restaurants at certain price points. When you charge thirty, forty dollars for an entrée, you have an accountability to justify those prices and you're fair game for journalists and their opinions, as well as the Michelin and Zagat guides and everyone else. But price still matters even if you have the stars—at Babbo, where we were trying to bridge the gap between being a hip restaurant and a fine-dining experience, all the entrées are under thirty dollars, except for the rib eye, which costs me almost that much to put on the plate.

But when you're a lower-priced restaurant, people will vote with their feet and their dining dollars. New York is a savvy town, and good food will always rise to the top in New York. I think there are very few examples of people serving great food at a great price and not succeeding in the city. They may not succeed wildly, but if you're really that good, people will seek you out and support you. There's no more of a meritocracy in the entire food universe than the New York dining scene.

People always ask me how I felt when Mario was becoming a TV star and a famous media personality while I was still mostly behind the scenes. I tell them I never minded. I was very happy, over the fucking moon about making some money with our business that was born completely out of our passion for Italian food and wine, and more comfortable with myself than I would have ever imagined when I was growing up a self-loathing wop. Between Bus Head and the bagel shop, some sort of seed had been planted, and now not only was I loving being in the restaurant business, I was loving my ginzo roots. All was right with the world.

This was also around the time of our first retail adventure. By now, any discomfort with my heritage that I'd wrestled with when I was growing up was long gone—in fact, I was wearing my pride on the sleeve of my Armani jacket. Our fortunes were tied to our passion for all things Italian, and it had occurred to us that, beyond our restaurants, a maniacal devotion to Italian wine could have some positive economic consequences on our lives. No one had really championed the category before; it was totally untrodden ground. We were kicking it hard—Babbo with the higher end, Lupa with more ready-to-go wines—but we had never been retailers.

America is still full of blue laws, a result of Prohibition residue and regional anti-alcohol sentiment. The idea originally was to stop people from having a monopoly in liquor. Back when those of a certain moral fiber thought that liquor was an evil thing, the fear was that if breweries could brew beer, distribute it, and own the pubs where it was drunk, then the beer companies would become a satanic monopoly that would turn the populace into monsters. That was the Prohibitionist mentality. After Prohibition every step in the commerce of alcoholic spirits in the United States needed to be separated. It was part hangover from the Volstead days and also part of an antitrust sentiment that doesn't really exist anymore: Back then there were also laws about movie studios owning distributors and theaters, and later about people owning television stations and newspapers in the same regions, but you've seen where that's gone. We live in a time of complete conglomeration—but when it comes to booze, there are still plenty of cranky old morality-driven laws on the books. We are still living in the shadow of Prohibition. For instance, you can't order a drink in New York City between 4:00 A.M. and noon on Sunday—between last call and lunch. That's kind of an amazing concept. Think about it: You can't order a Bloody Mary with your 11:00 A.M. brunch on Sunday even if you're staying at the St. Regis and spending two thousand dollars a night for your room.

We were successful at selling wine in restaurants, but we also knew that Italian wine had a long way to go. We believed that it was very undervalued. We saw all these wine collectors coming into restaurants—young wannabes who really didn't know anything about wine and would drop thousands of dollars, all of it on Bordeaux.

Italian wine, which we thought was the greatest wine in the world, had no play in this universe. It wouldn't be abnormal to find a guy spending a quarter million in a year on wine, all of it French and Californian. We thought that was wrong. We were running into this kind of aristocracy of wine people, and none of them were buying or collecting Italian wine. We thought, how many hundreds of millions of dollars was the collectible-wine market in the United States? What if we could convert 15 percent of all expenditures on overpriced Bordeaux and Napa Valley crap to quality Italian wines? Certainly it was merited. That was our business plan. And that's how Italian Wine Merchants was born. We had flourished in our restaurants with this laser focus on everything pure and Italian, so why wouldn't it be a reasonable assumption that we could take on retail, or the collectors of the country, and put what we thought were the greatest wines in the world into the big leagues? All we wanted was a small slice of the big pie.

Italian Wine Merchants was me and Mario, of course, and, unfortunately, a sawed-off Neapolitan prick named Sergio. He was a manager or a sommelier at San Domenico, and he used to hang around our restaurants.

Even before Babbo I had the ambition to do a retail business, but

I was running restaurants and had no experience on that level. Sergio's dad was a retailer up in some bumfuck town near Albany, and he had worked there and knew the bottle-shop business. He talked the talk. And this was my downfall—he had the 3 percent I needed at that moment, the retail experience I was missing, even if back then it was only brown-bagging pints of Popov for the town drunks—to get me to 100 percent and get the business started. I should always be smarter than that—that 3 percent, I can buy it or learn it—but we made him a full partner. Big fucking mistake. Eventually we'd be sitting out on the stoop at Babbo talking about whacking the short-dicked little fuck.

But meanwhile the Italian Wine Merchants was turning into another Joe and Mario fantasy camp. It wasn't exactly *Field of Dreams*—we built a four-thousand-square-foot showroom on Sixteenth Street off Union Square. The problem was, it was right across from some social-services building, and around the corner was a high school, so it was all very weird and wired, even though fifty feet in the other direction was Union Square, pure gold. But this block was not a good scene. There was almost no foot traffic, it was kind of scary— you had to want to come to see us. But it was cheap, and it was big.

The space was a showcase of Italian lifestyle, and we were very aggressive—you came in to talk about wine and we'd be in there curing a giant fucking prosciutto. We brought in pigs, five-hundred-pound pigs we would buy at farms, and we'd start carving and cooking the fuckers right there in the store. It was very avant-garde. We took it to the rawest element. We were giving cooking demonstrations and wine tastings—we were the first people to have a kitchen in a wine store. It was insane, conceptually out of the parameters of anything anyone had ever attempted when it came to wine retail. It was a store, but with big ambitions. It wasn't a bottle shop, it was a dream. It was barely legal, but we didn't care, we just did it. It's not that we didn't care about the laws—we did—but we were going to push it until someone called "Cut!" No one ever did.

It was very nonconformist. But what it was really all about was building a relationship with the customers to educate them about Italian wine and having them buy into the concept that as a wine buyer you need to make Italian wine a part of what you collect or own. And this is where my Wall Street experience really paid off: We were like portfolio managers. We had account executives, cellar managers—we took the model from the world of finance and applied it to wine.

Italian Wine Merchants led the way for everything else that has happened in the last ten years in very specific wine retailing and this insistent focus on *niche, niche, niche.* And it didn't happen just in New York. We were everywhere. We hit every wine festival and every wine collector. We were in Nashville, Portland, Los Angeles, San Diego—you name it. If you had a wine festival, we would come to town like fucking Vikings. We were out there on the national scene in a big way, saying, "Look, guys. Wake up. Italian wines are the greatest in the world. Get hip, get on board, or get run over." One great night we were in Nashville at the house of Tom Black, who is one of the great opinion makers and collectors of wine. We had every hotshot wine yahoo from Alabama to Florida to Arizona there, and we did a night with absolutely mind-fucking Barolos, like ten vintages, with agnolotti and white truffles right off the plane from Alba, and we blew these people away. One by one we conquered all these nouveau riche wine snobs who had no clue and had to be told what they should be drinking and buying. They knew our momentum. They knew Mario, they knew Babbo, they knew me, maybe they had an idea of what we were really about, but we would come in and we would kill these guys, millionaires who thought they were big wheels because they had a couple of cases of Bordeaux in their basement. We were rocking the whole American wine scene. Italian Wine Merchants went from zero to $12 million a year in five years. That's a big number for only Italian wine.

At the most basic level, we weren't selling wine, we were selling legitimacy. We were selling a slice to everyone who wanted to feel a little bit Italian. All those people who had the money went to Amalfi, went to Florence, rented the villas, but they didn't have access to the essence of Italianness. We were selling that passport.

I never lost money buying a bottle of wine. I may not make any money *making* wine, but buying and selling it, hell yeah.

I learned how to buy and sell it from my parents when they were loading up Felidia with great bottles. Then Pat Cetta at Sparks taught me to buy wine like Attila the Hun. Eventually that translated to my being able to do business with not only retailers but these insane wine collectors—there are about a hundred guys in this country who have multimillion-dollar cellars and who get together to drink obscene amounts of wine on any given weekend.

On a flight from New York to L.A., these guys can mop up half a million dollars of wine, no sweat. Happens all the time. You couldn't snort that much cocaine—Aerosmith and Mötley Crüe in midseason form couldn't even come close. It's complete lunacy. These are regular guys from New Jersey who are sitting on millions of dollars of wine. Think about having $20 million worth of wine in your basement. Can you imagine having that in your house? Start drinkin', baby—you can try, but you'll never drink it all in your whole life.

Of course there are a lot of people in the wine world who are full of shit—poseurs and wannabes, people with no taste, who just want to impress one another with their rented wine savvy, but there are also the truly great collectors, who can truly taste and who understand wine and who treat it as if they were collecting art, because, really, that's what it is. Except you can't drink a Warhol. And, at its best, is consumable art, there when you want it.

There's a hierarchy in the wine world. Thanks to Robert Parker, the critics are at the top. Below them are the professional wine intelligentsia—educated restaurateurs and their sommeliers and the people who create wine programs, and winemakers. On the other side is a *consumer* wine intelligentsia that is very powerful. These guys are not wine professionals, but they are knowledgeable, passionate, and they have resources beyond those of mortal men.

There are people who can raise simple wood whittling into high-minded sculpture by being sagely critical about it, or just publicly championing it, and it is the same thing with wine. A great wine collector takes the work of the winemaker and, through whatever gravitas or juice he has, can elevate its status, the same as in the art world. One guy can declare a bottle of Barbaresco a masterpiece and boost its reputation (and price) to that of a Botticelli.

The moat around the fortress that separates the wine elite from the masses is winespeak. It is a subculture of snobs, invented out of necessity to explain the unexplainable, but also created to dichotomize the wine world and keep the smart clique in and the masses out. It is learnable—I suppose Esperanto is, too—but basically we allow ourselves to make shit up, and if you have enough authority and the balls to say it with 100 percent confidence, you can call any wine pretty much anything and people will listen to you—notes of mother's milk and bananas Foster, rusty Moxie caps and damp 1969 National League baseball cards. Say it with enough gravitas and, for better or worse, people will accept it. And that's what makes you a master of *this* universe. We have been given free rein in the use of an imperfect system, and within that there is a lot of abuse, but most of it is hidden under the cloak of pomp and stature, so even if you're dead wrong, enough chutzpah and maybe a nice suit will let you get away with it.

But we were very earnest, we were true believers, and with Italian Wine Merchants we created Italy as a category in every major wine cellar in the country—before that it wasn't really taken all that seriously, which is odd, because Italian culture has had a bigger impact on America than that of most other wine-producing countries. Italy has always been popular with Americans, as opposed to France, which has always had a snooty, douchebag reputation. Spain has a great rep for being lots of fun, and the Spanish are maybe twenty years behind Italy in becoming real players in the global wine market. Of course, they don't have Rome, Florence, or Leonardo da Vinci—not that there's anything wrong with Madrid, Barcelona, and Goya, but it's just not the same.

We realized pretty soon after we opened Italian Wine Merchants that Sergio just wasn't our guy. Mario and I have always made partners of people who brought something to the party. We've turned waiters into owners, but they all had vision. Sergio didn't have shit. He was that 3 percent that we needed for the first forty-five days, and from that point on he was just in our way.

After a few years, we were ready to string him up with one of the hams that were hanging in the back of the shop, but we figured it would be better just to go our separate ways, which is what we did. We both had our hands full with our restaurants, and mine with actually making wine, and it was a good time to get out. If it was our goal to spread the gospel of Italian wine, we could declare success. We had opened many doors and created a lot of awareness that brought a great deal to every other part of our business.

We sold out right before the crash in '08—Sergio found some newly minted millionaires who were looking to buy some legitimacy in the wine world, and it turned out okay, because we made some good money on the deal, but not as much as it was worth. We gave away at least a couple of million dollars. But that's how badly we wanted to get away from Sergio.

Mario mistrusted him from the beginning. My mother told me not to do the deal—she told me never to go into business with a Neapolitan. Mario always defers to Lidia's advice. They really like each other, and for Mario, Lidia is like a higher-intellect version of me—we are a lot alike, but she's much smarter. They both warned me, but I didn't listen, which was another mistake, because not only is she always right, but Mario loves to tell me when she is. When we took a $2 million haircut on this, he told me, "You should have listened to your mother, you douchebag. Don't get into fucking business with a sawed-off Neapolitan fuck. Anyone with a small penis is no one you want to have business with. Only guys with big swinging dicks." He meant that existentially, of course.

CHAPTER THIRTEEN

Pirate Love

Dave Pasternack knew fishermen who had hooks for hands, real fucking *hooks,* metal hooks, like fucking pirates. These were guys who would come into a restaurant to sell you a bag of scallops that was hanging off the end of their arm. It was fucking awesome. When it came to authenticity, you couldn't argue with that.

Dave was the chef at Picholine. His wife, Donna, was a waitress at Po, which is how Mario knew him. Dave was a good guy, a tough guy who'd been around the block a few times. He was a real South Shore Long Island fisherman, a blue-collar Jewish guy who wasn't afraid to knock back boilermakers with roughneck crews that hung around the dock bars or throw a wrench at a Detroit diesel. He had worked as an ass kicker for Andrew Silverman at one of his joints. Mario thought he was a talented cook, and really one of us, and wanted to work with him. So we decided to open a restaurant together. We made the decision sitting on the stoop at Babbo, drinking wine out of our fancy Spiegelau wine stems—some things never change.

Given his background and our worldview, we thought it only natural to do an Italian seafood restaurant. I had the property, so the real-estate side was done. We had already opened a restaurant at Forty-third and Ninth, where Esca is now, called Frico Bar, which didn't really work out. I closed it down after three years. It was a wine bar, and we had wine on tap and a lot of *affettati* and antipasti. It was doing all right, but very obviously, to me at least, underperforming. We were just ahead of our time—wine on tap is becoming popular now, and a lot of what we were doing there became very successful later, when we opened Otto. But no one was hip to it back then, the preexisting wine culture wouldn't tolerate it, and it's one of the only places that we ever closed. As restaurants go, it rates up there with my Capezios in the "I don't like to talk about it much" department.

The first thing we did with Dave was take off on another research trip. That's always the best part of opening a new place—you're funded and powered to go out to have a wild time and find crazy shit. You're with your partners and friends, and it's a license to have fun. You're doing your job, but it's the crème of our business, the greatest perk of all, whether it's sourcing salmon in Nova Scotia, seeking out an unknown breed of oysters in Iceland, or chasing coastal food around Italy and meeting the people. It usually involved swimming at night and major hangovers. In this case we thought we would eat our way through the whole Italian coastline—Amalfi, Sicily, Naples, Bari, Ancona, Venice, Trieste—and find out what really inspired us about the local seafood culture.

Dave grew up with a lot of fishermen—he was a guy who could relate to that world. We went to local fish markets, usually after being up all night, and saw what was coming in and what the fishermen's culture was at that time, what *they* were cooking. We would go eat wherever they ate. To our surprise we found that the fishermen at the source were eating everything raw, which was counterintuitive at that point, because no one thought raw fish had anything to do with Italy. The concept of crudo, of raw fish, at least in America, was born on that trip.

They would take the best local fish, combine it with the best regional Italian olive oil. If you were in Venice, you would have an olive oil from the Veneto. If you were in Ancona, you would have one from Le Marche. If you were in Palermo, you would have a Sicilian oil and the perfect sea salt—or maybe black volcanic salt, pre–Ice Age pink Himalayan, or some flaky French—and it was brilliant. So we came back to New York and got with it, doing exactly what we'd seen.

When we opened Esca, Gael Greene thought it was a put-on. She thought we were making it up. *Italian sushi? What, are you guys inventing this stuff?* Ruth Reichl was a big champion of Esca—she got it from the beginning—but a lot of the food mafia were rolling their eyes and calling it bullshit. We didn't even bother trying to convince them otherwise. We very much had a fuck-you attitude, because we knew that it was no joke. We fucking lived it. We were over there, and it was an epiphany—holy shit, everyone is eating everything raw here! We thought we were going to come back with the latest risotto du jour and some concocted scallop-with-cauliflower appetizer. But meanwhile it was just fresh fish cut into manageable pieces with a little local olive oil on it, and that was it. Simple food served simply. What else did you need to know?

We had a few other early champions. Bill Grimes gave us a three-star review in the *New York Times,* and we subsequently got many three-star reviews, but his was the first major one. We didn't really know where we would land, two or three stars, and with Esca, unlike Babbo, we didn't really think about it. We knew that it was special, but it kind of flipped out the market—we'd created a new category that you now see everywhere. Maybe there'd been a tuna carpaccio popping up here or there, but now Italian restaurants open with entire crudo sections on the menu. When you change behavior, that's when you know you're doing something important, and doing it effectively.

Babbo changed things by dint of sheer imagination and audacity. Lupa changed behavior because it created a category of microspecific restaurants. Twenty years later everything is superregional and superfocused. Now you have restaurants that serve just meatballs—one-dish restaurants. Lupa and Esca are both testimonies to our ability to commit to something and bring it to economic fruition. I think where a lot of restaurateurs go wrong—and our success has a lot to do with Mario, because he is a stubborn fuck and when he is committed to an idea, you can't push him off with a monster truck—is that the first minute they hit a bump or a slow night, they have the instinct to add things to the menu and go off concept. You have to have the balls to put something out there and to stick with it and to be pure and not to feel that the minute you have two empty tables, you have to offer something for everybody, because that's how you dilute the product and it becomes a shitty experience.

To have the real vision, to take the bumps, to take the criticism, to take the people who walk out because you don't have veal parmesan, and stay focused, true to your concept, and pure over decades requires a certain kind of restaurateur. Drew always told me, "You know you're really a restaurateur when you're opening up restaurants with different themes. You're not opening up the same restaurant over and over again." And that's what we did, almost to a fault. I think we might be more successful, certainly richer, had we figured out how to do thirty Babbos and sold them at an IPO for $200 million eight years ago when the market was hot. Instead we're *figli d'arte*, as they say in Italian, "sons of art." We pursued restaurants born of our trips and passions and experiences in Italy, and that has remained our MO—to interpret the authentic Italian experience and make it economically viable in the American restaurant market.

But it would never work anywhere else. Babbo is so much about the building and the neighborhood—the West Village, Waverly Place, and the former Coach House building—it's a crossroads of uptown and downtown, it's where aristocrats meet bohemians, and it's crafted for a pretty sophisticated customer. Because it is such a small restaurant, maybe it could find its place in San Francisco. But does it work in Houston? No, because you'd have to have veal parmesan and fucking spaghetti with meatballs, and we don't do spaghetti with fucking meatballs. I'm painting in broad strokes, but to be true to its form, I think a place like Babbo needs the depth of the New York City restaurant customer base to thrive as well as it does. If your goal was to open up two hundred restaurants and sell them, you would have to have something with a broader market appeal.

Esca can't be duplicated because you just can't source the product. We have a hard time even in New York, which aside from Tokyo is probably the greatest fish market in the world. It would be impossible to drive that menu without having the local market there for you—we probably have over 150 different types of fresh fish coming through the door. In fact, in New York we are really in the wholesale-fish business. We have four buyers and two trucks in the market every day. We source fish from all over the world for our restaurants and sell to other restaurants, so we're very immersed in the fish business. But given the complexity and the range of what we serve at Esca, we would have a hard time sourcing that kind of product anywhere else. Just managing that inventory is nearly impossible, and if you didn't have the traffic we do in Manhattan, you'd really have to simplify it.

The best dinner at Esca always starts with the crudo. Usually it's an appetizer—you could eat a whole dinner of raw fish, but you know, when you eat sashimi for dinner, it comes with a carbohy-drate. You'd have to eat a lot of rice or something else with it, and that's not the point. So a good start is a flight of crudo—the best fish with the best olive oil with the best salt. Three pieces of fish, usually lighter to heavier, left to right on the tasting plate. Maybe Nantucket scallops with Maldon salt and a Liguorian olive oil. Next you might have tuna belly with Gaeta tapenade and some Tuscan olive oil, which is a little more peppery. The last flight might be Spanish mackerel with Sicilian black volcanic salt, sea beans, and olive oil from Trapani, ramping up the flavor. And then maybe a few things for the table, like a little *fritto misto* and *marinati*, maybe some anchovies and mackerel poached in olive oil. Then I would go with black tagliatelle with zippy tomato sauce and teeny cuttlefish for a pasta, followed by a tasting of whole fish, I think the branzino *in sale,* which has become an Esca classic, where we bury the whole branzino in salt and then bake it until it's like a fucking cinder block. And then spiny porgy on the grill, and a dorade patiently baked in seaweed. So three whole fish, filleted tableside and served with corresponding olive oil and salt. It's fabulous. And it makes you want to fuck—it's the Viagra of the Italian table, with no known side effects.

At Esca we always try to serve the best regional, simple wines. Simple wine for simple food. It's not somewhere you would have a hulking super Tuscan wine or anything like an "important" wine from Italy. We always had the concept of coastal food with coastal wines. So we served wines like Vermentino from Sardinia, and Fiano di Avellino from Campania. It got to the spirit of what they would do in Italy. Italian fishermen aren't drinking expensive wine—you eat the fish that comes from the dock and the grapes that are grown across the street, and you eat the olive oil that is made from the olive trees behind the grapes. In Italy it's ultraregionalism at its most natural, and we wanted to bring that spirit to our interpretation of fish at Esca. Thirty to fifty dollars will get you anything you want to drink. That's a pretty low average in this day and age. You get some mooks who want to order a fucking Amarone with their branzino—they just can't help themselves—but it's not meant for that type of wine consumption. At Esca we have the worst wine sales of any of our restaurants, because simple white wine is a nice idea and it's very poetic, but it doesn't add up to dollars on a check.

The real challenge at Esca was this creeping food-cost number, which is what you get when it is all about serving proteins—35, 37, 38 percent, which is eight points above what is acceptable in the normal line. And the wine sales, where we normally would make it up, were not going to be a hundred and twenty bucks of Barolo or Barbaresco. It was going to be thirty-dollar Vermentino, and that really put us under the gun to figure out how to make the margins work and get to the magical 20 percent bottom line.

We had an old lease, so we had low rent going for us, but what did it is even simpler than that—we figured out how to keep the place crowded, how to jam the place every day. Basically, people loved it. They loved the crudo, and they loved Dave, who brought some real flavor to the place. Name one other chef who would go fishing in the morning and then bring his catch to his restaurant to cook it for you for dinner. He was the real deal and completely unpretentious about who he was and what he loved.

A big advantage Esca had was being in Times Square, near Condé Nast and the *New York Times,* and it was the only decent, serious restaurant in a twenty-block radius, so we had everyone from Arthur Ochs Sulzberger Jr. and S. I. Newhouse on down coming by for lunch, although depending on lunch is always a risky business, because the lunch crowd is very fickle—expense accounts follow the leading indicators of the economy. From one day to the next, you could pretty much predict the lunch covers in an expensive restaurant in midtown based on the headlines in the business section of the *Times* coupled with the Dow Jones Industrial Average.

It helped that at some point we were in the wholesale food business and had effectively cut out the middleman. In other words we were buying in bulk, huge quantities—we began to cut out the distributor and source everything ourselves. We established a purchasing department and were buying enormous quantities of commodity items like olive oil, made for us, directly from the producer in Italy. We bring over containers of canned tomatoes and salt. We've got literally tons of cheese coming over. It's classic Restaurant Man, just brought to a higher level of sophistication and a grand economy of scale.

Restaurant Man has always been about going direct and creating more margin. But as much as you can make great margin by buying olive oil in bulk and cutting out the middleman, you'd still never want to be in the linen business, even as much as I hate paying for it. Linen is always the lowest-lying fruit, but it's full of worms. It's the nastiest, most disgusting, chemically driven, waste-spewing business you could ever imagine. If you spend a lot of money on linen, you can set up a small operation and save some dough, but no one has persevered, because it takes a certain kind of animal to run linens. It's an ugly, ugly business.

Regardless of all our successes, the Restaurant Man mind-set of being a cheap fuck always prevails. This is still a nickel-and-dime business, and you still have to strike the perfect balance of watching the margins like a motherfucker while being generous to your customers' quality of experience, and you can't cheat at it—customers can tell when someone is trying to throw something flashy at them, and it's really nothing. Customers are not stupid, especially in New York; they can smell a con job from a mile away. So you have to make sure your cheapness is invisible. You must always appear generous to the point of being opulent—like I always say, you give from the front, you pull from the back.

One thing you never want to do is compete on price point on menu items. You'll lose that fight every time, because someone will always be willing to do it for less. But on the other hand, price puts bodies in seats, and it's a marketing tool. It gives you the platform to create the art, to create the experience, the food, and the hospitality. But it has to be used judiciously.

We've modified prices strategically during major downturns in the economy, but we've never discounted. Discounting is kind of like degrading the quality of your service. It's undermining the professionalism of the restaurateur. Would you want your doctor to give you a discount? Would you go to a different doctor because he offered 25 percent off your next colonoscopy? I didn't think so.

And it weighs very heavily on me. Sometimes I can't sleep because I'm thinking about prices and about the check at the end of dinner and if my customers are going to look at it and say, "It was absolutely worthwhile. Let's do this again soon." We're in the business of taking people's money, but we are not in the business of ripping people off. We're in the business of exceeding expectations.

Ultimately at Esca we were able to drive a pretty substantial check average even though the food cost was high—fish is not cheap.

In Europe there's a culture of quality fish. Fish in American restaurants is ubiquitous, but a lot of it is farm-raised crap. The problem with a lot of farm-raised salmon, for instance, is that they feed them dead salmon parts. They're turning them into cannibals. It's disgusting. They don't give them fresh water to swim in, and their flesh becomes murky and tastes like shit. Branzino, which has become in the last ten years the standard menu item in an Italian restaurant, is farm-raised, usually in Greece or Turkey. They have large ocean farms, and they're good. But most of what you get in the cheap Greek and Italian restaurants in Queens and on the Upper East Side, it's not real branzino, and it tastes like mud. Of course, using cheap product is nothing new—how much veal parm being served do you think is really pork that's seen the business end of a mallet? How much fish in the fish and chips in your local pub that's being sold as Atlantic cod is really generic whitefish, or worse?

Sourcing fish is another hot topic. Delicacy fishes, which are really integral to Mediterranean seafood culture, to Spaniards and Italians and Greeks, these are all becoming endangered from over-harvesting. Ultimately, if we're going to preserve them for the future, we have to stop eating them. It's a sad but true fact. The future of feeding the world is almost certainly going to be some sort of farmed fish that are not cannibals, that are vegetarians. That eat moss—algae, basically. Tilapia is big now, and most people had never even heard of it five years ago. It eats everything, not including other fish. The yield is incredible. The meat tastes pretty good. It's kind of an innocuous whitefish, but it's cheap and good for frying. I think there are a lot of people who think tilapia can save the world. There are guys in Bushwick who are farming tilapia in bathtubs on their fucking terraces.

Coming from the Northeast, we have an incredible resource of fish in our waters. Occasionally we import fish for our restaurants, but we certainly don't serve anything that is in danger.

I am not going to rattle a political saber over every menu item, though. I make these decisions on a personal level. Mario has some strong politics and principles, too, and between what we believe in and what we offer on our menus, we're not so wound up. We can feel good about what we do. Mario is also very big into the Food Bank for New York City, which is a great cause—they serve hundreds of thousands of meals to the homeless and the hungry—and also "Meatless Mondays," promoting vegetarian consumption. Everyone agrees that if you eat more vegetables, it's good. And eating a lot of vegetables for us, quite frankly, is a very Italian way to eat anyway. There's no conflict there.

Fish is a big issue because as the world's demand for it and for more refined proteins increases, we're pinching the resources of the ocean. Sustainable fish consumption is a very hot political topic these days. In five years fish will triple in price from what we know now. In ten years fish might be five to ten times more expensive.

The golden age of cheap, abundant food, quality food in this country, is ending. Fresh foods that used to be staples are now becoming commodity items. We're really looking at the world where energy prices are driving up the cost of commodities. Flour doubled in price this year, and all dairy products—butter, milk, eggs—are greatly affected by transportation costs, so fuel, refrigeration, expiration dates all have a big bearing on price. And the kind of farming we do is so wasteful and unsustainable—industrial farming is a fucking nightmare. How many energy calories does it cost to make one potato compared with the yield? And once it goes through the commercial cycle, by the time it gets to the restaurant and served back to the customer, the cost is insane. There really are no economics to drive the farming model in this country—it's really about subsidies and the American petroleum agenda.

In 1992 I could put a twenty-eight-ounce porterhouse steak on the plate, not prime but choice, for nineteen dollars. These days it's hard to even find any affordable steak to put on the menu, quite honestly, considering what the product costs. That's why steaks are all forty or fifty bucks—a fifty-dollar steak in a responsible restaurant costs twenty-five dollars to put on the plate, and you still have a 50 percent food cost, enough to make Restaurant Man want to go on a killing spree. Steak houses try to make it up on big wines—they've got a higher margin on big reds to cover the shitty margin on food cost, and at the end of the day it should even out. Also, in the steak house, a major part of the model is that you're not fabricating as much product. You're not creating food, or really making food—you're buying meat and potatoes. You have less labor in the kitchen but higher food costs. In a pasta restaurant, making fresh pasta costs nothing, but you need the skill set to make the ravioli by hand, to fill them, to cook them. You need an educated, trained staff, on every level. A grill man is not even a fucking sauté cook. All he has to do is get a steak medium rare. It's not easy, but once you know the trick, it's pretty hard to fuck up.

It used to be that if you were really good, you could handpick beef. Sometimes the USDA inspectors miss, and you could pick out high-grade choice that kind of approaches prime. If you knew what you were doing, you could bring your meat hook up to Hunts Point and go one side of beef at a time, but those days are over.

The veal chop is the bane of every restaurateur's existence, because there's almost no margin; the food cost is just too fucking high. I lose money on it. If a four-top comes in and every one of them orders a veal chop, I might as well go to their table, give them twenty dollars each, and tell them to get the fuck out.

The primo end-cut veal chop, the one you dream about that's two inches thick and white on both sides and on that big, long bone, and it looks like it was drawn by Dr. Seuss? That veal chop costs almost twenty-five dollars to put on the plate. So even if I charge thirty-five for it, I'm way over my pain threshold. I have certain friends who know that when they come and order the veal chop at Becco, they have to put five dollars in an envelope and leave it for me. That's absolutely true. I've got them trained like monkeys. The classic veal-chop eater is a savvy New Yorker, a guy who knows his way around the dining scene, who is instinctively going to go for what is probably the highest-food-cost item. And veal is more delicate than steak, not quite as macho. It's a gorgeous, delicious, beautiful thing. But when you order it, please keep in mind that you are driving me out of business.

Frugality is exactly the core value that you need to be successful in this business. It's not even something you can learn—for me, being cheap is in my DNA. Well, honestly, I'm not cheap, but I am a frugal motherfucker. Come to my house, I'll open up a four-hundred-dollar bottle of wine for us, and I won't even think about it. But to see half a tube of toothpaste thrown out because you're not willing to roll it up right or to see lights left on . . . that kills me. I go around the house turning off lights after my kids. And the way they waste toothpaste—or food, for that matter—it just eats at me. Sometimes I come home at night and what the fuck, there are eighty lightbulbs burning in the house, and I'm counting them while I'm switching them off. The kids get the memo in the morning. At breakfast time I sit them down and tell them, "Last night I turned off eighty lightbulbs when I got home at one A.M."

I think that's really the nature of the beast. You have to think that way. It has to be a part of who you are. When someone wants to talk these highfalutin ideas about sustainability, I tell them, "Why don't we start by turning off the fucking lights?" You walk into a restaurant like Del Posto, you have eight hundred fucking lightbulbs that are running all day, from seven in the morning when no one is there, just because that's how things are done—open the front door, turn on all the lights. What if we just turn off the fucking lights when we don't need them? How about like in the old days, when the last customer left the restaurant you turned off the lights and everyone ate the family meal in the dark, because the people who work there don't need the lights? Lights are for customers.

When you're dealing in the world of forty-dollar entrées it's easy to be all green and wear the whole responsible-sourcing thing like a badge of honor, because there's so much money and margin on every level. And that's the problem with all the Alice Waters–isms and even Slow Food to a degree—it's expensive and fucking elitist. My criticism of it has always been, yeah, everyone should eat locally in a sustainable way and eat beautiful garden vegetables, but this shit is not cheap. And you have to live in certain communities to have access to it. Going to fancy restaurants like Blue Hill at Stone Barns and paying forty bucks for a local lamb that they slaughtered in the back served with carrots they're growing in their Rockefeller garden is a beautiful thing, but really, it's such a small percentage of the population who can afford to live in that ether that it's not applicable in any wide, mainstream way.

We source locally as much as possible. Not because we want to be so didactic, but because it's just better. If it's going to make the food on the plate better, or the wine in the bottle better, or the experience for the customer better, then of course that is what we're always aiming for. And using things that are geographically as close to the point of sale as possible, especially produce and dairy, generally equates to improved quality and better dining. So as far as that affects local consumption, less transport, less packaging, I'm all for it. But doing it for the sake of doing it and being held to some impossible, idealistic standard is crazy.

We're running into that in our retail business, Eataly. Some wiseass is always going to say, "Hey, you guys preach all this shit, but look, you have strawberries from fucking Florida." But if we were really going to have just local fruits and vegetables we might as well shut it down right now. We'd have four carrots and six beets—that's all that's strictly local right now.

And then there's the new wave of foodies—including a lot of people I genuinely like—preaching urban farming out in Brooklyn. Their intentions are good, but seriously, what I want to know is, for all their proselytizing, who is getting those vegetables? Are the people in Bushwick really getting those carrots, or are they just being served to hipsters who live in lofts and don't have jobs while the world around them shops at filthy, roach-infested superbodegas. It's so far from being economically viable as to be farcical. Hippie Joe loves it, but Restaurant Man Joe thinks these are just spoiled kids playing in the sandbox and they ought to get real jobs.

"Farm to table" became superhot and trendy, but it's not a new concept. Nothing is new. Everything is reinvented. Now they've stuck a whole bunch of fancy lingo on it, talking about carbon footprints and protein this and that—someone is always figuring out a different way of interpreting the cost of food—but it's still the same old concept of waste not, want not, use what's around you. And don't do things to people you wouldn't want them to do to you. Have a little humanity and morality. A little fucking respect. That's truly what it's all about, right? My grandmother has been living sustainably since forever, and she's been feeding her family from her urban garden and reading her paper by a forty-watt bulb since she came to America in the 1950s. She'd rather strip down to her bra than turn on the air conditioner. Her mantra is "Don't do nothing you don't want nobody to do to you." Consume what you need, act locally, don't waste anything, and turn off the fucking lights.

CHAPTER FOURTEEN

The Curse of Restaurant Man!

One of the great tragedies of being Restaurant Man is that I have a lot of trouble enjoying myself in a restaurant, any restaurant. I'm too wound up. I'm tweaked. I can't give myself up to the experience. Imagine being a scientist and every time you fucked your wife, all you thought about was the biology of it. It would be tragic.

I eat in restaurants all the time. But for me it's not simply another experience—it's like living or breathing. It just *is*. Restaurants aren't special to me anymore. When they're fancy and ambitious, they become a burden. When they're light, they become unsatisfactory. And when they're exactly right, the kind of experience that most consumers would die for, then it's like being alive to me, that's it. Like breathing. I love every one of my restaurants, and I strive to make them the best they can be, and I know how good they are, but I'm fucking jaded. Honestly, it's not a good way to be.

Actually, what I am mostly jaded about is that Eurocentric, New York, high-end thing. That's why I enjoy Asian food—Chinese, dim sum, Japanese, Thai noodles—food where the experience is so out of left field for me in a professional context. Cooking comes naturally to me, but I don't even like to eat what I cook. I like to sit around and steam dumplings that I pick up in Chinatown because

I don't know anything about them. Every plate of dim sum that comes is a surprise to me, and it's delicious. Dim sum makes me feel like a kid at a birthday party. I love Japanese food, too, because I don't know the business. I don't know how to make a fucking spicy tuna roll, I don't know what shumai costs; I'm completely lost at sea, and it's a good feeling. Otherwise every time I'm looking at a plate of food, I'm doing the math. I don't even have to glance at the menu. I know what food costs; I do the markup in my head, and I'm never wrong. Seriously, I can't help myself. Fucking Restaurant Man—the irony is that I can hardly enjoy the thing I love the most, because I can't stop thinking about it from the business side.

But then, going down to Drew's restaurant for me is not really about eating, it's about, "Wazzup, Drew?" When I go to any restaurant and there are three waiters there who used to be my busboys, that's the biggest high I can have. Because the busboys are really the heart and soul of the New York restaurant world. If I take people out to dinner with friends and three former busboys come up and say, "Hey, Papi! What's up? Good to see you, man," then I know I'm really somebody in the New York restaurant scene. They all have nicknames for me, and that's when you know you've made it.

But it's sad, being so oversaturated with the experience. It's like being a musician who can't enjoy going to someone else's gig, although he might still be into the records that got him into music originally. The first love never dies, right? I still like to go to Sparks and eat that shitty butter submerged in ice. I love the incredibly mediocre iceberg lettuce. It just brings me to that moment. It's not like I stopped loving food or wine, or that any of the real magic that inspired me when I started ever died. The simple stuff amazes me more than ever—every bite of salty prosciutto with some snappy Lambrusco, whatever—the magic will always be there. I am always amazed at the power of food and wine to transport you. But the trappings of a working restaurant are such that I just can't look past the man behind the screen, ever.

There is no detail that can escape the ever-vigilant gaze of Restaurant Man! I will often decide what restaurant I go to or don't go to based on stemware. To me it is a primal part of the wine experience. There are BBQ places I like but won't go to because I don't drink out of fucking mason jars.

Another thing that bugs the shit out of me is polyester napkins. Nothing worse than a fucking polyester napkin that doesn't absorb anything. A simple cotton napkin is one of the basic commandments of Restaurant Man. And I'd rather have a clean wooden table than a shitty, abrasive polyester tablecloth anytime. It's all about the sensibility of the tabletop. At Del Posto it's a padded, plush table where you press down on it and it's almost like lying on a mattress. It's like a Sealy Posturepedic table—it bounces back very slowly, and there's a richness to that. It ain't cheap, but it is very satisfying.

I'm not fanatical about silverware, as long as it's functional. I like Sambonet, an Italian company that makes good, simple flatware. In most cases we use stainless steel, but at Del Posto we actually have silver silverware. We kind of went crazy—we have Ginori china, which is this handmade Italian china that costs a hundred fifty dollars per plate. The handmade wineglasses cost me about thirty bucks a stem—and I'm importing them directly from Slovenia. For a civilian they'd be sixty bucks a glass, easy. And then, of course, we break them.

I put a bucket for broken plates and glasses in each restaurant. You think that's crazy? I mandated that because I want to see it all out—if they're just breaking plates and throwing them in the garbage, there's no control point. So we keep buckets in the kitchen where all the breakage goes, and you can look at it and see what your consumption rate is. You look in the bucket, you see ten Ginori plates, you're looking at more than a thousand dollars' worth of china. I want everyone else to see it, too, because I think it sends a message. It's the same thing I do with the dishwashers. I tell them every time they pull a fork or knife out of the garbage can in the dish station, I give them ten bucks. The fork usually costs only two or three dollars, but it's the point that you're making such a big statement to your dishwasher. He is never going to forget it. And every time he goes by, he says, "Hey, Papi. Come here. Ten pesos." It's the international language, and you're reminding them that silverware in the garbage is not a sock lost in the dryer and you just shrug it off. This is my fucking money. This is your salary.

And then of course we replace everything the second it gets tired—you see a lot of fatigued plates in restaurants, which is kind of gross. They get metal fatigue because all the surfaces in restaurants where food is plated and washed are stainless steel, and even though it's a superhard metal, it remits a little bit of resin after the friction with the porcelain. The bottom rim of the plates collects the resin, and when you stack the plates, it stains the plate you're stacking into. We bleach our plates once a month—throw them into giant garbage cans filled with bleach and hot water and soak them overnight. The problem is that after a few years of bleaching your plates, you basically eat away at the enamel. They become porous, and then you've got to throw them out, which is expensive.

Everything on the table sends a message. A big statement is not to put salt and pepper on the table. If you're a chef-driven restaurant, why would you allow the customer to alter the flavor of the food? Obviously, if customers request salt, we will bring it to them. Salt and pepper on request—although we've been fresh-peppered to death in this country. And no cheese on fish. That's for gavones.

We get a lot of people who come in and ask for olive oil, then balsamic vinegar. And then more bread. And then parmesan cheese. It's like a fucking free appetizer they're getting. Ever see those people who take the butter plate and put the balsamic vinegar in it? And the olive oil, red chili flakes, pepper, parmesan cheese. It's a fucking disaster. It is the scourge of our industry, these fucking Italian places where you're seated and they appear with the giant bottle of shit olive oil and fake balsamic vinegar, which is basically cheap vinegar colored with caramel and acid, and pour it on the plate for you. You know, for a dipping sauce for your bread.

It's deplorable. Places like the fucking Olive Garden are responsible for teaching America all this bullshit, all these bad habits. And then people come to real restaurants and expect it. Olive oil is expensive, but restaurants should always buy great olive oil. I have my own brand of olive oil, but a liter still costs me twenty bucks—my cost. Which means it would be thirty-five bucks at Whole Foods, for you. Which is an expensive bottle of oil.

We use different grades of olive oil—there's table oils, finishing oils, cooking oils. Olive oil is a big thing in restaurants, especially Italian ones. But good olive oil in cooking is what makes the difference between good restaurants and great ones. It's that level of detail. The type of olive oil you use, the type of salt you use—you'd better believe you can taste it. Why go to all the trouble of making and serving food and then screwing yourself with crappy salt? I know guys who have broken up with women because they served iodized salt at home. Some people don't think it makes a difference, but it does. Everything does. For men of taste, iodized salt is a deal breaker.

Just as important is the grated cheese. People expect you to give it away. And we do. But guess what? Real Parmigiano-Reggiano costs me more than ten dollars a pound. And then you're only getting like 70 percent yield. So the net product is costing me thirteen dollars a pound.

A lot of restaurants either don't use real parmesan and instead use cheese that costs 30 percent of the real thing, like an Argentinean knockoff, or they think they're smart and they'll blend it. Thirty percent real parmesan, and then they cut it with Stella. They step on it, like they're cutting cocaine. Good parmesan cheese is like snowflakes that melt on warm concrete. When the Stella hits your pasta, it forms these little waxy balls that don't really melt. That's how they cut corners. It's the equivalent of snorting baby laxative, and I won't stand for it.

But the number-one thing about a restaurant is, when you walk in, what does it smell like? Because in Manhattan at least, most restaurants don't have balanced air systems. They have hoods that suck out more air than is coming in, but they don't have makeup air, which is the way it should be done.

You know that smell of rancid grease? Ever clean the grease trap in a restaurant? The grease trap is the vilest, most disgusting thing you've ever smelled in your entire life. It's where all the water and the grease drainage from the kitchen go. By law you can't flush that grease into the sewer systems. So you have what's basically a giant iron box that traps the grease and sends the water into the sewer system. It's like a huge box of filth.

We used to pay someone to come and take it away, but now I run my car on it—it's biodiesel. We have a filling station at Del Posto, and we run two box trucks and my Ford Excursion off scrap oil. There's a whole greening aspect to what we've been doing. Being sustainable and green is nothing new to us, but we like to push it. Restaurant Man likes to come on like a tough guy, but he's still the same old hippie, running his truck the same way Willie Nelson runs his.

Speaking of smells, here's another reason Restaurant Man hates linen—dirt. Because linen is not just linen, right? It's food, coffee stains, grease. You ever see those motherfuckers who blow their nose in restaurant napkins? These guys should be dragged out into the street and shot. That is the nastiest, most disgusting thing I have ever seen. You walk into the restaurant, take the napkin, and blow your snot-filled honker into it. And we, as restaurateurs, have to pick up that napkin and refold it. It fucking should be illegal. That is some seriously gross shit.

The night's dirty linen goes into plastic bags and needs to be tied tightly, because it smells—foul. Usually linen companies don't pick up on Sundays, so you've got Saturday's linen festering until Monday. Sunday smells.

I also have a rule about changing toilet seats—I change the seats on every toilet once a month. Because I think having nice, clean, new toilet seats is a small investment that goes a long way. Toilet seats cost only twenty bucks apiece. Ever see a toilet seat in a restaurant with nicks on it? Again—revolting.

You would be amazed about the stuff that happens in restaurant bathrooms. Some people think that shitting in a restaurant is part of the dining experience. They do. Some people think that fucking in the restaurant is part of the dining experience. We get a lot of that. Babbo is where it always happens. I've found condoms, syringes, women's underwear, glassine envelopes—you name it, I've found everything in the bathroom. There is a woman blogger who fucks her date in the bathroom and reviews the sex and the food. I love her. Even my father was a fan.

And then there are bar smells. Bars smell because bartenders never want to clean them. And that smell is something you can pick up. When you walk through even a nice restaurant, have a drink at the bar and you can get a whiff of that bar stink. It's nasty shit.

We do a strip-down of the bar once a week. Take everything out. Bleach out the back and clean it up good, because everything behind the bar is syrupy and sticky. The bar just *wants* to be dirty. You have to be invested in it to keep it clean.

The thing about the bar that disgusts me most is the soda gun. Think about going into some shitty bar or restaurant in New York City—picture bags of syrup in some fucking roach-infested basement. That syrup comes through this tube that has twelve little plastic tubes in it that gets its water right from the tap, then goes through the carbonizer. And the gun is just oozing syrup from the cracks in it—the lemon-lime, the cola. . . . And the big thing in bars is fruit flies, because they breed in still water and feed on sugar. Some guns have cranberry juice, iced tea, fucking Gatorade. . . . You've got twelve different syrups coming through one gun, mixing with the same water. And you can fucking taste it. You can taste the sour mix when you order a Coke.

The good thing about ordering a Coke in one of my restaurants? You get a nice little bottle of Coca-Cola. You're paying five bucks for it, so why the fuck not? That's one of the biggest rip-offs in restaurants. Because soda out of the gun costs you eight or nine cents a glass, and you're charging four or five bucks. Restaurant Man likes the margin, but you're just killing yourself and the beverage program you pretend to be so proud of—that gun is a bastion of disgustingness. It sits in its little holster oozing syrup. It's the same with beer systems in restaurants. People do not maintain their beer lines, and you get yeast-fermented nasty skunk beer. Beer systems need to be cleaned like once every two or three weeks, but that costs money, and some people just don't get that it's worth it as an investment in your business and shows respect for the product and the customer.

Some soda guns are really Coca-Cola or Pepsi guns, and the syrup is actually a high-quality, controlled product. You buy their stuff and their guns are better, and they really do care. But a lot of restaurants are using these unbranded generic soda-system companies. They sell Jerry's Cola, complete shit, and they pass it off as Coca-Cola. Then it only costs ten cents a glass, but you're still charging five bucks, so what the fuck? The carbonation is never right. It's always too sweet. It's flat. And it's unsanitary. You know it the second you taste it. It tastes metallic. Chalky. It sucks because it's not Coca-Cola, and you should fucking send it back.

You can tell more about a restaurant by smelling it than by seeing it. From the entryway to the bathroom to the coat-check room to the bar to the table, it's just like wine: You can close your eyes and tell how good it's going to be, tell about the quality of the experience. A restaurant with delicious food that is run by people who really care has a good smell to it. It smells like deliciousness and love. The building might be five hundred years old, but it still smells right. That's when I'm not jaded. It's embracing. That's when Restaurant Man turns into a puppy dog.

CHAPTER FIFTEEN

If we had ever declared that we were going to open a four-star Italian joint, we would have been laughed out of town. Three stars at Babbo was already pushing it, especially since we'd been so libertine with regard to the old concepts of what an Italian restaurant could be. There were people who already suspected that we were nuts, and we were certainly supplying ample evidence to support that theory. There is smart and successful and creative, and then there is the overreaching hubris that kills a lot of people in this game, and that was the story behind what would become Del Posto. Eventually we earned the four stars, but it was a long journey, and in retrospect I would never do it again, no fucking way. Between creating this stratospheric experience and all the short-term failures, the tableside disasters, and then the years of fighting and battling with the most unlikable fucking New York douchebag landlords ever, it was like being dragged through a war. It was an endless, bloody campaign. But am I glad I did it? Well, if you'd asked me that before we got the fourth star, I really don't know what I would have said, but having gotten it, I can say that it is no doubt the most significant thing that has happened to Mario, my mom, and me in our professional lives. There are only five or six four-star restaurants in New York currently, and if you look back over the last fifty years, maybe there have been a dozen. It's the only four-star Italian restaurant in the country, and you can't put a price on that. But that's not the whole story.

Del Posto started as yet another real-estate deal, just after September 11, 2001. The corridor of West Chelsea where we built it was part of the extended Meatpacking District, a kind of no-man's-land out by the West Side Highway. There were actually tumbleweeds haunting the streets when we got there.

We knew a guy named Irwin Cohen. He had developed the Chelsea Market as a far–West Side concept five years before, and then he bought the Nabisco baking building at 85 Tenth Avenue, which is where we built Del Posto. He had a guy who worked for him, Jim Somoza, who was a customer at Babbo, and they were looking to do retail on the ground floor, and he came to us with a sweetheart deal. It had been a hard-core lesbian bar in the eighties, totally industrial, a very rough extension of the West Village. And that's how it started—once again we had the real estate before we had the concept. It was just too good an idea to pass up; there was no way that this was not going to become a great location.

So we carved out twenty-eight thousand square feet, which is a massive amount of space, on this corner, and then we got down to the business of how we were going to fill it with people.

My original idea was to do a retro red-sauce joint and re-create Buonavia, my parents' first restaurant in the 1970s in Queens. Given the horror show that we were about to enter, it might have been the right way to go.

A massive red-sauce joint on the West Side probably would have been successful. I was going to bring back my dad's combination plate—chicken scarpariello, shrimp parmigiana, and eggplant parmigiana—which is why my mother came on board. She loved the idea because she *was* Buonavia. This was the first business I was going to do with my mom since Becco, and she was great, totally along for the ride, even as the concept kept changing. When we did Babbo, she was a little suspicious of Mario's creativity, but now it is like a fucking love fest between them—they are completely crazy about each other, and sometimes I'm the one outside looking in, but it's all very good.

Gradually the concept changed from checkered tablecloths to something more authentically Italian, and then somewhere the ambition emerged to do something very high-end. I think when the restaurant started coming together and we saw how beautiful and grand the space would be, that's when we let our four-star ambition sneak in the side door—because the dream always was to do something at the top of the Italian pyramid. We always felt we were the guys to do it. We thought we could build the greatest, most opulent Italian restaurant in the world. We also had a chef in-house, Mark Ladner, who was then working with us in Lupa and Otto, and we knew he had the talent. When Mark came on board, things crystallized, and then everything snowballed: It was ambition fueled by money fueled by ambition fueled by opportunity.

The rent was so far under market that we signed a really long lease—the market value now is about twenty times what we're paying. Without the obligation of a heavy real-estate cost, you can be more creative and more flexible on the concept. And when we started poking around the basement, we discovered things we didn't expect, a netherworld of New York architecture. The first thing we learned is that all those buildings on the far West Side are basically built on landfill and the Hudson River runs underneath them. So what you see if you go through the basement floor is that they're built on pylons. And the river flows underneath the basement. Manhattan Island was widened to make the West Side Highway happen, and the bottom of the island, Battery Park, is landfill. As is often the case, our imagination started to get the best of us, and in what was just raw space we built a grand staircase that descends from a sprawling mezzanine when you come in, everything ultra-opulent and everything from scratch. Once again it was the Big Bang According to Mario and Joe—first nothing, then suddenly a brand-new galaxy. Pow.

Del Posto was the first time we went to outside partners to help us finance a project—we talked to a prominent financial luminary who had a little vision and to a couple of Goldman Sachs guys who were customers at Babbo. We raised $5 or $6 million from investors.

We pitched them on having the real estate sewn up—this was before all the condos, before the High Line, before everything, so it was really pioneering. We were pretty much the first restaurant out there. The only other one is the old Frank's Steak House on the south side of the block, which had moved from Fourteenth Street. I had my bachelor party at the original, and that closed in 1994.

We thought $6 million would do it, but it ended up taking double that. We had to get another bank loan, which we personally guaranteed for $5 million to finish the job and thought we'd do the Curly Shuffle on the back end to the tune of a million to float the thing. That's a lot of Curly and a lot of shuffling, but for $12 million, you get a twenty-eight-thousand-square-foot restaurant that looks like it's been there for a hundred years, that has more marble in it than a Medici palace, and is state-of-the-art, top to bottom. There's nothing quite like Del Posto; it's a restaurant that's going to be there forever.

We opened in 2005, and things got very bad very quickly. What happened was that our friend Irwin sold the building—he'd bought it for $40 million and sold it for $70 million to some hedge-fund jerk-offs who wanted to flip it again. Our deal with Irwin was a little soft, I admit, nothing earth-shattering, but there was some ambiguity about some building and technical details—the proper specs for vents and compressors, stuff like that—so the new landlords immediately launched a lawsuit. It was a full-on frontal attack with one purpose only: to chase us out of the building and close the restaurant.

No matter who owned the building, our lease was going to hold up at Irwin's super-friend-of-family rate, a big negative when you're trying to sell a building. Let me put it into perspective: Say I'm paying $200,000 a year in rent with my sweet friend-of-Irwin lease, but the market rent is really $2 million a year, so that's $1.8 million a year that the new guys are leaving on the table, times thirty-five years of our lease. See where I'm going with this? It was easily worth spending a few million to get us the fuck out. All they wanted to do was flip the building, and they did—they sold it a year later and made $100 million over what they'd bought it for—but maybe they would have made $130 million if they'd gotten us out, minus the few million they spent on the war with us.

They hired Warren Estis, who is like the fucking antichrist of landlord-tenant lawyers. L&T litigation in New York is notoriously vicious and public, and these guys were just pure fucking evil. They hired multiple law firms and the Hermann Göring of publicists—suddenly there were stories on "Page Six" about the troubles Mario and I were having, personal shit you would not believe—because they didn't really care about winning any lawsuit; that was never going to happen. They just wanted to close the restaurant, which was the only way to get us out, and that became their ambition—to ruin us. Personally. They went after Mario especially, because he is a celebrity. And the whole time we were open for business. Never mind that we were trying to keep our heads up and evolve a concept that really didn't exist, that we had 150 employees with hundreds of people who depended on them. I get it, business is business, and this is New York, but these guys didn't want to talk, they didn't care about the neighborhood, they had zero good faith. They were just complete fucking hemorrhoids.

It would have been the end of life as I knew it if I had to walk out. It was all built and paid for. Mario and Lidia and I all had personal guarantees on the loans—it was everything, our homes, our business, my wife's engagement ring. Everything in our lives would have gone to paying that debt if they'd been successful. Have you ever been served with court papers? You're served. Tag, you're it. And every time I turned around, I would get served. It was crazy. We spent well over a million dollars fighting this shit.

When does ambition get the better of you? Whether it's egotistical or professional, you think you're at the top of your game and you want to execute. But do you want to do it for yourself or do you do it to show the world what you can do? What is the cost if you don't succeed? Would I have been justified in trying to do something so ambitious, having to pay $5 million back to the bank, losing $6 million in partner money, and probably being responsible for the *Heaven's Gate* of restaurant failures? I can't even imagine how it would have affected our other businesses. It would have changed my life. Losing wasn't something we really knew. It was one of the worst times of my life—all I could do was think of what Winston Churchill supposedly said, and tell myself that when you are going through hell, keep on going.

Our partnership always worked because we were always unified in our success and in our failure. I think that ultimately what brought the restaurant to its fruition was our ability to hunker down together, dig in deep, live through the bad times, bite the bullet and throw in some more money, and believe. With my mom and Mario, I have the best partners in the business.

.   .   .

Meanwhile, we've got people coming in to eat, and they are super-tweaked, because every day they're reading in the paper that we're breaking building codes left and right, playing a game way out of our league, in cahoots with the devil, and on the verge of collapsing. It didn't help that aesthetically Del Posto *was* breaking all sorts of rules.

"Four-star Italian" is a category created by us. We were always uncompromisingly committed to making sure that we did not become another four-star *French* restaurant—everything we did had to be conceptualized in its *Italianness*. Luxury dining from the Italian perspective, from the culture of the Italian table. We were looking back into history and bringing all the greatest elements of Italian restaurants and dining and food into one contemporary restaurant. And that would be the ultimate Italian dining experience.

We took everything, even the tableside service, all the clichés about the French dining experience, and reinterpreted them to fit into the Italian vernacular and the sensibility of Italians. Italian four-star dining is different from French in the sense that, yes, it's opulent, luxurious, detail-oriented, but it's also a little bit more familiar, warmer, more family-oriented, a little bit more interactive, not quite as distanced. Eliminate the snob value and appeal to people's desire to eat pure food in a real way. But since there was no clear history of that, we were kind of making it up as we went along. There are the standard expectations of what a four-star restaurant is. You come into Daniel, you have amuse-bouches, which is the shit they send you for free when you sit down. But we couldn't call it amuse-bouche, and there's no Italian name for that. So we had to invent a name, which was *primo assaggio,* first taste, which doesn't exist in Italy because in Italy they didn't have to name it. But we did.

Now every aspiring Italian restaurant passes it off as old-school—anywhere you go, *primo assaggio,* compliments of the chef. We invented that term and convinced everyone it was legit.

In the beginning, people were slamming us—everyone said, "Hey, that's not a Joe and Mario place. We love Babbo, we love Lupa—what the fuck is this?" Not only did we have to create an Italian restaurant that played the game at such a high level, not only did we have to convince the dining market that it was even possible, we had to convince our fans who were calling it bullshit, and that's bad. There was no category for Del Posto, at least not here at home. That's why Del Posto, initially, was much more an easy sell for Brazilians, Mexicans, Europeans, people who really dine around the world. Del Posto is much more similar to dining in Paris, London, or Rome than it is to dining on the Upper East Side. And of course people who eat uptown don't always come downtown, and young people do not eat at the traditional four-star places, period.

So we set out to make Del Posto a transgenerational restaurant. Lidia was a full-on partner because she was there for the original concept, but beyond that we thought that she, Mario, and I would be the three best people from three different perspectives to come together to create a four-star dining experience. Lidia brought some history and gravitas to Del Posto. And Mario brought more of the edgy-chef thing. I brought a lot of ideas and concepts. Sometimes I think creating a restaurant is almost like putting on a play: You build the set, you decorate the set, you put in the players and then it goes. And a big role of mine at Del Posto was being the set designer.

When I was conceptualizing the restaurant, I was watching a lot of Fellini movies. If you look at *8½* or *I Vitelloni,* you can feel that marble-meets-wood, Old World, masculine vibe, but really it's where the Old World meets sixties and seventies design. There are a lot of restaurant scenes in *And the Ship Sails On*. It definitely made an impression on me. It's a little bit mod yet classic at the same time.

More than anything we have done, Del Posto took time to evolve—over five years—which culminated with a four-star review. The initial menu was not only impenetrable for the customer, it was unexecutable. It was quite literally delusional—we couldn't even serve what was on it. We did "friends and family," but where we usually do it for two, three days, at Del Posto we did it for two fucking months.

The menu was ambitious to the point of being counterproductive, and it almost ruined us. We were cooking whole animals and bringing them out and finishing them tableside. So the cooks weren't really cooking, and you had captains and waiters carving the shit up—it was like the Three Stooges. We were doing whole loins of veal and selling entrée items that cost three hundred dollars. It was so far out of the paradigm of any New York dining experience, just pure insanity. Once in a while when a critic came in, we could fake it and make it seem as if it worked, but it didn't—there'd be an entire fucking lamb on the floor, juice spilling out of the kitchen like a murder scene, something was always burning, and we'd have these ladies from the Upper East Side, dressed in white Chanel suits, who would sit down and get splashed with lamb blood. It was fucking biblical. They'd get black paint all over them because we'd painted that day and forgotten to put up a sign. We didn't tell them. We just kept bringing them more wine so they'd get drunk and wouldn't care.

I remember we were flambéing some crepes, and we set the tableside cart on fire. There was tons of bad shit happening—a lot of food went on the floor. Unfortunately, when you're in front of customers, the ten-second rule doesn't apply, unless it's a whole roasted suckling pig, in which case we just pick it up, dust it off, and keep on hacking at it in front of the customer. If Michael Bay remade *I Love Lucy* starring Mario Batali, featuring Joe and Lidia Bastianich, this would have been it.

Our intentions were good, but it was ludicrous. And people knew it. The first reviews were mixed. We snuck out a three-star review from Frank Bruni, but we totally played it. We knew he was there. We created the best experience we could within the context, but it didn't even matter, because this was also around the time the blogosphere was starting to cook, and word was out that Del Posto was some kind of elaborate joke.

For a while we tried to create a more casual menu and worked on the bar business, but that was sending mixed signals about the restaurant. We were losing our focus. Then, at a certain point two years ago, we realized that it would just take a while for a restaurant with that level of ambition to gain its stride. In our case it took us four years, but that's not completely unjustified. I think that we were extra fucked up in the beginning, but we've become extra good and superrefined in the end. Maybe you could start a little closer and not have to go as far. A three-star review in the *Times* was great—amazing, really—but honestly, it wasn't what we wanted. Babbo was three stars. We were batting .300. Lots of guys do that. We wanted to bat .400.

Early on, we also became pretty well known for being the de facto hosts of what I like to call "Cops 'n' Robbers Night." At one end of the bar are the robbers, and at the other end of the bar are the cops. They're all drinking the same drinks, they're all trying to pick up the same cocktail waitresses, or pretty much any random broad within eyeshot. Sometimes it's hard to tell who's who. Good guys? Bad guys? Whatever. I think if you go far enough to the left and far enough to the right, you come around to the same place again. It's not just Del Posto—think Rao's. There's always been these places where opposites attract.

When I first met the wiseguys in the early days, I said to one of the bosses, "You guys ready to eat?" He looked at me and said, "Eat? We don't eat. We dine." And his sidekick goes, "Yeah, yeah. We don't eat. We dine." And they were very fucking serious about it. They make a big deal of being gourmands, and quite frankly they know more about food than most people do, even though they have particular dining habits. They're not into too much democracy. At Del Posto we can facilitate their need for tyranny.

There's one group that'll come in with the roll of hundies—a hundred to the coat-check girl, a hundred to every hostess, a hundred for the maître d', a hundred to the bartender, a hundred to the bar back, a hundred to the piano player, and suddenly our piano player, Fat Tony Monte, turns on a dime and puts the brakes on the Sondheim mid-fucking-measure and starts twirling tarantellas like he was working Don Corleone's wedding reception. They're ordering double vodkas on the rocks in wineglasses. Whatever the capo drinks, everyone else drinks—and it's usually double vodkas in big wineglasses. Now, I am of the opinion that double vodkas should be served in rocks glasses, and I feel pretty strongly about that, but they feel very strongly about the opposite. And then their big thing is, they won't sit down at the table and wait for the food—the food has to be on the table. They don't want to waste time at the table waiting for food. The food is on the table, then they make the move from the bar. What the fuck do I know? I mean, you can drink at the table, too. I'm a wop from Queens, and I do it all the time, but this is some kind of bizarre subculture that goes way beyond Bus Head and Astoria.

It kind of feels like a movie from the 1940s—they're all looking for one another, but they're all right fucking there, hiding in plain sight. The wiseguys are at one end of the bar, and the cops drink down at the other. Not beat cops. I'm talking about NYPD detectives, FBI agents, DEA. Those guys like to "dine," too. As much as they're on opposite ends of the law with their counterparts, they have a similar aesthetic and sensibility. They like Del Posto; they think it's their kind of place.

My dad was never in love with the Idlewild crew. I remember when I was a kid, those guys used to come into Buonavia. *Goodfellas* is pretty accurate, actually—they were doing the airport runs, driving Monte Carlos and Cutlass Supremes, had insane taste in clothes. There's that one scene with the helicopter chase—that's all in Bayside, where I grew up—and it was a pretty fair representation of what life was like down there. Gotti was a customer of Buonavia in the early days, but my father always told me, "If you treat them like everyone else, they'll never come back," because once you bought them a free round, you became *their* place, and then you were in the fold. You became beholden to them, and that was a scary place to live. My father successfully avoided them—Restaurant Man came from the Old World, and he had seen it all. Those guys spent money, but it wasn't money he wanted, which tells you a lot.

These days you can have a healthier customer relationship with the double-vodka gang. And a lot of them are incredible restaurant customers, because they're very respectful and enjoy and appreciate what you do, and they totally participate in the restaurant experience. They pay attention and react. Whether you're talking about a food-and-wine pairing or a particular bottle of wine, or a dish, they're always chiming in with their recipes, their experience, how good it is. They're very much participants in the process of dining, which makes them fabulous customers, aside from the fact that they're pamphleting the place with hundred-dollar bills on the way in, so it's a party for everyone. They spend, they tip, they have a good time, they always befriend the staff. I don't know what they do in their professional lives, but they're awesome restaurant customers. Their sensibility and their aesthetic run very deep, the way they look, the way they carry themselves, what they know about food and wine and the details of style—their nails are always perfect, their shoes are like fucking mirrors, they have the best suits you have ever seen. You can call these guys whatever you want, but don't tell them they dress bad or don't know a fucking good plate of linguini. That would be a mistake.

After the economy collapsed and the market went to shit—I always mark it as the day Lehman imploded in September of '08—the world changed and all our corporate business vanished. Ever walk into an empty dining room, where it's just staff looking at you like hurt puppies wondering what's coming next? It makes you want to shit your heart out. And in the middle of it all, Fat Tony was still playing the piano, boring the shit out of us with some somnambulistic version of Gershwin or watered-down Andrew Lloyd Webber. I can't explain why exactly, but we could never get rid of him. Even when we were shuffling to pay the electric bill, we somehow came up with Fat Tony's three hundred bucks, but don't ask me how. We were very committed to the piano thing. Later, when we started making some dough, I got rid of the rental piano and bought an antique Steinway. He was mildly impressed.

And then we did some soul-searching—we spent a half million dollars, renovated the bar, got rid of the bar trade, and focused in on one level of service. We still had that extra star in our eyes. We eliminated tables, gussied up the place, and brought in staff to execute the final vision of what we thought an unambiguous, kick-you-in-the-ass, four-star restaurant should be. Which was the experience that Sam Sifton, the food critic at the *New York Times* after Frank Bruni—and a good guy—had.

But there were some real lows. Dark meetings in the private party rooms in the Del Posto basement, with mounting legal bills and no reservations coming in, a bad review from Adam Platt in *New York* magazine calling us "Vegas on the Hudson," and another from jack-of-all-tirades Steve Cuozzo at the *New York Post,* their puffed-up real-estate columnist who moonlights as a restaurant critic. He wrote a two-page review of Del Posto and Morimoto's Chelsea restaurant, and the headline was "Dumb and Dumber." That was his review of the two restaurants. After I read that, I sent him an e-mail: *"Are we dumb? Or dumber? That's all I need to know."* Seven years later, with combined sales between Morimoto and Del Posto of something like $40 million, I just want to ask Steve, "Are you a real-estate reporter, a restaurant critic, or just plain fucking stupid?"

Bruni came in a couple of times while we were in this transitional mode, and we missed him, which is inexcusable. I still can't believe we let that happen. He flew in under the radar, and he dogged us on the experience. He said a few things about us in the *Times* that really hurt, not that we were such a terrible restaurant but more like, "What the fuck are they doing there? What are they even thinking about?" It was gut wrenching.

When you're as visible in that world as we are, and you tell the most important critic in town that you think you have a four-star restaurant, he's going to respond. When Bruni left and Sam Sifton came in, that was our cue; we knew we had a chance. It was a clean slate. We knew that Sifton was already a fan of the restaurant, or at least he wanted to like it. He had come to Del Posto a few times and celebrated some anniversaries there with his wife. So we figured, this was it, we'd better jump on it and bring him over to our side.

This was no joke, what we did for a fourth star. It was like a manned mission to Mars. We really went all out. We did less business for a year—we just stopped doing the volume, cut down the tables, and fine-tuned the experience. Every day we found some new edge to polish, every day we talked about how to make the food better. We were brutal in our self-critique. And then we put it out there and waited. It's like fishing. We said, "All right, Mr. Sifton, this is New York's first four-star Italian restaurant. . . ." We waited and waited, and one year went by . . . and then a year and a half. Seriously, we *could* have been to Mars and back in that time. He came in once, came in twice, came in three times—and then the whole thing just fucking exploded. We had it nailed. And we got that fourth star. We were crushing it, but it took that much time, that much work and extreme focus to make the grade. There's a reason they don't just give those stars away.

On the level of complexity where Del Posto operates, there is no faking it. And when Sifton came in again, what he got is exactly what the experience is for everyone. The menu kicked ass from top to bottom. Even the dessert program was like something from another planet—we found this kid, Brooks Headley, a punk-rock drummer who was a genius savant pastry chef. And it all clicked.

Ironically, the fourth star means less profit, even as it gains you serious national and international recognition, because that fourth star is a responsibility. You want it like nothing else in your life, but it's a burden. You carry it like a weight. Every day when you make decisions, when you think about expanding, all you can think about is that fucking star. We lost a Michelin star through the years, and that was a big loss. When the Michelin guy came to New York our opening year, he gave us two stars. It was the first two-star Italian restaurant in the country—we had three two-star years, and then we lost a star. We're still working to get it back.

It sounds crazy just talking about it. Fucking stars. It's all an illusion, I suppose, but it brings a lot of international clientele, not to mention bragging rights, which none of us are beyond, except maybe my mom. We work in a field with some very competitive motherfuckers, some of whom like to rib us about the fourth star—because we generally root for other restaurants to do well. We like it when our friends succeed. We think it's good for everyone when New York restaurants shine and reach new levels. We're competitive, sure, but it's good for everyone's business when it happens. And then there are the others who don't see it that way, they see us as the enemy, and then we'd just as soon take that star and beat them over the fucking head with it.

CHAPTER SIXTEEN

Don't Shoot the Piano Player

Either you believe that the pope is the Vicar of Christ or you don't, but I will say that meeting him and being around him turned out to be one of the most powerful experiences I've ever had. Being blessed by him, talking to him, singing "Happy Birthday" to him, spilling wine on him—there is an otherworldliness to him that I cannot even begin to describe.

When Pope Benedict came to New York in 2008, they needed someone to cook breakfast, lunch, and dinner for him for two days—"they" being the Vatican apostolate of New York—and they asked my mom, who agreed to curate all his dining for the whole weekend that he was here, to source the food, make the menus, bring the wine, hire cooks and a service staff, everything. She put me in charge of the wine. I didn't ask for that job. My mother told me what I was going to do, and I listened. Sometimes that's just the way it is.

Lidia had been grand marshal of the Columbus Day parade in 2007, which is a very big deal in New York City. Through this she became friendly with Monsignor Celestino Migliore and the archdiocese, who were naturally very involved in the Columbus Foundation, and the apostolate, who were in charge of planning the pope's visit, and of course one thing leads to the next, and that's how she got the gig cooking for the pope.

The apostolate's residence is on Seventy-second Street between Fifth and Madison, an old embassy building, and, as you might imagine, it is beautiful and very rich in detail. The dining room is this extremely ornate affair with one giant oval table set up so the pope can have dinner with the Vatican secretary of state, who travels with him, and all the cardinals in the United States—there are about thirteen of them. The details are incredible, from what he wears—that crazy pope hat and those funky red Prada shoes—to the smell of the house. There is a lot of whispering. The church is so mysterious and cryptic, and there are all these freaky nuns running around, and it is all supercultish and weird. At first I was kind of like, hey, this is bullshit, a lot of pomp and circumstance, a real waste of time. It was my usual smart-ass way of rejecting dogma and conformity—it just seemed like a masquerade party. But when I got there and got into it, I changed my mind. The experience was just overwhelming.

When the pope comes to town, they block off the entire Upper East Side of Manhattan. Security was presidential *times three*—you had to walk everywhere for those few days; Midtown was pretty much closed to traffic. You could not drive anywhere in the remote vicinity of the pope.

Benedict had some particular issues about what he likes and doesn't like to eat—he was definitely not going downtown to have the calamari at Babbo. His mother had been a cook, too. She came from southern Germany, from the Munich area, and of course there is a very similar sensibility in food styles between that area and northeastern Italy, so my mom designed menus that could have played on either border, to be true to her *patria* but also to invoke memories of his mother's cooking. So she made insalata di fave, asparagi e fagiolini con pecorino fresco, ravioli di cacio e pere, risotto con verdure di primavera e schegge di Grana Padano, but also tenerone di manzo brasato, which is a beef goulash served with smoked potatoes, sauerkraut, and sour cream, and for dessert a classic apple strudel with honey-swirled gelato. And he totally got what she was doing and loved it. I remember there was a long discussion about his mother's cooking—Lidia's food reminded him of what his mom made. It was all very sweet.

It was an intense couple of days. The access was extremely intimate. Lidia was toasting homemade Easter bread for him for breakfast and bringing him coffee and milk, and he's there in his robe, reading the paper. He wakes up, he has coffee, and he looks at the headlines just like every other man on the planet, and then he gets going with the pope thing. He may be infallible, but there is a real humanity to him. At this point he hadn't been the pope for that long, and he had kind of a PR problem, especially following such a popular pope as John Paul II, but he turned out to be an okay guy.

The first night was His Holiness entertaining a group of American cardinals. There is a very specific dining room setup, and there is a protocol for everything. The pope always gets served first. He gets the food first, then the wine, and everyone waits for the pope. Pope, secretary of state, the cardinal of New York, and then the rank and file. Everyone else had normal service, but he had his own dedicated waiter and wine guy, and that was me.

The pope liked to work the room; he was a real schmoozer, talking to everyone at the table, and of course everyone kisses his ring, just like in the movies. He has kind of a sweet tooth, and my mom brought him this special dessert wine we made for her sixtieth birthday. She never shares it, but she brought some for the pope, and he really loved it. He's not a huge drinker, although he indulged a bit and was having a good time.

It was Cardinal Bertone who asked me about how this wine was made, and then the pope jumped in, and it turned into a thirty-minute conversation, a very technical discussion, with everyone speaking in Italian. I'm explaining to them about picking the grapes in Friuli and the style of winemaking there, and the pope stayed right with me, asking questions and offering opinions. The pontiff knew a few things about grapes.

The second night my grandmother put on her best Lidia hand-me-down dress from the eighties and came to dinner with the pope. He had an audience with all the cooks and all the help. It was his birthday, and my mom made a cake—a giant replica of the papal mitre, aka that crazy pope hat. It reminded me of Monty Python, something between *The Holy Grail* and *Life of Brian*. And then after dinner, we went to some room that was either a study or the parlor, and he sat down at the piano and banged out some concert-level Mozart. The pope played a mean piano. Who knew? At one point I spilled some wine on him. Just a drop of red wine, but thankfully he didn't notice, and I didn't tell him. It was when I was filling his glass and pulling the carafe back, and one drop of red wine hit his shoulder. I saw it in slow motion. Bing! And it stained his vestment. Until now that moment has remained between God and me.

Every night the pope went out on the street to greet the public. There were tens of thousands of people, an ocean of people, waiting for him to come out onto the balcony. You could look down Fifth Avenue or Seventy-second Street in either direction, and all you saw was people. There were so many babies—babies with cancer, just horribly sick children—and they were passed through the crowd on the tips of people's fingers, to the pope. And he would kiss them and send them back. Maybe they were healed, I don't know. But crowd-surfing babies? It was the craziest shit I ever saw.

After the initial insanity of Del Posto had leveled out a bit, I realized that I wasn't sleeping well and that it had nothing to do with the stress of having the sword of Damocles hanging over my career. I had severe sleep apnea. I figured it out because the only time that I would actually rest was sleeping on airplanes, sitting up. I would take a flight to California for six hours, or to Italy, and when I landed, I'd be as refreshed as I could ever remember being. I was basically doing the head-bob thing, which wasn't ideal, but I was breathing more or less normally and getting into deep REM territory, so it was actually better sleep than I was getting horizontal in a bed.

I went to sleep clinics, I went to the doctor. A lot of my lifestyle was finally catching up with me, and I was told in no uncertain terms to lose some weight. I was as heavy as I had ever been, 260 pounds.

I was always a chubby kid. I'd struggled with weight my whole life. And I was always an eater. In my family, eating—this started for me with my father, but it also came from my mother and my grandmother—was a reward for behaving properly. It came from my father's mentality where, when you're facing starvation, what you eat validates who you are. Eating a lot meant you were doing well.

In addition to this food-as-reward scenario, there was also the unwritten commandment never to leave any food on the table, all of which came directly from my parents and grandparents, their having grown up in abject poverty. My grandmother wouldn't eat until everybody else at the table ate, for fear that there wouldn't be enough food for the rest of us. This went on even after my mom and I had become successful restaurateurs. This whole wartime mentality—

that it represented your social standing and was a reward for a job well done—fostered this absurd, unhealthy relationship with food.

My mom's approach to food is basically very healthy, as is the sensibility of the Italian table, but even now I think that there's certainly an element of speaking out of both sides of our mouths when we preach it. We just eat too fucking much. Even if you're eating things that are fresh and healthy, you don't need to act like every meal is going to be the last one.

When I was young, a reward for a good grade in English might be a two-ton plate of hot antipasto. Later it was a suckling pig with Barolos among cousins in the house. When I was working on Wall Street, it was going out to a restaurant and having a helping of pasta and a thirty-six-ounce veal chop, followed by chocolate mousse for dessert, washed down with the best of the wine list. My whole life I have been buried in all the excesses of eating and what it meant on so many different levels, from big family dinners to holiday feasts, and the sheer quantity and hedonism of it were not only accepted, they were encouraged as a sign of wealth in the New World. I was very prone to unhealthy eating—when I was a kid, I would eat a fucking boxful of Count Chocula in a salad bowl with a quart of milk while watching cartoons on a Saturday morning, and let me tell you, if my wife caught my kids doing that, she'd probably have a coronary. In New York there are the warriors who go out to Balthazar to celebrate their conquests in the big city over a côte de boeuf at three in the morning. That's food as a reward in another sensibility, and I was right there, along for the ride. It was all part of the living-large ethos of New York City, but I was turning into a complete disaster.

Del Posto was the apogee of elegance, and I was fucking slovenly. I'd given up the cigarettes, except now I was immersed in this trendy cigar lifestyle and was inhaling four Cubans a day. I had expensive humidors and boxes of contraband Commie cigars being delivered. I loved it; it was part of being the successful Restaurant Man.

I had a neighbor, a guy named Hank, who was a total aficionado of cigars and had these pre-Castro, aged masterpieces of the cigar maker's art. And when someone gives you a cigar like that to smoke in his Greenwich mansion, in his perfectly humidified cigar room with some 150-year-old French cognac, after you have wet your palate with a sip of 30-year-old vintage Champagne while looking at his Monets and Cézannes hanging on the wall, that can turn your head around. It was all part of the same indulgence. And then we'd have another drink, another cigar, and head out to eat another cow.

The doctor told me if I didn't stop I would have full-on type 2 diabetes in five to ten years and either die of a heart attack while I was sleeping or begin to go blind from glaucoma and start losing limbs. It was a nice picture he painted for me. He told me to take a look at my father—he had type 2 diabetes, which he did not control. He had glaucoma. He had poor circulation and neuropathy. I knew I had to change my life.

The real aha moment is when I stopped looking at food as an indicator of my social status or as a reward and started looking at it as fuel for my body.

People can eat any way they like. I still think everyone should drink wine every day and eat pasta every day, and I'm lucky to have found a good balance for myself. I am an advocate of consumption—cocktails, wine, a Roman food orgy with steaks bigger than New Jersey and bowls of pasta that could sink a ship—but I can't do it anymore. I love it when fat people come into one of my places and eat five courses. There's a yin and a yang to it, of course, as with everything. I love gusto, but for me at least, that kind of eating had to end. Certainly I had done my fair share, more than twenty people will eat in a lifetime.

No more marathons of the Mario-and-me variety. Enough. And I had to sleep with this mask on that regulated oxygen, this Darth Vader contraption, and you can imagine what that was doing for my romantic life. But it stopped the apnea temporarily.

I started running. Well, first I started walking, but a walk became a jog, which quickly turned into a 5K run, which became a 10K, which became a half marathon, and then I was running in the New York City Marathon and eventually took it to the extreme and completed the world-championship Ironman triathlon in Kona, Hawaii, which was one of the most powerful experiences of my entire life.

In Italy over the summer, I met this guy Luca, a marathon runner, who helped me train and got me into some very good habits, and once I became a runner, then everything else took care of itself. It just improved every part of my life. I think there is a whole book to be written about how people look at me and treat me differently now versus when I was sixty pounds heavier. The world changed.

Now I am hooked—I've fallen in love with running. It has become a part of my life. Running for me is the most Zen thing you can do to begin your day. For me it's a way to meditate, it keeps me aligned, keeps my weight off, keeps my eating regimen established. I had high cholesterol, I had high blood pressure, and all of that went away. Now I have to consciously remember to eat enough so that I don't lose too much weight. Breakfast is a banana, maybe a piece of toast with a scrambled egg on it. The days of the thirty-six-ounce veal chops are gone. I'm not a big meal eater; these days I snack a lot more. I eat a lot of carbs and a lot of protein and try to stay away from processed food, although I eat a lot of chocolate and drink too much red Gatorade.

And then there is wine. I had to laugh recently when a blogger thought that he was being a smart-ass by writing that the secret to my success was drinking a bottle of wine a day, as if that were some sort of scarlet A for excessive alcohol consumption.

Which is complete bullshit.

The part about my drinking a bottle a day is true, but being snarky about it is uninformed, paranoid, puritanical, pedantic, and frankly just pathetic. Wine and food are definitely in the same category when it comes to their being used in reward scenarios, and of course many people have very unhealthy relationships with the bottle. But seriously, drinking a bottle of wine every day is completely moderate consumption, and if you have a sound philosophy about living life and enjoying your meals, about elevating the experience of eating every time you get with the knife and fork, you should be able to see that without my coshing you over the head with an empty quartino. If you have a glass of wine with lunch, and two with dinner, you could drink a bottle a day for the rest of your life and not only never be drunk but not even feel the effects of alcohol. A bottle of wine is nothing, hardly even a middle finger to the old ghosts of Prohibition. It's actually good for you. Wine promotes balance and beauty in life.

I was thinking after I read that blog that maybe I should write a book called Joe's Bottle-of-Wine-a-Day Method for Success. But now I'm thinking that one bottle isn't nearly enough—especially if you're drinking Bastianich wine.

CHAPTER SEVENTEEN

No, You Can't Sit Down

Restaurants go bad when you stop paying attention to them. Of course, there are things that go out of style, but as I've said, we try not to be trendy. As long as you are committed to a restaurant and to keeping it fresh and vibrant, as long as you know what you're doing and are watching those margins, you should be able to continue. Exceed expectations and people will always come back.

And if you do get hot, you have to be very careful not to get caught up in the whirlwind of your own success. It's easy to let the swagger of the restaurant in its big moment affect you. It actually requires a lot of discipline to operate a hot restaurant. You have to step away just a bit. An immature or inexperienced operator might be high on the fifteen minutes of glory and forget the basic rules—when you're hot, there are a lot of things that the market will forgive. What you have to do is keep the standard high and overdeliver on the market perception even when you're the toughest reservation in town—*especially* when you're turning people away—and then you'll be able to survive once the spotlight fades. People coming into a trendy restaurant are usually so eager to like it that they're willing to overlook a lot—shitty food, shitty service—because they know it's hot and they think they are, too, for even being there. You need to announce that you're in it for the long run, and you do that by leaning on value, quality, and the overall experience. People will get the message that you're no flash in the pan. The graveyard is filled with the hottest restaurants in town.

Gramercy Tavern is a great example of a restaurant that has gone on for fifteen-plus years and has never been really trendy but is always fantastically consistent. Personally, I don't like the hokeyness of it, I don't like the Americana-purebred patina that the whole place is wrapped in, but it's an incredibly well-run restaurant, and I do enjoy eating there. It's a benchmark in New York City dining. It created a category, actually an entire genre—the American, quasi-farm-to-table, überhospitalitarian, make-the-customer-feel-great-at-any-expense experience. The food is honest and good and they make people feel very comfortable. Everything about it delivers.

In the long term, what keeps restaurants viable is just consistency. That's what people want. This is a big Mario thing. People come back to your place and expect to have what they had last time. They don't want to go to a new restaurant—people are creatures of habit. If they find something they like, they want to reexperience it. They want to bring their friends and show their friends how smart they are because they've found this great place. The minute you start changing too much, you spook them. Successful restaurants don't close themselves; it takes a little push, like bad decisions, trend chasing, or willful indifference from the owner.

One Fifth Avenue was a historic restaurant with a fabulous location for years and years, but at some point it just drifted into obscurity. In the seventies it was a great hangout—John Belushi and the early *Saturday Night Live* crew spent every wrap party there, every week. There was a piano bar in front, and it was a classic Village joint for a long time, but it changed too often—it opened and reopened, and no one seemed to know what to do with it.

One second it was a gay cabaret scene and then it was a seafood restaurant. I remember eating there when it was Clementine, a restaurant/discotheque. There was no consistency, but that address, that location, was fucking magic, if only someone knew the trick. And we did.

Mario actually lived next door, and at some point he got wind that Clementine was going to close. He knew the head of the co-op board of the building, and we were able to get the inside track on it before it went to the market and grab it at a nice price. Once again it was a New York deal—we had the real estate before we had any solid idea of what we wanted to do with it. Frankly, we were making it up as we went along.

One of the ballsy things we did was to take the bar, which was in a very weird place in a corridor toward the back, and move it right up front. To move a bar in a historic restaurant is bad karma, but it worked. It all happened organically, and the space felt really good. We were physically very close to Lupa and Babbo, so it felt like home. This would become Otto.

We were fooling around with the idea of doing pizza—what we really wanted was a pizza-and-wine bar, which believe it or not was somewhat heretical. If you went to a pizzeria in Italy, you drank beer. No one drinks wine—eat pizza, drink beer, it's like religion. Drinking wine with pizza really wasn't very authentic, at least not for street-level Italians.

We went to Naples, to Da Michele, which is the most famous pizza place in the heart of the ghetto. We were eating pizzas where there were literally crime scenes just outside. You see another side of Italian humanity there. It is not the enlightened rolling hills of Tuscany's countryside, with guys in suede vests riding horseback and drinking Chianti Classico. This is gangs, violence, Mafia—the real deal. Everyone is on the take. It's serious shit. People getting shot and knifed. If you want to see a ghetto, go to Naples. That is as urban as urban gets.

At Da Michele they make two pizzas, tomato and cheese, or just tomato. And that's it. It's a time-honored tradition. They use the same oven that's been there for like two hundred years. It's very minimal. And that's the beauty of Neapolitan pizza: It is absolutely the poorest food in the city of Naples, it is peasant food, but it has to be done a specific way. The pizza has to have a big crust—they call it a frame—and it has to be blistered perfectly. And the inside needs to be soft. A *cuore dolce,* a soft heart. You go, you see these women, the way they eat pizza, they just fold them up and eat it like that, kind of like John Travolta in *Saturday Night Fever,* now that I think about it.

Speaking of Queens, home-style pizza for me was two slices and a small root beer for ninety-five cents at Jack's in Bay Terrace, next to the Bagel Den. Even though the tomato sauce is industrial and the crust and cheese are kind of chemical and sourced from a landfill or an oil spill, there's a certain pleasure in a great, dried, crusty, overcheesed slab of gooey junk food. And I like garlic powder, which is still a complete mystery to me. I have no idea what's in it.

In Rome the pizza would be crisper and cooked through. You could take a slice with a superthin crust, and it might even hold up. And there's also the whole concept of focaccia from Rome, which are basically what we call the Sicilian pizza, the square one baked in the pan. That's really just a focaccia with cheese and sauce on top.

We wanted to do a pizzeria at One Fifth, but here's the thing: We couldn't put in a pizza oven, because it was this old, historic building and there were serious venting issues. It seems counterintuitive to make pizza at a place where you can't have an oven, but we were stuck on the idea. We thought that sliced meats, cheeses, pizza, and wine together were the magic combination for a two-hundred-seat restaurant near NYU in Greenwich Village. So we came up with the idea of cooking pizza on a griddle or a flattop. You cook the bread, put the toppings on it, and then finish it in something like a convection oven. In Providence, Rhode Island, we had seen great pizzas made on the grill, so we figured why the fuck not?

The pizza was a compromised product from the very beginning. We were so tortured, we ate so many pizzas trying to get it right— hundreds of pies coming out of the oven. We'd be there all night trying all sorts of timing and combinations and cooking techniques until we thought we had it right. But we were fucking lambasted when we opened. Reviewers were calling it "matzo pizza." They said it was like Swedish flatbread. It was brutal. Ed Levine, the pizza king of New York, said our pizza sucked. Even our friends were slapping us over our pie. But Bill Grimes came in, gave us a nice *New York Times* two-star—I don't know how the fuck he figured that was a two-star restaurant, but God bless his soul.

Truly, Otto isn't really about the pizza—the success of Otto was a combination of this very winecentric, accessibly priced experience, a quality Italian-food experience that pizza happened to be a part of. The place was flooded with tables of twenty-year-old girls. Third-year NYU students. Droves of them. The success of Otto lies in the fact that it is a lot of people's first real experience with these products, done right—good prosciutto, a good piece of cheese, a good glass of wine—and consuming everything together in the culturally right setting. People are blown away by it.

And if it isn't a new experience for them, then they're thinking about that summer they spent in Tuscany when they were sophomores or the trip they made to Italy with their parents. But there's something about the impact of those flavors on young palates that really opens up their minds. Otto is entry-level authentic Italian flavors. We have ten pastas for nine bucks a bowl. People got hooked.

A lot of what makes Otto so great isn't even good cooking, it's good food handling. Easy stuff—make sure your cheeses are not oxidized and never too cold. We make sure the prosciutto is the right thickness. We use antique slicers. Everything counts, everything communicates. Even the condiments—extra-sticky truffled honey; tangy, crunchy amarena cherries; and a hot and sweet apricot mostarda—are little Otto-isms, snippets of Italian wine-bar culture and Italian food culture, all adding up to a great experience.

The gelato is another thing that really helped Otto. It's made by a crusty, West Village hippie lesbian. She's probably sixty years old. I don't like her very much; she hasn't been nice to me. She's crotchety. But her ice cream is unbelievable—she's obsessively consumed. She's a genius, a true artisan in the classical Italian spirit. She uses only seasonal fresh fruit, and everything is worked by hand. The Otto ice-cream experience is truly amazing. It's a work of art. There's nothing quite like it. No one in the United States of America is even fucking close.

At first the high tables in the front room at Otto were a disaster. The restaurant is divided into two spaces, the front room with a bar and some tall tables, and then a larger dining room behind that. People would come in and not know what to make of these tables, which were chest-high and completely alien to American diners. They would complain, "What is this? We can't eat here! There are no chairs!" Otto was the first quality New York restaurant that forced people to consume food at a table without chairs. You couldn't even get one if you asked.

We got the idea from the Autogrill, a chain of restaurants out on the highways in Italy, where people would stand up and eat at tall counters. We actually measured how high the counters were, and that's how high we built our tables. The design came from the card tables in a trattoria back in Trieste, where the old men played *scopa*, drinking and slamming cards down on the tables. The tables had a little cubby underneath where you put your ashtray and cigarettes, your car keys, and your money. So you come into Otto, you can put your cell phone and shit inside the little drawer, and then eat on top. At first there was a lot of resistance—because it was different. But that was our business plan, to create a venue for people to eat up front while waiting to have tables in the back. Have some antipasto and vino standing up, then sit down in the back and order pizza or pasta. That was the idea: spend some money, then sit down and spend more money.

Eventually everyone got used to it, and now it's considered part of the Otto experience. And the train board is part of the trip, too; it really adds some fun and maybe a bit of romance. When you come to Otto, you get a train ticket to one of the fifty-two largest cities in Italy, and then while you're standing and eating and drinking, you have to watch the board. When your city comes up, you go to the front with your ticket and they seat you. That was my idea.

Opening day of Otto was New Year's Eve 2002, and the place was still a mess. Typical Joe and Mario chaos. Oh, and I wound up in jail.

I had to go return a floor sander to this shop up on Lafayette Street. I double-parked, dropped the thing off, and then I was waiting outside, standing by my truck so I could move it if I had to, smoking a cigar. A Partagás No. 4 Robusto—I will never forget that cigar.

I was just waiting for the guy to bring out the receipt, and a cop came up behind me, gets out of his car, and comes over to me. "License and registration."

I said, "I can move, no problem."

"License and registration."

"I'm just double-parked, I can—"

But he wasn't having it. "License and registration."

I'm standing there puffing on my cigar, a little bit annoyed. It's New Year's Eve, and I have to get back and open my new restaurant, and I'm thinking, *Why is this guy breaking my balls? I'm just double-parked.*

I stood on the sidewalk steaming my stogie for a full five minutes. I figured I was going to get a ticket for double-parking, but he turned me around. "Sir, please stand up against the wall." He frisked me, cuffed me, put me in the back of his cruiser, and called a tow truck.

"Sir, you've been driving with a suspended license."

"You gotta be fucking kidding me. I'm opening a restaurant tonight!"

"Nothing I can do, sir. Mandatory arrest in the state of New York."

I mentioned that I was a restaurateur. Babbo, Becco, Lupa, partners with Mario . . . but he clearly was not a fan. The next thing I knew, I was heading for the Lower East Side—Elizabeth Street, I think. They put me in a holding cell, took my belt and my shoelaces, and locked me up with this young transvestite prostitute, a junkie in sore need of a fix and some fresh mascara who was completely strung out and puking in the New Year.

I got my one phone call—I called our CFO, Mark Coscia, and told him that whatever he was doing, stop and come get me the fuck out of jail. He gets my assistant on the phone, and for whatever it's worth (zero), they figure out that my license was suspended because I'd gotten a seat-belt ticket that my former assistant had paid with a credit card, or tried to—she put the credit-card number down wrong, and the ticket was never paid. And then I moved into a new house, and they kept sending the no-payment notices to the old address, and I never saw any of them and never knew that my license was suspended.

After I'd spent three hours in the precinct, the police van comes to bring us to Central Booking. They chain me to the junkie, who is now totally cold and shaking. They put us in the paddy wagon and take us down to Centre Street, where I'm booked, fingerprinted, have mug shots taken, and undergo the medical interview. *Do you have AIDS? Are you an addict?* I didn't get the finger search, but that was probably just because they were starting to get busy. It's New Year's Eve, so they're bringing in bloody drunks, guys who've been in fights, and a guy in a full-body, red-fur Elmo suit, crusted in shit from rolling around in the gutter. A real mess of humanity.

Then we were moved into a big holding pen, a real shithole, just like on television, with the stainless-steel toilet bowl in the middle of the room. There is piss and vomit everywhere, and every few minutes another drunk or drug dealer gets tossed in with us. I end up standing for the first four hours, because not only am I scared shitless, I'm wearing a thousand-dollar suit, and fuck me if I'm going to sit in a puddle of piss. Hours later some matron comes by with completely disgusting cheese sandwiches wrapped in plastic and little containers of warm skim milk. The first six hours go by, then the next six hours, and nothing. There's this bizarre contraband-cigarette business going on that I can't figure out, but it's obviously sanctioned by the cops who run the place, and all I can think about is what the margin is, what's the cost of the cigarette versus the markup. Fucking Restaurant Man can never shut it off.

I was there for over forty-eight hours in the same cell. By that time I'd made friends with a couple of gangbangers. And everyone asked me what I was in for, which was a really interesting question, because you're in here with these guys who are drunk and covered in blood and there's no law down there, and I'm obviously some sort of yuppie. I can't tell these guys I'm in for a fucking seat-belt violation—that would be the end, I could feel it. But I heard one guy say he was in for multiple warrants, so I figured that was vague enough. When somebody asked me, I told the guy, "I'm in for multiple warrants," and tried to scowl. It seemed to work.

Later that night Ray Kelly, the police commissioner, was at Babbo, and word got back to my mom, who called and had the maître d' bring the portable house phone to his table—while he's eating dinner. With a journalist. She told him, "My son is in Central Booking. Can you get him out?" He didn't like that very much.

Mario called a detective friend of his, and he came down with some brass, all the way down to my cell—there were like four cops and two detectives, and they called me over. I looked up from the swamp of squalor and stench and was thinking, *Thank God,* but they really couldn't do anything. Once you're in the system, you're in the system, and they have the legal right to hold you for seventy-two hours before you even see a judge. But they promise to get me in front of a judge as soon as they can. If I'd had a hundred thousand dollars in my bank account and someone had asked me to sign a check for a hundred thousand dollars, I would have signed it on the spot. I was that fucking horrified and sick from the experience.

There was this one young black kid who kind of became my buddy in there. I think he was arrested for dealing crack. He'd been down there for a day or two before I even got there, and when he saw the cops come to talk to me, he said, "Yo, this guy's like a John Gotti motherfucker. He's all mobbed up an' shit, and he's gonna get us all outta here!" And now everybody in the cell thought I was connected, what with a whole slew of cops coming down and talking to me, at which point I became the celebrity of the cell, because maybe I had some pull and I was going to help them get out of there. Which is a double-edged sword, because either they're scared to fuck with you and want to be nice to you or they want to kill you because they think you're getting some sort of special treatment.

Night turns to day and then night again, and finally they put me in chains and drag me up to see the judge. One of the friendly cops managed to get me bumped up in the line, which probably saved me another thirty hours down there. I pled guilty to driving with a suspended license and was sentenced to time served and a thirty-five-dollar fine.

I missed the opening of the restaurant. I missed New Year's Day with my kids. It was the worst experience of my life. It was like living in the fifth circle of hell. It was really that bad. Just the smell— it made me miss my grandmother's piss jug in Yugoslavia. It made me want to be doused in rancid chicken water just to freshen up.

One thing I found out was that after being in jail, you don't just walk into your house. You have to stop at the doorstep and take all your clothes off and walk in naked so you don't bring in any bad luck.

It was January and fucking freezing in Connecticut, and there I was standing buck naked in front of my big, fancy house. My wife went from complete disbelief to panic to just making fun of me. Pretty normal for us, actually.

●

CHAPTER EIGHTEEN

That's Right, the Women Are Smarter

Women are better cooks than men. April Bloomfield is a great example of why—she cooks to nourish your soul and your spirit, not to impress you with how clever and smart she is. It's very evident; it translates directly into her food, which is both very comforting and unfancy and yet exquisitely executed. Her cooking is unapologetically a reflection of her personality—that of an ambitious, young, extremely focused woman who cares very much about her art and craft. Men construct and create. I think women just extend who they are into their food.

Cooking is a male-dominated profession, very chauvinistic, and it can be very antiwoman just because it's a difficult job being in the extreme heat in the kitchen, and what's demanded of you physically is like being in a rugby scrum. You have to be a tough bastard in there just to deal with these other macho men who are breathing down your neck, happy to see you burn or fail.

The women who rise to the top in this profession have fucking brass balls. Start with my first partner, my mother. In the early Felidia years, she was hard-core—she was back there cooking up a fucking storm and taking shit from no one. She was never the chef-whites, *oui-oui* French kind of chef. She was always cooking more the way a mom cooks in the kitchen, and she never really lost her presence. She would cook the food and bring it into the dining room. That was the great transition she was able to make—cooking for you not as a chef but as a mother would cook for you, then bringing the food to your table. That's how people still relate to her.

April is British, a policeman's daughter who was raised in some soot-filled industrial town, and she came up by working her ass off—I think she actually was going to be a cop but somehow got a gig in a kitchen and cooked her way into the royalty of London restaurants. She is truly a cook's cook. Her style and approach remind me of my mother's, and that really struck a chord with me. April and my mother are the perfect examples of why women are simply inherently better at creating and sharing food. Everything she does is with flavor and taste and not with hype. She doesn't return critics' calls; she never pandered to the media, so they started chasing her. The way she promoted her food was with exactly the same integrity as what she put on the plate. She is the real fucking deal. She is famous for refusing to take the Roquefort off her signature burger; I don't necessarily agree with that. I don't like it that way, but I respect her willingness to deal with the flak she gets for it and for her belief in her own vision. It takes a lot to be so committed, and that speaks volumes. If she won't take the cheese off the burger, imagine how she feels about the rest of the menu.

Gabrielle Hamilton is another hard-core chef who has been fantastic in translating her sensibility to the table. Barbara Lynch in Boston is amazing; she cooks like a ninety-year-old grandmother. There are a lot of women chefs in San Francisco—Traci Des Jardins and Alice Waters, of course. I like Waters and her overall message, but I think there's an inherent contradiction in her attempt to be so egalitarian and populist; ultimately, she lives in a haze of idealism.

Mario found April when we were working on opening the Spotted Pig. She was working at the River Café in London, a very famous

Italian restaurant, and he recruited her to come over to New York and join the team.

The Spotted Pig, April's entrée into the maelstrom of New York, was born of Ken Friedman, who had enjoyed a pretty good career in the music business. He started with Bill Graham and worked with U2 back in the late seventies—the urban legend is that he worked his ass off, literally stapling flyers to telephone poles in San Francisco. That kind of grassroots DIY promotion was central to their success, and they didn't forget that. They brought him along for the ride, but I guess at a certain point in the music business, once you reach a certain age, you're kind of too old to be swimming in that pool and you need to find something else to do. Paul McGuinness, U2's manager, was good friends with Ken and one day said to him, "Well, you like food and you're a good host. You should be in the restaurant business." And Ken said, "Okay, I'd like to be in the restaurant business." These, of course, are all the wrong reasons to start a restaurant. Paul told Ken that he should recruit some people who could help him and give him a bit of legitimacy, and so he called Mario, and Mario started by hiring April. Ken really knew nothing about the restaurant business, nothing about construction, so I was coaching him and Mario was coaching April on the food and the menu, and I worked on the wine program and getting the restaurant built. Ken is a very smart guy and paid very close attention to everything happening around him—and pretty soon he was flexing Restaurant Man muscle.

In 2003 we were looking around for a location. We wanted it to be pubby, with a casual vibe, but also with food that was exceptional and not run-of-the-mill bar grub. Ken had spent a lot of time in London, had seen the birth of the gastropub and certainly the Spotted Pig was the first gastropub in New York. He found the old Le Zoo space in the West Village. It was a famous restaurant that had been there forever on the corner of West Twelfth and Greenwich.

The Pig was our first sort of side project—we were given equity because of our role in helping launch it. Ken knew lots of heavy hitters—the money came from the U2 boys and various other people in the business: Michael Stipe, Jay-Z, Eminem, Fatboy Slim. We helped them as much as we could. Because of Ken's quirkiness and his gang of rock-star investors, it was mayhem right out of the gate, but the mayhem led to incredible success. It was like a free-form party that went on until six in the morning, every night. Ken hosted, the music people started showing up, then they were showing up every night, and the party would just go on and on. Eventually we took over the second floor, which wasn't really part of the restaurant. It became more like the private club.

The Pig is an amazing study in New York restaurants, because what any normal person was sure wouldn't work, or anything that was instinctively a bad idea to a restaurant professional, always seemed to fuel the fire of its success. Intuitively, to run a good restaurant, you create order and systems, and Ken was intentionally plunging everything into total entropy—from staffing to hierarchy to how the books were run to how the menu was written to how the pricing was done. I would tell him exactly what to do, and he would do the opposite, and it would work.

He wasn't *hiring* people, he was *casting* them—he brought in tattooed lesbian punk rockers who had never tended bar before to be his bartenders, and then he had them write the wine list. The maître d' was the pizza-delivery boy from down the block. You would think that this sort of Bizarro World cherry-picking would have led to complete chaos. And it did. But that's exactly what drew people to it; it really had that feel of the West Village gone wild. In the third month open, I was there with Mario, and we look around, and it's fucking Bono, Bill Clinton, Robin Williams, and Jay-Z having burgers together, talking about saving the world. That's the kind of shit that went down there. It had that magic of putting people from different worlds, of high influence, together over beers and burgers at 2:00 A.M., and suddenly everyone is talking about the Pig and reading about it in tabloids from New York to London.

We never hired a publicist—that's something I learned from Mario. His view of publicists and PR people was that they're just useless cretins who live off the fumes of people who actually do shit. In the beginning I didn't necessarily agree with that, coming from a more formalized, structured world where if you had a restaurant, you hired a publicist, but now I agree with the fact that if you're doing the right thing and your message is clean and pure, you can just pick up the phone and call whoever the fuck you want and tell them what you're doing yourself. If you're a stand-up person and you're not a douchebag, you don't have to distance yourself from the media. In fact, they'd usually rather hear it from the person who's creating the mayhem.

Anyway, we didn't need the hype—every band that came to town had its afterparty at the Spotted Pig, along with the groupies, the celebrities, the strippers, and everything else that comes with the package. Ken hosted that party all these years. To his credit, he has gone on to leverage it to major success. A lesser man could have wound up dead. Or worse.

Nancy Silverton, our partner and the chef at the Mozza restaurants in Los Angeles, is a very powerful cook. I'm kind of in awe of her. Nancy is incredibly talented, a master chef, and a very passionate and inspired baker. She also makes the best grilled cheese you've ever had in your life. It's amazing. She uses brioche and sour breads and butters them with a brush and grills them till they're caramelized and crunchy.

She started Campanile in Los Angeles with her then-husband, Mark Peel, then opened La Brea Bakery, which she eventually sold to some multinational conglomerate. She got divorced and left Campanile.

We trusted her implicitly—we never even would have gone into Los Angeles without her. She was a hometown hero; they loved her, they knew her, they trusted her as we did. She was a known entity in the critical community and in the public community. She was amazing to have as a partner. Her palate is as good as it gets. Actually, I don't think I've ever seen her eat, but she tastes continuously all day long, and her quest for purity and flavor is unrelenting. She's obsessed. And it shows, because the food is great. Also, she was very inspired—opening a new restaurant with us was like a big fuck-you to the life she'd left behind.

It is a complete pain in the ass to open a restaurant in L.A., because there's no center—it's like a conglomeration of five cities, and there's no one obvious hub. We looked in Culver City and Santa Monica, which I love, and Venice Beach, which was still too hippie, too left, too out there. We considered Beverly Hills for about a second, but that place makes me want to barf every time I go there. It's the most antiseptic, sterile, faux-luxurious place—it's just the worst of humanity, the worst of retail, and the worst of eating all wrapped up into one. Except for Spago. Wolfgang Puck is great. For an Austrian guy who speaks like Helmut Kohl to become the number-one chef to the stars in this country is amazing. He's a very savvy guy—he created this aura, everyone knows who Wolfgang Puck is. He never really had a regular TV show, and he's still a celebrity chef. It's kind of amazing if you think about that.

We settled on West Hollywood, because we knew we had to be near the main business of L.A., which is the movie business. We wanted to be close to the studio lots; we thought those were the people who could drive the business. We found our location, a restaurant called Amelio's on the corner of Melrose and North Highland. It turned out to be two restaurants that were attached. One was a more traditional restaurant, and the other had been run as a pizzeria. It was already laid out that way, so we went with that and opened Pizzeria Mozza on one side and Osteria Mozza on the other, which is kind of like Babbo minus 10 percent, or Lupa plus 30.

We got the concept of the mozzarella bar when we were in Rome with Nancy. We went to Obika, which is a famous mozzarella bar in Rome. We loved the idea of the interactive—pulling fresh mozzarella in the dining room in a classic osteria setting, with a pizzeria next door, where all the wines were under fifty bucks.

In a city where it's said that people eat only between seven and eight-thirty, we were full at six and full at ten. We had lines of people at eleven-thirty in the morning waiting to have pizza for lunch. L.A. has never really been known as a great restaurant city—everyone drives everywhere, so people don't really drink much when they go out to eat, and they're more worried about who's in the room than what's on their plate. Those are the classic L.A. stereotypes. But we found there was a real groundswell of people who wanted to eat good food and cared enough to take a 6:00 P.M. or 10:00 P.M. reservation. It probably started with transplanted New Yorkers and Europeans, and then Jeffrey Katzenberg started coming in, and then Steven Spielberg, and all of a sudden we had this whole wave of L.A. luminaries.

Nancy's vision is counterintuitive to any normal standard of Italian pizza—it's some sort of pizza she invented. It's basically a long bake. Whereas classic Neapolitan pizza is usually a ninety-second, two-minute bake tops, this is like a twelve-minute pickup. There's a very particular recipe for the dough. It's crunchy, light, it's very ingredient-driven in the topping.

Classic Neapolitan pizza is about mozzarella, tomato, and bread. Period. The top-selling pizza at Mozza is a fennel/onion/sausage job. It's really more of a pizza *concept* than an actual pizza, but it's awesome. People say it's the best pizza they've ever had.

So now I've got two restaurants that serve pizza, neither very traditional—basically we disrespected the old Italian traditional pizza paradigm and really went off road on both Otto and then Mozza. It's not until we get to Tarry Lodge in 2009 that we have our first wood-fired oven to make our own Roman-style pizza.

Tarry Lodge was, again, a real-estate-driven deal. My wife was driving to Costco to buy me a case of red Gatorade. Port Chester, where Costco is, is the working-class town between Greenwich, Connecticut, and Rye, New York. It's where the movie theater is and where all the best Mexican, Peruvian, and Chilean restaurants are. And she saw this burned-out building, the old Tarry Lodge, with an auction sign on it, and she told me she loved the location and that I needed to buy it. I went to the auction and bid, and bid, and bid. Some guy finally outbid me by a hundred thousand dollars. On the way out, I gave him my number and said, "If you choose not to go with the sale, give me a call. I'd still be interested."

Weeks pass, the guy closes on the building, but then he freaks out because he learns that some serious baggage comes with it—it was built on top of a foundry, which meant that there were potential preexisting environmental hazards, and you had to quantify them in order to develop the property. There was a lot of risk involved, and when he realized it, he had a meltdown, called me, and I wound up buying it from him for a hundred thousand dollars less than he paid for it.

For a century the Tarry Lodge was the watering hole for a foundry on the Byram River, which like most big foundries had its own bar where the guys would drink after work. Following World War II, some Italian family took it over, and it became a dark-paneled, pool-table-in-the-back-with-the-Budweiser-lampshade-over-it kind of place that had a shuffleboard bar and served pan pizza. A real townie bar, and very much loved. I started asking around, and people told me they'd been there on Pearl Harbor Day, and on their birthdays and anniversaries and after their weddings. There was a lot of nostalgia.

We had to knock it down because the place was a mess, gutted by fire. We razed the structure and rebuilt it to look as if the new place had been there for a hundred years. Our vision was to cater to the sentimentality of everyone who lived in Port Chester and the surrounding, swankier communities, everyone who had real or imagined memories of the place. It was a very romantic notion, and even if some of it was a bit fabulistic, we were very sincere, and it was quickly embraced. So now Tarry Lodge is a trattoria. It serves great brick-oven pizza, plus steaks, fish, and pasta—kind of like the greatest hits of Lupa and Otto.

And this is when our worlds collided and the Tarry Lodge became a crossroads for us—before that we were more dogmatically committed to single styles of restaurant, very true to one concept or style of Italian restaurateuring.

One of the great problems in the business of Italian restaurants is that making pizza creates a huge internal conflict. It's all about labor and disparate check averages. Running a good pizzeria and a good trattoria in the same restaurant is almost like having a back of house for two restaurants, with only one revenue point. In other words, you have a pizzeria kitchen and a restaurant kitchen in the same place with only one set of tables, and to do it right you have to staff them both with qualified people. But you're getting the revenue from just one set of tables, so classically that's a big no-no. But at a certain point we realized with the Tarry Lodge that . . . you know what? People want pizza, pasta, and steak all in the same place. Fuck it. Let's just give them what they want. It was like when we went out to Las Vegas a few years earlier and realized that there were some battles that were just not worth fighting. It took us a while to figure it out: Even though we are fundamentally right, and caving in to the requests for deviations from our menu and the experience we wanted to deliver stood firmly against every moral principle we have as Restaurant Men and hospitalitarians, it was still not worth fighting, at least not in Las Vegas. We just had to let it go.

There's an underlying concept that we all struggle with; it's at the very heart of what we do. We came out of Babbo and went to Vegas with the idea that you should listen to us because we know what the fuck we're doing. The customer is not always right. Good customers, sophisticated customers, understand that. It might seem ironic, genuinely, but in New York City, the toughest place on earth, with audiences and customers who are relentlessly demanding, they understand that better than anywhere: *The customer is not always right.* There is an openness and an earnest desire to be surprised here that makes it the best place to practice any kind of art or culture.

Our instinct is to protect our art form, and when customers try to take us so far astray from the fundamental concept that they came to us for, then they must be stopped. We have to be able to say no. You can't come into one of my restaurants and think that you are going to reimagine our menu with substitutions or your special needs. You want to bring *your* wine to *my* restaurant? I don't think so. The million dollars of inventory I bought and selected for my restaurant is not sufficient? Why not bring your own food, too? The wine we choose is part of the dining experience, and that's just the way it is. If you didn't want it, you shouldn't have come here. Can we turn the music down? No, we can't. This is how we play the music. In fact, let's crank it up.

And that's all great if I'm saying it or Mario is saying it. But once we've given a paid employee two thousand miles away in Vegas that kind of power over an enormous and very populist transient customer base, we're creating monsters. So we've had to bend on some of the classic Joe and Mario rules. And that was a big learning curve. It works in New York, where we have the leverage based on our reputation and the loyalty of our longtime customers, but in the world of Las Vegas where it's once-a-year diners, if we want to play in that league we have to be willing to give the people what they ask for and learn to suck it up.

In Vegas the dream was to open something like Babbo, which became B&B. We also opened Otto there as well. We didn't do a classic Vegas management deal, which generally involves licensing the name and giving up some control. We wound up being able to own the restaurants, which made it much more attractive to enter the market. We had a good relationship with Rob Goldstein, who was the head of casinos at the Las Vegas Sands, which also owns the Venetian and the Palazzo. Rob is a fit, fiftysomething Jewish guy from Philly with remarkably perfect hair, five-thousand-dollar French suits, and belts and shoes that were obviously skinned from the same very handsome crocodile. He was a classic Vegas casino guy, and he was a foodie and a fan of our restaurants. At first we were courted by Steve Wynn to do something—he wanted Babbo in the first Wynn casino resort. Keith McNally was going to do

Balthazar there, and that was a big thing, but Wynn was impossible to deal with. He wanted us to work for him, but he had crazy demands on how much we had to be there. There was no way we could sign that deal. We met Rob Goldstein, however, and the Venetian was one of those hotels that were open-minded to our ideas—they were very proactive in creating incredible restaurants.

At first we proposed to do just one restaurant. And of course they wanted us to call it Babbo, but we thought there should only be one Babbo, and so we decided to call it B&B—Batali and Bastianich. And the fact that there is still just one Babbo is a good thing. I think the only other city that might warrant another Babbo might be London. One day.

In the beginning we had a great deal of resistance from the spaghetti-and-meatballs crowd. They came in and didn't really understand what we were doing—the menu was very similar to Babbo's and outside the realm of experience of most Vegas diners. But Vegas has really changed in the last five years; the market has become more sophisticated, a lot of hip New York restaurant brands have moved in, and B&B is doing better than ever. It is clearly the best authentic Italian dining experience in all of Vegas, and people search it out. There's only so much bad spaghetti and meatballs you can eat, even in Vegas.

But B&B is only 92 seats, very small, very boutique by Vegas standards, so once it caught on, it wasn't that hard to fill. It was an anomaly, though—we learned very quickly that people who come to Vegas mostly just want to eat steak and drink gigantic red wines. So four years later we opened up Carnevino Italian Steakhouse, which has 280 seats.

We hired Adam Perry Lang, who is a master butcher and a very talented meat sourcer. We spent a lot of time analyzing the supply chain of beef—our ambition was nothing short of being able to control the source of the meat from genetics through cow-calf, through feedlot, through slaughtering, through aging, and right to the plate. Because truly, the only thing that distinguishes one steak house from the next is the quality of the beef. It does not take a master chef to deliver charred and rare; it's all about the product. We built a twenty-thousand-square-foot dry-aging facility in a bunker in the middle of the desert, and we put a million dollars of beef in there, all of it handpicked by our team. We have porterhouse, rib eye, filet, and we also focus on carne crudo, raw beef Italian style.

Everyone in Vegas wants the best. At Carnevino the rib eye costs a hundred sixty dollars, but believe it or not, more than half of that is the actual food cost, which as you now know is not the kind of margin I would ever look for.

In the eyes of Restaurant Man, the yield on dry-aged steaks is just a complete fucking tragedy. It's the *King Lear* of menu items. Look at the math—the shrinkage on dry aging is horrifying. You could lose 30, 35 percent of the weight in a month's time. In other words, a thirty-two-ounce steak, by the time I serve it, might be twenty-two ounces. And then you've got to cook it, and you lose another 25, 30 percent of the weight. It's constant shrinkage. From the moment you take in the prime cuts, you trim them, cull fat, and when you dry-age, you have to trim off all the oxidized parts, take off the mold, and you are shrinking it again. And then you shrink it on the grill. By the time it gets to the customer, it's a miracle there's anything left.

We're talking about meat that might cost thirty dollars a pound—that is, it costs *me* thirty dollars a pound. So if you have a twenty-ounce steak, it costs me fifty bucks to put it on the plate. It's massively expensive. It's an extreme level of hedonism—sourcing these proteins and aging them. And then there's the time value of money, holding a million dollars of meat inventory while it's rotting in the middle of the desert. I should be paid interest for holding it, never mind the cost of the facility I built and the talent I hired to choose it and care for it. I think everything we serve is dry-aged at least thirty days—we don't serve any fresh meat. Personally I like a thirty- to forty-day steak. I like some age on it, I like the richness. I like a little bit of funk on it. We have some kinky steaks that have been aged up to sixty, seventy days, which is really kind of out there. I don't know if you've eaten a steak that old, but it's very heavy, very rich, and stinky like gorgonzola. It's a bit fetishy, definitely not for everyone. But many people will swear it is the best steak they've ever eaten.

All this übermeat is superfucking expensive, and that's why there's never anything else on the plate. We need you to cough up some more cash for some overpriced broccoli—and where else would you pay ten bucks for creamed spinach? And that's why the markup on wine is also a little bit more. Your net, your profit as a percentage of gross, might be lower, but your cost is higher, so in absolute dollars coming through the door you make more money. In other words, you're getting a smaller piece, but it's a bigger pie. Your check average is higher, because people are inclined to spend more in a steak house—it's the one place where you can count on the customer's knowing the game going in. Steak houses exist for one reason only: for you to spend money.

●

CHAPTER NINETEEN

Game Changer

Eataly is the game changer, a fifty-thousand-square-foot emporium, which could be intimidating in scale, but really it is just born from a very simple idea: to put restaurants and grocery stores in the same building and to make the food accessible and attractive. Shopping while you eat and eating while you shop is a very powerful experience. Everything about Eataly makes you hungry.

Eataly has already changed behavior in New York. Where else are you going to find hipsters from Brooklyn, bluehairs from the Upper East Side, *New York Times* liberals from the Upper West Side, and everyone in between, interacting, buying, and consuming food in a communal space? It's that kind of diversity and egalitarian mentality that drives Eataly. In its very own Italian way, I think Eataly became New York's first piazza for food and wine, and if we're successful, we'll change behavior all over the country.

Everyone is there for the same reason—the passion for Italy doesn't know any economic, political, religious, or demographic boundaries. Who doesn't love Italian food and wine? I think that's why the Eataly thing was so viral—every walk of New York life was ignited by that passion, and Eataly was able to create this magical world where all of New York came together. I don't think there are many other examples of that kind of environment in the city.

The Eataly project came along through my connections in the wine world. I had met a guy named Oscar Farinetti, who was a successful Italian businessman—he was like the Crazy Eddie of Italy, selling consumer electronics, stereos, washers and dryers, air conditioners, and whatnot, and he became very successful creating a big-box retail model in Italy that never really existed before.

You have to remember that when it came to any sort of modern conveniences, Italy was always a little behind. People were buying their first washing machines in the seventies. It wasn't that long ago that Italians were still gathering to watch television in bars, because not everyone had a good set at home. Oscar came along and helped change that, and when his business was peaking, he sold out to some huge conglomerate and began investing in his true passion— he comes from Piemonte and loves wine and food. He began buying wineries, cheese producers, mineral-water companies—everything he loved about Italy—and then he opened the first Eataly, in Torino in an old Fiat factory.

Eataly is not about trudging to the supermarket, it's about becoming part of this great experience, maybe have an *aperitivo* or a glass of Prosecco in the piazza, and if you decide that you're hungry, you can think about pizza, pasta, or fish, then sit down and enjoy whatever you like. Or shop for the best ingredients and re-create the experience at home.

Eataly is a revolution in how food is sold. It's a giant grocery store where every department has its own single-themed restaurant. The vegetable department has a vegetarian restaurant. There is pizza, pasta, espresso, gelato—all have their own dedicated areas. For instance, there is no pasta in the fish restaurant; it's all fish. If you'd like something sweet, there is a dessert bar, or great gelato. There are two espresso bars. By the meat area, we have a steak house called Manzo, which is the only restaurant with tablecloths and a complete menu and the only one that takes reservations. Everywhere else it is first come, first served, so you can move around, check out various offerings, flirt with what you want, and just have a blast eating and shopping. It's a great way to spend an afternoon.

Eataly was an immediate success in the city of Torino. It created something of an uproar, because no own had ever done this before. Oscar expanded to Japan, but of course he wanted to bring it to New York. Every Italian's ambition is to be a success in New York, and he was smart enough to know he needed a local partner. He found our group—me, mom, and Mario. Who better? We went over to Torino to meet him, and we were all very impressed.

When we got back to New York, after two years of searching, we finally found the perfect location at 200 Fifth Avenue, the old Toy Building. We signed the lease in the middle of the banking crisis of 2008, so we had a great deal on the real estate. It was a courageous move to do it; honestly, it took some balls given the environment. And there were a million challenges—we were retrofitting the lobby of a hundred-year-old building, a landmark space, and leases of this nature are generally very complex. This one was no different. It was hundreds of pages of tech stuff and building codes, insanely detailed regulations. And it was a union building, so all the construction was union—and trust me, the Italians didn't really understand what union labor means in New York. Managing the whole process was like building a city from scratch, and yet somehow Eataly opened up in 2010, a year and a half after we began.

It was like the perfect storm. The Italians brought this aggressive, intelligent approach to retail, to which we added our practical and effective way of running restaurants. It was that "your chocolate is in my peanut butter, your peanut butter is on my chocolate" kind of moment. Dave Pasternack came down from Esca to run the fish restaurant. And we brought Liz Benno, who was a cook at Babbo and a sous-chef at Casa Mono, to run the vegetarian restaurant. We brought some great talent in from Vegas—Zach the narcoleptic gave us a hand—and we brought some cooks from Del Posto for pasta. Michael Toscano, who was the sous-chef at Babbo, became the chef at Manzo. This was a big deal for us, and there was no room for error. The whole world was watching. And Oscar knew how to crank up the publicity machine. The opening was incredible— Mayor Bloomberg was there eating pizza margherita and prosciutto. We cut a pasta ribbon. It was high Italian camp. For the first couple of months, we had lines of people waiting to get in. Twenty-thousand-a-day head counts.

As New Yorkers we are kind of defined by where we eat. If you tell me which restaurants you like to frequent, I'll have a pretty good idea of where you come from and how much money you make. I can profile anyone based on dining habits alone. But Eataly is a wild card. I can't categorize it. As at an Italian piazza, not only does the richest man in town go there, so does the poorest. Eataly can be a two-dollar espresso or Eataly can be a hundred-and-fifty-dollar meal at Manzo with steak and Barolo.

There are a lot of people who are not happy with Eataly. Some of the old guard went public, whining that the ambition of Eataly wasn't authentic or it somehow wasn't done right, but meanwhile they were still hustling overpriced veal Milanese and tired *frutti di mare* pasta specials to blissfully unsophisticated Park Avenue rubes.

The truth is, Eataly threatens many people in the Italian food and wine world, because once they saw how incredibly powerful and dominating it was, they realized we were going to be taking away a big chunk of their business. They said we'd be eating them, from Little Italy to Agata & Valentina, and all the Dean & DeLucas in between, but as it turns out, that cannot be further from the truth. Eataly has become the showroom for Italian culture and keeps customers returning to the Italian table.

Eataly celebrates the producer of each product and acts as a link between the customer and the maker. There are no private-label brands in Eataly. It's counter to the fundamental essence of the concept, which is communication about the product and about who makes the product and where it comes from. It is all very authentic and very transparent. If Eataly is successful, it creates a conduit. The objective is to know the people who grow your food. Know the people who make your chocolate. Know the guy who roasts your coffee. I think Eataly is a fundamentally better experience than other retailers who private-label everything and stamp it "organic," which it very well may be, but we're not about putting a screen between the producer and the customer by wrapping everything in our name. Eataly is all about communication—why wouldn't you want to know who makes that granola you're going to buy? Or that milk or that yogurt? Not telling is like lying to the customer. Eataly is a brand, but that brand represents a culmination of artisanal food producers. They create everything that is inside Eataly. Eataly represents the culture of the Italian table.

I'm sure that Trader Joe's is not delighted with our moving into the neighborhood, either. They are a very impressive operation from a retail perspective, but as a wine purist I find their wine mission statement to be just kind of sad, because it takes away what I believe to be the purity of wine, the art form of making wine. Everything we've discussed in this book about what wine should be, Trader Joe's wine doesn't do. They buy huge vats of leftover wine and put their label on it, and even though those bottles cost only between seven and fifteen dollars retail, they are probably 95 percent of the wine market—actually, maybe Trader Joe's *doesn't* give a shit about Eataly—but to me what they're doing is just reinforcing the industrial wine complex, which is bad for everyone.

There are five hundred restaurant seats in Eataly. It did $40 million in food and beverage and $40 million in groceries in its first year. These are huge numbers, and to a certain extent it is going to hurt someone, although I never believed that the market is a zero-sum game—I don't believe that if a customer goes to eat somewhere else, that's one less customer coming to me. I honestly think that every time customers go out and have a good experience, that's going to reinforce their habit of going out, and they'll do it again and tell a friend, and then more people are going to be eating out. I truly believe that influencing behavior as we do has a positive impact on our industry as a whole. But I also know that when you get to something with the dimension and scale of Eataly, something that's sucking so much out of the economy, you've got to be pissing people off. If I walked into Eataly and had not created it myself, I'd have to walk right back out, vomit on the sidewalk, and shoot myself in the head.

We've been incredibly fortunate, but there have been a few hiccups here and there. Frico Bar is a good example of a mistake, but was it really a failure? I think Frico was just a decade ahead of its time—basically, Otto is the evolved version of Frico Bar, and it does about $12 million a year, so our vision was eventually accepted in the marketplace. Sometimes you just have to wait for the public to catch up to you.

But a few years later, we did a project on Forty-second Street called Bistro du Vent, which was our foray into French bistro dining, and for our effort we got thoroughly spanked, financially and editorially. It was a complete fucking failure, with a capital *F*.

Dave Pasternack had the idea to open his own bistro. He had

come from this culture of bistro cooking, at Steak Frites for Andrew Silverman and later for Terrance Brennan at Picholine, and at the time there really were no good French bistros in Midtown. Dave was kind of smitten with his success at Esca, but this turned out to be a fucking nightmare. I'm not saying whose fault it was, but it sucked. Hard.

Again, it was one of those deals that was more real-estate-driven. There was a space that came up in the Manhattan Plaza, where Esca is. This is right before we began Del Posto, and we had the time and energy for a new project. Dave would be just around the corner; he would oversee both restaurants. But it was categorically a disaster, from conception to layout to design. The first mistake was listening to Dave and placating his ambition. Doing a French restaurant was a stupid idea, and, unfortunately, I didn't have the discipline or vision to say no.

Actually, the food was great, but no one wanted French food from us. No one. It got a good review—I think Bruni gave it two stars—but it didn't resonate with our customers, who wanted to know what the fuck we thought we were doing making French food. That's a good example of where a solid two-star review didn't even matter. The place was destined to go over like the *Hindenburg*. There was no saving it. I don't think Dave really knew how to create a spirited bistro menu, and that showed. The wine list was kind of silly. The service sucked. Simon, who was the manager, was sprinting between the bistro and Esca trying to run the front of the house in both places, and it was a joke.

We've done Spanish restaurants—Casa Mono and Bar Jamón— and they worked, but Mario has lived in Spain, and he really feels it. Trying to be French, though, was a huge mistake. The attempt was totally contrived; we simply weren't capable of doing it. The customers sniffed it out and stayed away.

It was a very frustrating situation. We wound up asking Dave to give up his kitchen in the new place. It was not a nice meeting, but we thought at the end that pulling Dave out might give us some chance of saving our investment and getting him back to being 100 percent Esca, where he was a complete stud. We hired the biggest gun we could find, a fancy-pants French chef, Laurent Gras. He was a rock star; in fact, he just received three Michelin stars for a restaurant in Chicago. Supertalented chef but a complete nutcase—he was like the insane, screaming French chef from some old comedy, or an X-rated version of the Muppets, clanging saucepans, cussing like a Gallic sailor on a meth jag, and scaring the shit out of anyone who came near him. The only good thing about the experience was when we finally admitted to ourselves that we were going to shut it down and we had to go there every night and try to drink out the entire wine inventory. That was fun, because we knew once we drank it all, we could walk away. But seriously, I felt terrible. It cost a year of my life and a million dollars.

What worries me now is that everything I've talked about in this book, every message, every lesson, is going to be completely foreign to my kids. They have it too good, and I don't know what to do about that. I bring them back to Italy and force them to spend time with the people who run our vineyards, and Grandma Lidia, of course, but they live in a world of prep schools and PlayStations. Their reality is Greenwich and Manhattan. Where is their piss jug and chicken water? Where is their Restaurant Man to kick their pasty white asses?

I know I can't replicate my experience for them—they don't even believe me when I tell them I'm a cheap fuck, because I spoil them too much.

My kids will never have to deal with buying papers from a fingerless fuck like Turtle, and I hope they'll never be delusional enough to think they're going to make money selling toilet paper in the Balkans, or feel that they have to. They're never going to get stoned and bake bagels, thankfully. And they will never get to enjoy the miracle of seeing a contraband copy of *The Analist* on clunky home video—the irony here is that they can't even sneak watching porn on their computers at home, because my wife is pretty savvy about that stuff and keeps the filters on, but when they're at Grandma's house, there's no firewall and they can watch whatever they want.

I hope that I can inspire them through my hard work and that they will excel in school and work just as hard as I did to get whatever it is they want. They are privileged, there is no question about it, but I can't and I won't hand them the kinds of victories that are bought purely with a family name, inheritance, and connections. I try to share every part of my experience with them, and even if they don't always get it, they will never be part of the culture of skimmers.

My biggest fear is that they won't be risk takers. We live in a nation of pussies, but for me, playing it safe was never an option. It's a funny way to live, but I'm still a slave to the turn of the card, taking the kinds of risks that fuel growth, and that's become the difference between running three restaurants in New York and more than twenty-five all over the world. You double down knowing that there are no guarantees. Failure and victory really aren't so far apart.

Even though they are two generations away, they need to feel the influence of my mom. Lidia has been the greatest influence for me. She supported me with her fame and infrastructure but was never afraid to let me succeed or fail in my own glory. She shared everything, she was incredibly generous, but she knew when to back off, and thanks to her I have this limitless ambition, meaning I truly believe that I can do anything I want to do in the world, and that confidence has never failed me. The flip side is, I'm not as risk-averse as I sometimes should be; while some other people are conservative and will do anything to protect their business, I feel I can draw outside the lines and take chances. Mario deserves credit for that, too, but mom is number one. It was she who instilled in me, on a very practical level, the passion for authenticity and honesty, for being true to our heritage and translating it without taking shortcuts when bringing it to the plate. She knew that sometimes you have to give up a few bucks to make money next week. She was never about the fast buck or instant gratification, which takes real brains, discipline, and vision. And that's what I try to instill in my kids—looking at the long term. You might not make it this week, but the long game is where it's at. One of the best things Lidia taught me is this: "Never make decisions on your best day, and never make your decisions on your worst day. Make all your decisions on medium days."

My parents' marriage and relationship mirrored the evolution of their restaurants and in many ways the restaurant world on the meta level, from a blue-collar business run by immigrants to the state of the art today: My mother became a superstar, Restaurant Man became a dinosaur.

When they started in the sixties, my mom was a pregnant bartender. She'd never cooked in a restaurant in her life; she was just working there because she married Restaurant Man. Mostly she was behind the bar dealing with the drunks and my dad was in the back—cooking, chopping, doing everything. But he wasn't a chef; he was just running the kitchen with two Mexican guys and maybe some guinea fresh off the boat, and he was running it no differently from the way a Russian-Jewish immigrant would have run his hardware store or plumbing-supply shop.

You know the story: There was product, you bought it, fixed it up, sold it. You watched the margin like a fucking hawk and tried to make as much money as you could. You tried to buy cheap, sell high. It was more like a commodity-driven business that could make you a decent living if you played by the rules—Restaurant Man rules—and the harder you worked, the more money you made. And in time that changed, but that was the role my father relished. He was a hardworking, pragmatic guy, and when my mom suddenly became an artist, someone known for being creative rather than being some kind of workaday animal who sweated it out in the kitchen like a blacksmith or a coal miner, there was a lot of resentment on his part. And my mother, being a very strong and opinionated person, also had her opinions about him and what he did. He was the sort of guy who liked to play his accordion and go to the Istria Club on Sundays, knock back a couple bottles of white wine and sing till two o'clock in the morning with his buddies, all these guys who owned their own businesses—contractors, plumbers, and other restaurateurs. They were successful immigrants, and this is how they celebrated. They went to their social club in Astoria and got drunk and sang songs that were meaningful for them. They played boccie and ate lamb and drank to their relative success.

That was not the life my mother wanted to live. Although she always respected it and would go and do her time with my father's friends, they were a largely uneducated, blue-collar, pointedly simple crowd, and they really resented my mother for her ambition, for being upwardly mobile and successful. My mother is wicked smart, and no shit, she worked for everything she has, but there was always this attitude from my father and his friends: Who the fuck does she think she is?

That kind of bitterness will kill you, and I'm not exaggerating or projecting any hippie good-vibes-and-positive-energy theories onto the situation, but you have to know that walking around with that kind of senseless anger is a formula for rapid decay, and it ran its course over the years. It didn't help that my father drank on top of being a lifelong diabetic. If you've ever been to his social club to see him at it with his friends . . . well, these were not guys who made healthy lifestyle choices even when everyone knew better. They were like a giant hangover from the Old World.

He didn't take care of his blood-sugar levels, just kept doing what he did, what his family had done for generations, and eventually he died. There isn't much more of a story to it than that, except for the heartbreak. We never had a great relationship, and it didn't end as a great relationship. He was bitter toward my mother's success, and our relationship was strained because he wasn't the kind of father I thought I should have had, the kind of dad who took his kids to ball games and played catch with them. Simple stuff like that.

Sometimes I think that in my own mind I glorify the story of the Restaurant Man more than it deserves to be, but it resonates with people, especially anyone who knows about the business, because it's all true, it's all there, none of it is made up or fabricated. The lessons are very real, sadly right down to my dad's never having time for his kids because he was constantly working. I always wondered, is that part of being Restaurant Man? But you know what? Fuck that—I took the good part of Restaurant Man, the part that made me work like a deranged obsessive to make Becco and Babbo successful, and if anything I am guilty of doting too much on my kids. My love and passion for them are boundless, but occasionally my time is limited, because this year's model of Restaurant Man is always on planes, so every now and then I bring them to work. Instead of a ball game with peanuts and hot dogs, they might wind up at a food-cost meeting, a shakedown with a building inspector, with maybe scraps of family meal at Babbo scarfed down before the dining room opens up for dinner—although I don't throw my kids out when customers come in the way my dad used to do.

I believe that my kids can be anything they want to be—and I tell them that every day, which is contrary to what my father told me. But at least one of them is already showing signs that the Restaurant Man DNA is taking control of his destiny. Every time I catch him pulling loose change out of the couch or speaking Spanish in the kitchen, I have to smile.

My dad was absent when I was in school, at college, on Wall Street. He was never there. It was my grandmother who raised us, and she hated him because she thought that at the end he lived off my mother's success and never contributed, although in the beginning he probably worked harder than she did. It was a very unfair way to look at him; he was the product of a war and of having lived under Communism, and she knew that, but still there was no love lost between those two.

Ironically, Grandma has a lot in common with Restaurant Man. She's a very intense, hard-core woman. She worked hard. She is very practical. She has that war mentality, intent on saving money so we could survive the next big crisis. She did a great job of raising me and my sister.

At some point the paradigm shifted and Restaurant Man became obsolete—at least in the eyes of the new generation of hotshot chefs and fancy restaurateurs. Restaurant Man, the guy who ran the business with the no-bullshit, buy-it/cook-it/sell-it simplicity of an immigrant trying to earn a living, was suddenly not as important as the chef as artiste, not to mention the whiz kids who were graduating from hotel-restaurant school with degrees in menu marketing and strategic hospitality theory. But he brought a sensibility and a hard-edged reasonableness to operating restaurants that had a lasting impact on me and still affects how I run all our restaurants today. In many ways my mom contributed more to helping me find success—especially partnering with me on my first restaurant and then again later with Del Posto and Eataly—but Restaurant Man forged me in iron. He gave me the balance of running restaurants as a real workingman's job. I don't think there is anyone out there in today's world spreading that message—all you see these days is the zest of restaurants, these media-driven, star-driven, made-for-TV experiences that somehow exist without all the backbreaking hard work that goes behind it—and I think the loss of that aspect of restaurateuring, the loss of an avatar who knew the real score, is a loss for everyone. The passing of Restaurant Man—the original gangsta Restaurant Man, my father—was the passing of an era. No one can replace him.

•

CHAPTER TWENTY

Closing Time

Closing time is that magical time in a restaurant when the worst debauchery, thievery, and the absolutely most destructive behavior happens. Much food and much wine have been served, everyone has worked hard, people have been made happy, and now everyone wants to blow off a little steam and play a little. Closing time is when the first bottle of wine that you stashed halfway through the night gets consumed. It's when the first waiter grabs a Mexican busboy's ass and calls him a *maricón*. It's when the dishwashers start feeling itchy to get the hell out.

This is when Restaurant Man has to keep his eyes open—this is where most customer complaints come from, too. You're cutting teams, moving people out of the restaurant, maybe waiters are switching tables or covering for one another. Chaos is imminent. Bad shit happens. Running a restaurant is like driving a locomotive, and all of a sudden you're bringing it to a grinding halt, and it requires the sage eye of management to make sure that the momentum you worked so hard to cultivate doesn't drive the thing off the tracks the second you put on the brakes.

The most important time at the end of the night is when you've gotten to the last three tables. That's the final countdown. And I always mandate that all managers have to touch the last three tables, because the customer who eats at ten-thirty is really your best customer of the night. He is spending as much as the customer who came in at eight o'clock, but at eight you don't really need him. You're full, he'd just be waiting anyway, and a guy who actually wants to sit down and have dinner at ten-thirty, if he comes back again, he's going to come at ten-thirty, exactly when you want customers, right? You love your before- and after-peak regulars.

When I say "touch the tables," that's not a joke. I mean physically touch the tables, talk to the people, buy them an after-dinner drink, some dessert wine, whatever. Once again we're pulling from the back to bring to the front, and our generosity must be seamless. Ask them how their experience was and make them feel some ownership—they should feel as though it is their place. If I'm there, I do it every time. I personally thank them for coming by, and more often than not that's money in the bank and I'll see them again.

Something that really burns my ass is when the last tables are getting up to leave and the maître d' is flirting with the coat-check girl or eating leftover pasta in the kitchen. He's already called it a day, and then my customer is not getting the proper good night and good-bye. Walking out of an empty restaurant when no one acknowledges you makes you feel like you didn't even eat there. It ruins the whole trip. It sucks. It's important for the bartender to acknowledge the customers, to look them right in the eye and thank everyone. The bartender is going to be your fail-safe, because in any good restaurant the bar is the first thing in the restaurant, and you can catch the customer coming and going. A good Restaurant Man maxim is that restaurants that don't have bars in the front generally fail.

And the maître d' should be there, too, right up front until the very end. At least two people have to say good night to every customer who leaves. Especially the last customers. You want to create a good experience with continuity so they feel appreciated. We don't chase them out; we let them linger for a while and enjoy the experience.

I love being the last customer. You feel like you're part of the family, right? I think fostering that feeling is important. Because at the end of service, an empty restaurant doesn't have the buzz and energy of a full restaurant, so you have to compensate for that. Instead of offering them the thrill of the peak of the evening, you offer them a bit of an insight into what the restaurant family is about. Sharing a little of that experience. That's what we try to make happen at the end of the night.

And then there's all the other Restaurant Man stuff that has to happen while you're getting ready to close—walking through the bus stations and making sure the place doesn't look like a shithole, checking the bathrooms often, because they're going to be the dirtiest at that point. Everyone is trying to rush to get all their jobs done, and invariably someone is pulling the linen bag through the dining room when he shouldn't be. Or pulling out some garbage from the kitchen when he shouldn't be. People want to leave, so they're trying to do what they have to do. But is it at the cost of the customer experience? It is if you're dragging bags of crap through the dining room.

Restaurant Man's greatest vulnerability is in those closing hours. You're really doing damage control, both from the customer's perspective and against the destructive nature of the people who work there. Theft, horseplay, fighting—that's when it happens. People are tired. Maybe she had a shot of tequila she shouldn't have had. He's got to go home and meet his girlfriend. She's in a rush because she wants to go to the disco. He didn't sleep the night before. It's when things go bad. Things are stolen or broken, and the restaurant loses money. It's the time of badness. It's the time when Restaurant Man has to pay the most attention.

My usual spot at the end of the night would be the end of the bar. I indulge in a glass of white wine, a slice of cheese, and a couple of grapes to fortify myself, but also because I want to enjoy those last moments. I put Zeppelin on the stereo and turn it up a little.

The most important thing is being present. Letting the customers and the staff know you're there. You get a good pulse on the night. Maybe you query two busboys. What's going on? Who was working hard? Who wasn't working hard? You get the inside scoop from the bartender, find out which regulars were in. Talk to the maître d'. See how many covers he did. See how your VIP list was. Any complaints. Any feedback. After opening, closing is what separates Restaurant Boy from Restaurant Man.

It used to be after closing we'd go a bit crazy, lock the doors, let the party really get started. Actually, the whole business used to be a lot crazier—every dinner was like a mini-fiesta. Nowadays it seems as if everyone feels that they have to act so buttoned up. Totally obvious sloppiness is not appreciated the way it used to be. People aren't fucked up. People don't create a scene anymore. We get rock stars in constantly, and they're better behaved than the people from the philharmonic. They're all foodies—they want to know where their beef cheeks are sourced. No one is chasing the dragon anymore.

It's a whole new paradigm, a new hierarchy for the aristocracy— the braisers of the beef cheek will inherit the earth! The dope smokers are relegated to college radio and limited-distribution indie releases. It's kind of sad. I'm not sure how much we had to do with it. We always tried to encourage both—the focused experience and the wild abandon. That's been our whole trip, but these days people are always on their best behavior, and I don't mean me, I mean the customers! Since when don't they get shitfaced at dinner? I'm not saying I want Babbo to look like a scene from *Satyricon,* but there is a reason we play the Rolling Stones at volume. You should be able to let loose a little without losing control. That's the whole secret of living in New York City. And if you do lose control once in a while, who the fuck cares, as long as you don't make it a habit?

This is a business that lives and dies on excess—every night is a celebration for someone, and with celebration comes the booze and the drugs. When you're the Restaurant Man, it's tempting to think that you should be part of the party every night, when what you really need is to be able to separate yourself and understand, yeah, sometimes you're part of the party, but mostly you're hosting the party, facilitating the party, giving real estate to the party. That's been kind of my demon—it is hard not to be the cheerleader. I feel that as the guy who wanted to be successful in this racket, not only do I have to kill it on the business side but I also have to be the champion of the party. It's just recently that I've been able to step away from that, feeling that just maybe I don't have to be the last one there every night. I don't have to open the last bottle of wine. I guess that just comes with twenty years of being on the floor— that's a hard way to live your life. And this is where many people in our business go wrong. Hosting the party is a big part of what you do, it's your job, and then all of a sudden you can't distinguish what's work and what's play. The downfall comes when you get so confused you slip too far in one direction and either become too uptight or get too loose. You can't party every night and still function as Restaurant Man. Maybe you can when you're twenty-four, but even then you'd better have your shit together. Nailed down. Tight.

Restaurant Man is in the entertainment business. Every night I put on a show. The meal is just the visible part of the iceberg. There's so much behind it—from conception to execution to kitchen maintenance and dealing with staff and vendors and watching margins and praying that the stock market doesn't tank again or that we don't get douched by evil landlords. But the main thing is that every night hundreds or even thousands of people come to a dozen different restaurants thinking they know what to expect, and I blow their minds and leave them looking forward to the next time they can come back.

And then I get up in the morning and do it all again.